Quantitative Value

Founded in 1807, John Wiley & Sons is the oldest independent publishing company in the United States. With offices in North America, Europe, Australia and Asia, Wiley is globally committed to developing and marketing print and electronic products and services for our customers' professional and personal knowledge and understanding.

The Wiley Finance series contains books written specifically for finance and investment professionals as well as sophisticated individual investors and their financial advisors. Book topics range from portfolio management to e-commerce, risk management, financial engineering, valuation and financial instrument analysis, as well as much more.

For a list of available titles, visit our website at www.WileyFinance.com.

Quantitative Value

*A Practitioner's Guide to
Automating Intelligent Investment
and Eliminating Behavioral Errors
+Website*

WESLEY R. GRAY, PhD, AND
TOBIAS E. CARLISLE, LLB

WILEY

John Wiley & Sons, Inc.

Library of Congress Cataloging-in-Publication Data:

Gray, Wesley R.
    Quantitative value + website : a practitioner's guide to automating intelligent investment and eliminating behavioral errors / Wesley R. Gray and Tobias E. Carlisle.
        pages cm. — (Wiley finance series)
    Includes bibliographical references and index.
    ISBN 978-1-118-32807-1 (cloth); ISBN 978-1-118-42000-3 (ebk);
ISBN 978-1-118-41655-6 (ebk)
    1. Investments--Psychological aspects. 2. Investments–Decision making. 3. Quantitative research. I. Carlisle, Tobias E., 1979- II. Title. III. Title: Quantitative value and website.
    HG4515.15.G73 2013
    332.6—dc23   2012032321

Printed in the United States of America
10 9 8 7 6 5 4 3

For Nickole, without whom none of this is possible, and with whom anything is possible.

—Toby

To all my girls: Katie, Alice, and Glenda. Semper Fidelis.

—Wes

Contents

Preface

This book is first and foremost about value investment—treating stock as part ownership of a business valued through analysis of fundamental financial statement data. Benjamin Graham established the principles of value investing more than 75 years ago. Today, they are widely employed in the investment industry and generally accepted in academia. Its success as an investment philosophy is largely due to the investment performance of Graham's most famous student, Warren Buffett, whose shareholder letters have inspired multitudes to follow in his footsteps. Despite the widespread adoption of the philosophy, the exponential growth in computing power, and the ubiquity of financial data, the value phenomenon persists. It seems to defy logic. Why does the efficient market leave a free lunch on the table? The best answer is that the value phenomenon persists for the same reason it existed when Graham first conceived it: human beings behave irrationally. While investment tools have advanced, humans remain all too human, subject to the same cognitive biases that have plagued us since time immemorial. We may not be able to conquer these intrinsic behavioral weaknesses, but we can adapt our investment process to minimize them. The means to do so is the second aspect of this book: quantitative investment.

While the term *quantitative* likely conjures images of complex equations churned by powerful computers, it's best understood as the antidote to behavioral error. Our apparatus for reasoning under conditions of uncertainty is faulty, so much so that we are often entirely unaware of how imperfect it is because it blinds us to our failure. We are confidently incompetent. We need some means to protect us from our cognitive biases, and the quantitative method is that means. It serves both to protect us from our own behavioral errors and to exploit the behavioral errors of others. The model does need not be complex to achieve this end. In fact, the weight of evidence indicates that even simple statistical models outperform the best experts. It speaks to the diabolical nature of our faulty cognitive apparatus that those simple statistical models continue to outperform the best experts *even when those same experts are given access to the models' output.* This is as true for a value investor as it is for any other expert in any other field of endeavor.

This book is aimed at value investors. It's a humbling and maddening experience to compare active investment results with an analogous passive strategy. How can it be that so much effort appears to be wasted? (We use the word *wasted* euphemistically. A more honest expression might be "value destroying.") The likely reason is that active managers unconsciously—but systematically—introduce cognitive biases into the portfolio, and these biases lead to underperformance. It's not, however, our destiny to do so. There are several quantitative measures that lead to better performance, and these metrics will be familiar to any value investor: enhancing the margin of safety, identifying the highest-quality franchises, and finding the cheapest stocks. We canvass the research in each, test it in our own system, and then combine the best ideas in each category into a comprehensive quantitative value strategy. It's not passive indexing. It's active value investing performed systematically.

Acknowledgments

We are a lot like a turtle on top of a fencepost—it's obvious we didn't get here alone. We have had enormous support from many colleagues, friends, and family in making this book a reality. First and foremost, Dr. Gray would like to thank Jack Vogel for his outstanding research and amazing dedication to accomplishing the mission. David Foulke played an integral role in the development of the book and made the book more accessible to "nonquants." Carl Kanner and the rest of the crew at Empiritrage, LLC—Cliff Gray, Yang Xu, Tao Wang, and Shenglan Zhang— read and reread the manuscript, ensuring it was democratizing quant at every step along the way. Katie Gray also played a key role in drafting the initial manuscript, ensuring it was easy to read and free of errors. Dr. Gray would also like to thank Drexel University's LeBow College of Business, and particularly his colleagues in the Department of Finance, for supporting his research agenda. Jared Wilson served as a dedicated research assistant and offered excellent advice and insights throughout the book-writing process. A number of colleagues at other institutions, notably Hui Chen at MIT, Steve Crawford at Rice University, Gil Sadka at Columbia, and Richard Price at Rice University, also provided valuable insights along the way. Robert Kanner and Edward Stern have been unfailing mentors in many of Dr. Gray's endeavors and particularly supportive in the development of the book, for which he is eternally grateful. When Dr. Gray's Popsicle stand finally takes flight, Bob and Eddie will be the reason for its success.

Legendary Australian ad man John "Singo" Singleton once said, "Anyone who reckons luck doesn't have anything to do with success has never been successful, and never will be, unless they're bloody lucky." It's a worldview to which Mr. Carlisle subscribes, and so, first and foremost, he'd like to thank his own personal Goddess Fortuna, Nickole Carlisle. Nickole helped to make the manuscript as compelling to the lay reader as we hope it is to the quant. Mr. Carlisle would also like to thank Michael and Heather Craft, Steve Baxter, Pete Latham, Chris Hughes, and Roger and Wendy Carlisle for the support; Troy Harry for the opportunity; Dougs, for teaching him that you don't play Ping-Pong if you can't take a punch; Em, who taught him that if you can keep your head when all about you are losing theirs, you have not fully grasped the gravity of situation; and Pete Love and Ross Johnson for the thoughtful discussion. Finally, he would like to thank the loyal readers of greenbackd.com, who inspired him to push beyond the boundaries of the online world.

Finally, we are deeply appreciative of the entire team at Wiley Finance, most especially Bill Falloon and Meg Freeborn, who provided guidance and advice all along the way.

One

The Foundation of
Quantitative Value

This book is organized into six main parts. Part One sets out the rationale for quantitative value investment and introduces our checklist. In it we examine several simple quantitative value strategies to illustrate some key elements of the investment process. In Part Two we discuss how to avoid stocks at high risk of sustaining a permanent loss of capital—those suffering from financial statement manipulation, fraud, and financial distress. Part Three contains an examination of the indicia of high-quality stocks—an economic franchise and superior financial strength. We go bargain hunting in Part Four, looking for the price ratios that best identify undervalued stocks and lead to the best risk-adjusted investment performance. We look at several unusual implementations of price ratios, including long-term average price ratios and price ratios in combination. Part Five sets out a variety of signals sent by other market participants. There we look at the impact of buybacks, insider purchases, short selling, and buying and selling from institutional investment managers like activists and other fund managers. Finally, in Part Six we build and test our quantitative value model. We study the best way to combine the research we've considered into a cohesive strategy, and then back-test the resulting quantitative value model.

CHAPTER 1

The Paradox of Dumb Money

"As they say in poker, 'If you've been in the game 30 minutes and you don't know who the patsy is, you're the patsy.'"
—Warren Buffett (1987)

In the summer of 1968, Ed Thorp, a young math professor at the University of California, Irvine (UCI), and author of *Beat the Market: A Scientific Stock Market System* (1967), accepted an invitation to spend the afternoon playing bridge with Warren Buffett, the not-yet-famous "value" investor. Ralph Waldo Gerard hosted the game. Gerard was an early investor in Buffett's first venture, Buffett Partners, and the dean of the Graduate School at UCI, where Thorp taught. Buffett was liquidating the partnership, and Gerard needed a new manager for his share of the proceeds. Gerard wanted Buffett's opinion on the young professor and the unusual "quantitative" investment strategy for which he was quietly earning a reputation among the members of the UCI community.

Gerard had invested with Buffett at the recommendation of a relative of Gerard's who had taught Buffett at Columbia University: the great value investment philosopher, Benjamin Graham. Graham had first published the value investor's bible, *Security Analysis*, along with David Dodd, in 1934.[1] He was considered the "Dean of Wall Street," and regarded Buffett as his star pupil. Graham's assessment would prove to be prescient.

By the time Thorp met Buffett in 1968, Buffett had established an exceptional investment record. He had started Buffett Partners 12 years earlier, in 1956, at the tender age of 26, with initial capital of just $100,100. (Buffett joked that the $100 was his contribution.) By 1968, Buffett Partners controlled $100 million in capital, and Buffett's share of that was $25 million.[2]

For the 12 years between 1956 and 1968, Buffett had compounded the partnership's capital at 30 percent per year before his fees, which were 25 percent of the gain over 6 percent per year. Investors like Gerard had compounded at an average of 24 percent a year. Before taxes, each original dollar invested in Buffett's partnership had grown to more than $13. Each of Buffett's own dollars, growing at the greater prefee annual rate of 30 percent became before taxes over $23. By 1968, however, Buffett was having difficulty finding sufficiently undervalued securities for the partnership, and so had decided to wind it up. This had led Gerard to find a new manager, and Gerard hoped Thorp was the man. He wanted to know if Thorp's unusual quantitative strategy worked, and so, at Gerard's behest, Thorp found himself sitting down for a game of bridge with Buffett.

Buffett is a near world-class bridge player. Sharon Osberg, international bridge player and regular professional partner to Buffett, says, "He can play with anyone. It's because of his logic, his ability to solve problems and his concentration."[3] Says Buffett, "I spend 12 hours a week—a little over 10 percent of my waking hours—playing the game. Now I am trying to figure out how to get by on less sleep in order to fit in a few more hands."[4] Buffett presented a daunting opponent. Thorp observed of Buffett's bridge playing[5]:

> *Bridge players know that bridge is what mathematicians call a game of imperfect information. The bidding, which precedes the play of the cards, conveys information about the four concealed hands held by the two pairs of players that are opposing each other. Once play begins, players use information from the bidding and from the cards as they are played to deduce who holds the remaining as yet unseen cards. The stock market also is a game of imperfect information and even resembles bridge in that they both have their deceptions and swindles. Like bridge, you do better in the market if you get more information, sooner, and put it to better use. It's no surprise then that Buffett, arguably the greatest investor in history, is a bridge addict.*

Thorp was no stranger to the card table either. Before he figured out how to beat the market, Thorp wrote *Beat the Dealer*, the definitive book on blackjack card counting. William Poundstone recounts the story of Thorp's foray into card counting in his book, *Fortune's Formula*.[6] In 1958, Thorp had read an article by mathematician Roger Baldwin, who had used U.S. Army "computers"—which actually meant "adding machines" or the people who operated them—to calculate the odds of various blackjack strategies in an effort to find an optimal strategy. Over three years, he and three associates found that by using an unusual strategy they could reduce the house edge in blackjack to 0.62 percent. Amazingly, prior to their paper, nobody, including the casinos, knew the real advantage held by the house. There were simply too many permutations in a card deck of 52 to calculate the casino's edge. "Good" players of blackjack, other writers had claimed, could get the house's edge down to 2 or 3 percent. Baldwin's strategy, by reducing the house edge to 0.62 percent, was a huge leap forward. The only problem, as far as Thorp could see, was that Baldwin's strategy still lost money. He was convinced he could do better.

Thorp's key insight was that at the time blackjack was played using only one deck and it was not shuffled between hands. In the parlance of the statistician, this meant that blackjack hands were not "independent" of each other. Information gleaned in earlier hands could be applied in subsequent hands. For example, in blackjack, aces are good for the player. If the dealer deals a hand with three aces, the player knows that only one ace remains in the deck. This information would lead the player to view the deck as being less favorable, and the player could adjust his or her betting accordingly. Thorp used MIT's mainframe computer to examine the implications of his observation and found something completely counterintuitive—the "five" cards had the most impact on the outcome of the hands remaining in the deck. Fives are bad for the player and good for the house. Thorp realized that by simply keeping track of the five cards, the player could determine the favorability or otherwise of the cards remaining in the deck. Thorp found that his improved strategy gave the player an edge of 0.13 percent. That small edge, Thorp reasoned, given enough hands, could add up to a lot of money. He published his new strategy first in a paper and then subsequently as *Beat the Dealer* in 1962, which went on to become a classic in gambling literature. The book detailed how Thorp had used his card-counting strategy for a period of several years, making $25,000 in the process. The casinos didn't like players counting cards to gain an edge. They immediately started taking "counter-measures," including adding more decks, randomly shuffling the cards, using "mechanics" (dealers who cheated by manipulating the cards in the deck), threatening Thorp with physical harm, and then simply barring him from the casinos. By 1964, Thorp no longer found blackjack fun or profitable. He had found a new obsession, the stock market, and he was already hunting for an edge.

Thorp started working on the key element of what would become his quantitative investment strategy when he moved to UCI in 1964.[7] There he met Sheen Kassouf, another professor at UCI, who had been working on the same problem: how to value a warrant, an unusual security that converted into stock on a certain event. They started meeting together once a week in an effort to solve the warrant valuation conundrum. Thorp found the answer in an unlikely place. In a collection of essays called *The Random*

Character of Stock Market Prices (1964), Thorp read the English translation of a French dissertation written in 1900 by a student at the University of Paris, Louis Bachelier. Bachelier's dissertation unlocked the secret to valuing warrants: the so-called "random walk" theory. As the name suggests, the "random walk" holds that the movements made by security prices are random. While it might seem paradoxical, the random nature of the moves makes it possible to *probabilistically* determine the future price of the security.

The implications of the random walk theory are profound, and they weren't lost on Thorp. He saw that he could apply the theory to handicap the value of the warrant. Where the warrant's price differed from Thorp's probabilistic valuation, Thorp recognized that an opportunity existed for him to trade the warrant and the underlying stock and to profit from the differential. While any given warrant might expire worthless, given a large enough portfolio of warrants Thorp was likely to make money. These two insights—a probabilistic approach to valuation and the construction of portfolios large enough to capture the probabilities—formed the bulwark of Thorp's "scientific stock market system," one of the most consistently profitable trading strategies ever developed. In 1965, Thorp wrote in a letter to a friend about his strategy[8]:

> *I have finally hit pay dirt with the stock market. I have constructed a complete mathematical model for a small section (epsilon times "infinity" isn't so small, though) of the stock market. I can prove from the model that the expected return is 33 percent per annum, and that the empirical assumptions of the model can be varied within wide limits (well beyond those dictated by skepticism) without affecting this figure much. Past records corroborate the 33 percent figure. It assumes I revise my portfolio once a year. With continuous attention to the portfolio the rate of return appears to exceed 50 percent gross per year. But I haven't finished with the details of that, so I can only be sure of the lower rate at present. A major portion of my modest resources has been invested for several months. We once "set" as a tentative first goal the doubling of capital every two years. It isn't far away now.*

As he had with his blackjack betting system, Thorp was again seeking to steadily exploit a small edge—epsilon times "infinity"—to beat the market.

Thorp put the strategy to work in his hedge fund, Princeton-Newport Partners, which went on to become one of the most successful ever formed. For the 20 years from its inception in 1969, the fund compounded at

15.1 percent annually after fees. By the time it was wound up, Princeton-Newport was managing over $270 million. Each dollar invested in the fund in 1969 had grown to $14.78. By way of comparison, the Standard & Poor's (S&P) 500 averaged 8.8 percent annually over the same period, which means that Princeton-Newport outperformed the market by more than 6 percent per year. But that's only half the story. The fund was much less volatile than the market itself. In fact, Princeton-Newport never had a down year or down *quarter*. Thorp closed Princeton-Newport in 1988 following an investigation by Rudy Giuliani into stock parking on behalf of Drexel Burnham Lambert in which Thorp was not accused of any wrongdoing.

Unable to stay away, Thorp relaunched in August 1994 as Ridgeline Partners. From the get-go Ridgeline outperformed Princeton-Newport, averaging 18 percent per year after fees. In 1998, Thorp reported that since the inception of Princeton-Newport in 1969 he had returned 20 percent per year for nearly 30 years, with a standard deviation of just 6 percent[9]:

> To help persuade you that this may not be luck, I estimate that ... I have made $80 billion worth of purchases and sales ("action," in casino language) for my investors. This breaks down to something like one and a quarter million individual "bets" averaging $65,000 each, with on average hundreds of "positions" in place at any one time. Over all, it would seem to be a moderately "long run" with a high probability that the excess performance is more than chance.

As Buffett and Thorp sat down for the 1968 game of bridge, it appeared that a deep philosophical chasm existed between each man's investment strategies. Buffett, the value investor, used fundamental analysis on individual securities to carefully calculate their "intrinsic value," and find those trading at a market price well below that intrinsic value. Thorp, the quantitative investor, valued securities on a probabilistic basis and relied on the statistical phenomenon known as "the law of large numbers"—the law states that the more observations we make, the closer our sample will be to the population, and hence greater the certainty of our prediction—to construct portfolios of securities that would, in aggregate, outperform the market. There were other apparently irreconcilable differences. In his 1992 Berkshire Hathaway, Inc. Chairman's Letter,[10] Buffett said of value investing:

> The investment shown by the discounted-flows-of-cash calculation to be the cheapest is the one that the investor should purchase—irrespective of whether the business grows or doesn't, displays volatility or smoothness in its earnings, or carries a high price or low in relation to its current earnings and book value.

Thorp had a different view of value investing, spelled out in *Beat the Market*[11]:

> *My attraction to fundamental analysis weakened further as practical difficulties appeared. It is almost impossible to estimate earnings for more than a year or two in the future. And this was not the least difficulty. After purchasing an undervalued stock it is essential that others make similar calculations so that they will either purchase or wish to purchase it, driving its price higher. Many "undervalued" stocks remain bargains for years, frustrating an owner who may have made a correct and ingenious calculation of the future prospects.*

Buffett spoke in his 1987 Shareholder Letter[12] about the use of computer programs in the investment process:

> *In my opinion, investment success will not be produced by arcane formulae, computer programs or signals flashed by the price behavior of stocks and markets. Rather an investor will succeed by coupling good business judgment with an ability to insulate his thoughts and behavior from the super-contagious emotions that swirl about the marketplace.*

Thorp countered in the introduction to *Beat the Market*[13]:

> *We have used mathematics, economics, and electronic computers to prove and perfect our theory. After reading dozens of books, investigating advisory services and mutual funds, and trying and rejecting scores of systems, we believe that ours is the first scientifically proven method for consistent stock market profits.*

While the philosophical differences between Thorp and Buffett were vast, over a game of bridge they were able to find common ground chatting about their shared interests in statistics and finance. For his part, Thorp was thoroughly charmed by Buffett, writing later that Buffett was a "high speed talker with a Nebraska twang and a steady flow of jokes, anecdotes and clever sayings."[14] He also observed that Buffett had a "remarkable facility for remembering and using numerical information, plus an adeptness in mental calculation." At the end of the evening, Thorp told his wife that he thought Buffett would one day be the richest man in America. Buffett's subsequent trajectory through life is well chronicled, and Thorp's prediction has been true, or within spitting distance, since the 1990s. Buffett's opinion on Thorp is unfortunately lost in the sands of time. We can, however, guess that it was favorable. Gerard, who had made a fortune with Buffett, went on to invest with Thorp. As we have seen, it turned out to be another great investment for him.

At first blush, each man's strategy seems diametrically opposed to the other, and irretrievably so. They agreed, however, on one very important point: both believed it was possible to outperform the stock market, a belief that flew in the face of the efficient market hypothesis. While it is true that Thorp's strategy was grounded in the random walk, a key component of the efficient market hypothesis, he disagreed with the efficient market believers that it necessarily implied that markets were efficient. Indeed, Thorp went so far as to call his book *Beat the Market*. Buffett also thought the efficient market hypothesis was nonsense, writing in his 1988 Shareholder Letter[15]:

> *This doctrine [the efficient market hypothesis] became highly fashionable—indeed, almost holy scripture in academic circles during the 1970s. Essentially, it said that analyzing stocks was useless because all public information about them was appropriately reflected in their prices. In other words, the market always knew everything. As a corollary, the professors who taught EMT said that someone throwing darts at the stock tables could select a stock portfolio having prospects just as good as one selected by the brightest, most hard-working security analyst. Amazingly, EMT was embraced not only by academics, but also by many investment professionals and corporate managers as well. Observing correctly that the market was frequently efficient, they went on to conclude incorrectly that it was always efficient. The difference between these propositions is night and day.*

On this most important point, Buffett and Thorp agreed: the market was beatable, if you held an edge.

VALUE STRATEGIES BEAT THE MARKET

> *[It] is extraordinary to me that the idea of buying dollar bills for 40 cents takes immediately to people or it doesn't take at all. It's like an inoculation. If it doesn't grab a person right away, I find that you can talk to him for years and show him records, and it*

doesn't make any difference. They just don't seem able to grasp the concept, simple as it is.

—Warren Buffett, "The Superinvestors of
Graham-and-Doddsville"[16]

*Corporate gold dollars are now available in quantity at
50 cents and less—but they do have strings attached.*

—Benjamin Graham, "Should Rich but
Losing Corporations Be Liquidated?"[17]

It is difficult to overstate Benjamin Graham's impact on Wall Street. He arrived there in 1914 fresh from Columbia College, where he just had turned down offers to undertake doctorates in the philosophy, mathematics, and English departments. He was employed on Wall Street as a "statistician" (as analysts were then known) and observed in this role that the "mass of information" available from the data services like Moody's and Standard Statistics was "largely going to waste in the area of common-stock analysis." Graham found Wall Street "virgin territory for examination by a genuine, penetrating analysis of security values."[18]

Graham wasn't exaggerating about the lack of genuine analysis on Wall Street. At the time, stock market statisticians had a deservedly poor reputation. A 1932 paper by Alfred Cowles III had asked, "Can stock market forecasters forecast?" and concluded that they could not. With the aid of an IBM punch card machine, Cowles examined the investment performance of 16 statistical services, 25 insurance companies, 24 forecasting letters, and the Dow Theory editorials of William Peter Hamilton over the period from December 1903 to December 1929. Only a handful beat the market. Worse, Cowles concluded of the performances of those few who had beaten the market that their results were "little, if any, better than what might be expected to result from pure chance."[19]

Graham took it upon himself to form a rigorous analytical framework for the scrutiny of securities. In 1927, he started teaching his philosophy at Columbia in a night class called "Security Analysis." By 1934, Graham, with the assistance of David Dodd, a student who had taken his first night class in 1927 and was by 1934 a Columbia Business School professor, converted his lectures into *Security Analysis*, his magnum opus.

Graham and Dodd's 1934 publication of *Security Analysis* laid out the first well-reasoned and comprehensive approach to analyzing securities. As each new edition was published, and with the subsequent publication of *The Intelligent Investor* in 1949,[20] Graham refined his approach, but the philosophy remained the same: equity securities should be regarded as a part share in a business. An investor should thoroughly analyze a security's financial statements to determine a conservative valuation for the security. If the price of the security is available in the market at a sufficient discount to the rough valuation to provide a margin of safety, the security could be purchased. This was "value" investing. More than any other book, *Security Analysis* ushered in the era of the professional financial analyst. But does it work? And how can we know?

The arguments for value investing fall into two categories: logical and empirical. The logical argument is that value investing seeks to exchange one sum of value (money) for a greater sum of value (the "intrinsic value" of the security), which Buffett more pithily states as "price is what you pay; value is what you get."[21] Value investors seek to pay less than the security's value. They realize the profit when the price reverts to the value, but the gain is made at the time of purchase because the purchaser has exchanged a smaller store of value for a greater one. Implicit in this assertion is the concept that price and value are distinct. There are many examples of stocks trading at a discount to intrinsic value, but the most transparent case is in a liquidation scenario. In the 1934 edition of *Security Analysis*, Graham argued that the phenomenon of a stock selling persistently below its liquidation value was "fundamentally illogical." In Graham's opinion, it meant that the stock is too cheap. In a liquidation, an investor can identify a transparent difference between market value and intrinsic value. After all other liabilities have been met, common stockholders are the residual claimants to the company's assets. As Seth Klarman, legendary chairman of the Baupost Group, elegantly demonstrated in his hugely popular out-of-print 1991 book *Margin of Safety*[22]:

> *A liquidation is, in a sense, one of the few interfaces where the essence of the stock market is revealed. Are stocks pieces of paper to be endlessly traded back and forth, or are they proportional interests in underlying businesses? A liquidation settles this debate, distributing to owners of pieces of paper the actual cash proceeds resulting from the sale of corporate assets to the highest bidder. A liquidation thereby acts as a tether to reality for the stock market, forcing either undervalued or overvalued share prices to move into line with actual underlying value.*

To say that price and value are distinct in theory is not to say that we can profit from this distinction in practice. The problem is that in the real world we cannot observe intrinsic value. Rather we must estimate it through some proxy, a model populated with imperfect, backward-looking information, and must make certain assumptions about the future. Change the assumptions, and we change our estimate of "intrinsic value." Klarman discusses the use of the "net current asset value" or "net-net working capital" model to calculate liquidation value[23]:

> *In approximating the liquidation value of a company, some value investors, emulating Benjamin Graham, calculate "net-net working capital" as a shortcut. Net working capital consists of current assets (cash, marketable securities, receivables, and inventories) less current liabilities (accounts, notes, and taxes payable within one year). Net-net working capital is defined as net working capital minus all long-term liabilities. Even when a company has little ongoing business value, investors who buy at a price below net-net working capital are protected by the approximate liquidation value of current assets alone.*

All well and good, but let's not forget that this assessment must be made with imperfect information. There are a number of assumptions embedded in the model, which amply demonstrates why the calculation is often difficult[24]:

> *As long as working capital is not overstated and operations are not rapidly consuming cash, a company could liquidate its assets, extinguish all liabilities, and still distribute proceeds in excess of the market price to investors. Ongoing business losses can, however, quickly erode net-net working capital. Investors must therefore always consider the state of a company's current operations before buying. Investors should also consider any off-balance sheet or contingent liabilities that might be incurred in the course of an actual liquidation, such as plant closing and environmental laws.*

Critics of this approach—typically adherents to the *efficient market theory*—focus on the deficiency of the information available to investors. They argue that price and value cannot be distinct in practice because all information about a security's value is immediately incorporated into the price. Any new information that might affect the value of a security is immediately reflected in its price by arbitrageurs trading away the differential. It is therefore not possible to profit from the difference. This argument reminds us of the old joke about the two professors of finance who while walking one day spot a 10-dollar note lying on the ground. One professor turns to the other and says, "Is that a 10-dollar note lying on the ground?" The other says, "Impossible. If that were a 10-dollar note, someone would have picked it up already."

The other argument in favor of value investing is empirical. Numerous studies demonstrate that a variety of price ratios find stocks that outperform the broader market. In Chapters 7 and 8, we examine in detail the performance of various value metrics. Figure 1.1 sets out a brief graphical overview of the performance of the cheapest stocks according to common fundamental price ratios, such as the price-to-earnings (P/E) ratio, the price-to-book (P/B) ratio, and the EBITDA enterprise multiple (total enterprise value divided by earnings before interest, taxes, depreciation, and amortization, or TEV/EBITDA).

As Figure 1.1 illustrates, value investing according to simple fundamental price ratios has cumulatively beaten the S&P 500 over almost 50 years.

Table 1.1 shows some additional performance metrics for the price ratios. The numbers illustrate that value strategies have been very successful (Chapter 7 has a detailed discussion of our method of our investment simulation procedures).

The counterargument to the empirical outperformance of value stocks is that these stocks are inherently more risky. In this instance, risk is defined as the additional volatility of the value stocks. Prolific finance researchers and founders of modern quantitative asset management analysis Eugene Fama and Ken French made this argument most forcefully in their 1992 paper, "The Cross-Section of Expected Stock Returns." Behavioral finance researchers Joseph Lakonishok, Andrei Shleifer, and Robert Vishny argue

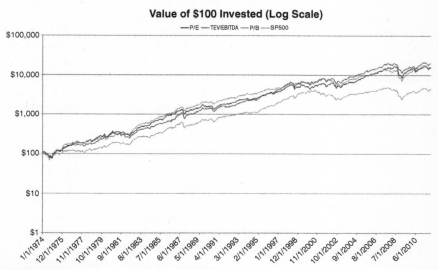

FIGURE 1.1 Cumulative Returns to Common Price Ratios

TABLE 1.1   Long-Term Performance of Common Price Ratios (1964 to 2011)

	P/E	Enterprise Multiple	P/B	S&P 500 TR
Compound Annual Growth Rate (CAGR)	12.44%	13.72%	13.11%	9.52%
Standard Deviation	17.62%	17.25%	17.39%	15.19%
Downside Deviation	12.17%	11.49%	11.12%	10.66%
Sharpe Ratio	0.46	0.53	0.50	0.33
Sortino Ratio	0.68	0.82	0.80	0.50
Worst Drawdown	−49.01%	−43.45%	−49.20%	−50.21%
Worst Month Return	−22.02%	−18.66%	−22.37%	−21.58%
Best Month Return	25.75%	16.95%	28.59%	16.81%
Profitable Months	60.42%	62.85%	61.63%	60.94%

in their 1994 paper, "Contrarian Investment, Extrapolation, and Risk,"[25] that value strategies produce better returns, not because they are fundamentally riskier, but because they are contrarian to the "naïve" strategies followed by other investors. Naïve investors extrapolate poor earnings performance too far into the future, assume a downward trend in stock prices will persist or simply overreact to bad news, leading them to oversell stocks to the point that they are undervalued. Contrarian investors bet against these naïve strategies, investing disproportionately in underpriced stocks and, consequently, beating the market. It might be more accurate to say that individual value stocks *appear* to be more risky to the naïve investor, but are, in the aggregate, no more risky than other stocks. We're not going to linger on the arguments. Instead, we'll give the last word to Buffett, who said in 1985[26]:

> *Most institutional investors in the early 1970s, on the other hand, regarded business value as of only minor relevance when they were deciding the prices at which they would buy or sell. This now seems hard to believe. However, these institutions were then under the spell of academics at prestigious business schools who were preaching a newly-fashioned theory: the stock market was totally efficient, and therefore calculations of business value—and even thought, itself—were of no importance in investment activities. (We are enormously indebted to those academics: what could be*

more advantageous in an intellectual contest—whether it be bridge, chess, or stock selection than to have opponents who have been taught that thinking is a waste of energy?)

Graham's Simple Quantitative Value Strategy

Security Analysis in 1934 was a weighty and ambitious tome focused on the analysis of individual securities. Graham and Dodd wrote in the preface to the original edition[27]:

> *The scope of the work is wider than its title may suggest. It deals not only with methods of analyzing individual issues, but also with the establishment of general principles of selection and protection of security holdings.*
>
> *...*
>
> *[We] have stressed the technique of discovering bargain issues beyond its relative importance in the entire field of investment, because in this activity the talents peculiar to the securities analyst find perhaps their most fruitful expression.*

Some 40 years after the publication of *Security Analysis*, Graham modified his approach in an important way. When asked in one of his last interviews whether he still selected stocks by carefully studying individual issues, Graham responded[28]:

> *I am no longer an advocate of elaborate techniques of security analysis in order to find superior value opportunities. This was a rewarding activity, say, 40 years ago, when our textbook "Graham and Dodd" was first published; but the situation has changed a great deal since then. In the old days any well-trained security analyst could do a good professional job of selecting undervalued issues through detailed studies; but in the light of the enormous amount of research now being carried on, I doubt whether in most cases such extensive efforts will generate sufficiently superior selections to justify their cost. To that very limited extent I'm on the side of the "efficient market" school of thought now generally accepted by the professors.*

Instead, Graham promoted a highly simplified approach that relied for its results on the performance of the portfolio as a whole rather than on the selection of individual issues. Graham believed that such an approach "[combined] the three virtues of sound logic, simplicity of application, and an extraordinarily good performance record."

Graham said of his simplified value investment strategy[29]:

> *What's needed is, first, a definite rule for purchasing which indicates a priori that you're acquiring stocks for less than they're worth. Second, you have to operate with a large enough number of stocks to make the approach effective. And finally you need a very definite guideline for selling.*

Graham proposed two broad approaches, the first of which he had discussed in some detail in the original edition of *Security Analysis*—"net current asset value"[30]:

> *My first, more limited, technique confines itself to the purchase of common stocks at less than their working-capital value, or net-current-asset value, giving no weight to the plant and other fixed assets, and deducting all liabilities in full from the current assets. We used this approach extensively in managing investment funds, and over a 30-odd year period we must have earned an average of some 20 per cent per year from this source. For a while, however, after the mid-1950's, this brand of buying opportunity became very scarce because of the pervasive bull market. But it has returned in quantity since the 1973–74 decline. In January 1976 we counted over 300 such issues in the Standard & Poor's Stock Guide—about 10 per cent of the total. I consider it a foolproof method of systematic investment—once again, not on the basis of individual results but in terms of the expectable group outcome.*

While this strategy was "almost unfailingly dependable and satisfactory," it was "severely limited in its application" because the stocks were too small and infrequently available. Graham had a second strategy with an application much wider than the first. Based on his own research over a 50-year period, Graham believed that a "portfolio put together using such an approach would have gained twice as much as the Dow Jones Industrial Average over the long run," or about 15 percent a year or better.

So what did Graham believe was the simplest way to select value stocks? He recommended that an investor create a portfolio of a minimum of 30 stocks meeting specific price-to-earnings criteria (below 10) and specific debt-to-equity criteria (below 50 percent) to give the "best odds statistically," and then hold those stocks until they had returned 50 percent, or, if a stock hadn't met that return objective by the "end of the second calendar year from the time of purchase, sell it regardless of price." Graham said that his research suggested that this formula returned approximately 15 percent per year over the preceding 50 years. He cautioned, however, that an investor should not expect 15 percent every year. The minimum period of time to determine the likely performance of the strategy was five years.

Graham's simple strategy sounds almost too good to be true. Sure, this approach worked in the 50 years prior to 1976, but how has it performed in the age of the personal computer and the Internet, where computing power is a commodity, and access to comprehensive financial information is as close as the browser? We decided to find out. Like Graham, we used a price-to-earnings ratio cutoff of 10, and we included only stocks with a debt-to-equity ratio of less than 50 percent. We also apply his trading rules, selling a stock if it returned 50 percent or had been held in the portfolio for two years.

Figure 1.2 shows the cumulative performance of Graham's simple value strategy plotted against the performance of the S&P 500 for the period 1976 to 2011. Amazingly, Graham's simple value strategy has continued to outperform.

Table 1.2 presents the results from our study of the simple Graham value strategy. Graham's strategy turns $100 invested on January 1, 1976, into $36,354 by December 31, 2011, which represents an average yearly compound rate of return of 17.80 percent—outperforming even

FIGURE 1.2 Graham Simple Value Strategy Performance Chart (1976 to 2011)

TABLE 1.2 Performance of Graham's Simple Quantitative Value Strategy (1976 to 2011)

	Graham	S&P 500 TR
CAGR	17.80%	11.05%
Standard Deviation	23.92%	15.40%
Downside Deviation	16.26%	11.15%
Sharpe Ratio	0.59	0.42
Sortino Ratio (MAR = 5%)	0.88	0.60
Worst Drawdown	−54.61%	−50.21%
Worst Month Return	−28.84%	−21.58%
Best Month Return	40.79%	13.52%
Profitable Months	59.95%	61.57%
Rolling 5-Year Win	—	90.35%
Rolling 10-Year Win	—	95.53%

Graham's estimate of approximately 15 percent per year. This compares favorably with the performance of the S&P 500 over the same period, which would have turned $100 invested on January 1, 1976, into $4,351 by December 31, 2011, an average yearly compound rate of return of 11.05 percent. The performance of the Graham strategy is attended by very high volatility, 23.92 percent versus 15.40 percent for the total return on the S&P 500. The strategy would also have required a cast-iron gut because only a few stocks qualified at any given time, and the backtest assumed that we invested all our capital in those stocks. The Graham portfolio averaged 21 positions for the full period, but Figure 1.3 illustrates that the portfolio was frequently heavily concentrated in only very few stocks, and was fully invested in only one security in 2004. In practice, portfolio risk considerations would prevent us from investing "all in" on one stock.

Table 1.2 sets out the performance statistics for Graham's simple quantitative strategy over the period from 1976 to 2011.

Graham said that the minimum period to determine the likely performance of his strategy was five years. Table 1.2 highlights that Graham's simple strategy beats the S&P 500 90.35 percent of rolling 5-year periods, and 95.53 percent of rolling 10-year periods. Figures 1.4 (a) and (b) show

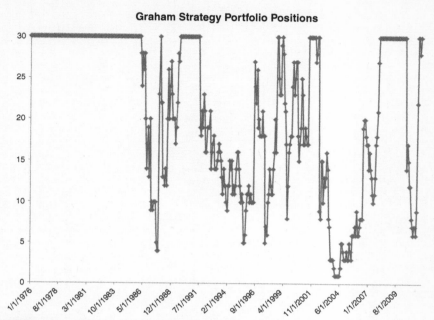

FIGURE 1.3 Graham Strategy Portfolio Holdings over Time (1976 to 2011)

the rolling 1-, 5-, and 10-year returns for the simple Graham strategy for the period 1976 to 2011. As the figures illustrate, Graham's simple value strategy has underperformed in several periods; however, over long periods of time, it has proven to perform exceptionally well and in accordance with Graham's prediction.

The evidence suggests that Graham's simplified approach to value investment continues to outperform the market. It's useful to consider why. At a superficial level, it's clear that some proxy for price—like a P/E ratio below 10—combined with some proxy for quality—like a debt-to-equity ratio below 50 percent—is predictive of future returns. But is something else at work here that might provide us with a deeper understanding of the reasons for the strategy's success? Is there some other reason for its outperformance beyond simple awareness of the strategy? We think so.

Graham's simple value strategy has concrete rules that have been applied consistently in our study. Even through the years when the strategy underperformed the market, and even though it forced us to put all our capital into one stock in 2004, our study assumed that we continued to apply it, regardless of how discouraged or scared we might have felt had we actually used it during the periods when it underperformed the market. Is

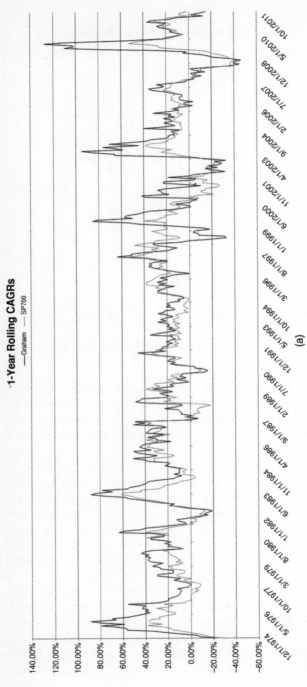

FIGURE 1.4(a) One-Year Rolling Period Performance Statistics: Graham Strategy (1976 to 2011)

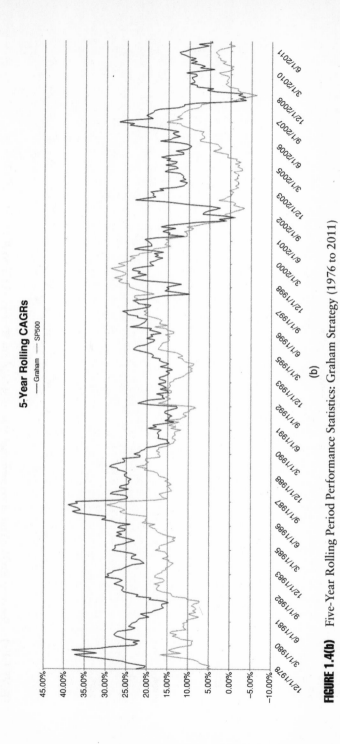

FIGURE 1.4(b) Five-Year Rolling Period Performance Statistics: Graham Strategy (1976 to 2011)

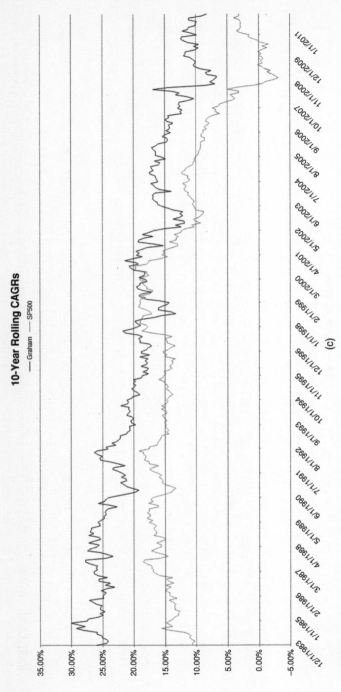

FIGURE 1.4(c) Ten-Year Rolling Period Performance Statistics: Graham Strategy (1976 to 2011)

it possible that the very consistency of the strategy is an important reason for its success? We believe so. A value investment strategy might provide an edge, but some other element is required to fully exploit that advantage. Warren Buffett and Charlie Munger believe that the missing ingredient is *temperament*. Says Buffett, "Success in investing doesn't correlate with IQ once you're above the level of 125. Once you have ordinary intelligence, what you need is the temperament to control the urges that get other people into trouble in investing."[31]

HOW QUANTITATIVE INVESTING PROTECTS AGAINST BEHAVIORAL ERRORS

In the decade to December 31, 2009, the *Wall Street Journal* reported that the best-performed U.S. diversified stock mutual fund according to fund-tracker *Morningstar* was Ken Heebner's *CGM Focus Fund*. Over the decade, the fund had gained 18.2 percent annually, beating its closest rival by 3.4 percent per year, which is exceptional. The typical investor in Heebner's fund, however, *lost* 11 percent annually. Investor returns, also known as "dollar-weighted returns," take into account the capital flowing into and out of the fund as investors buy and sell. The investor returns were lower than the fund's total returns because investors bought into the fund after it had a strong run and then sold as it hit bottom. Heebner's fund surged 80 percent in 2007, and then investors poured in $2.6 billion. The following year, the fund sunk 48 percent, and investors yanked out more than $750 million. Said Heebner[32]:

> *A huge amount of money came in right when the performance of the fund was at a peak. I don't know what to say about that. We don't have any control over what investors do.*

This behavior caused the investor returns in Heebner's fund to be among the worst of any fund tracked by *Morningstar*. Amazingly, this means that the worst investor returns were found in the decade's best-performed fund. We are each our own worst enemy.

Reason Is the Slave of the Passions

Behavioral finance researchers have found that investors behave in a predictably irrational manner. The reason? Humans are flawed decision makers. Sure, at our best we're capable of amazing things like logic, humor, deduction, abstract reasoning, and imagination. But our brains were adapted for life in the wild, where split-second decision making meant the difference between life and death. We developed mental shortcuts—called heuristics—that enable us to identify a snake and jump away before we are conscious of the snake's presence.[33] When we realize moments later that the "snake" was in fact a stick, we are a victim of the heuristic that avoids snakelike objects. These heuristics—useful as they are for survival—give us a number of *cognitive biases* that impede us in our efforts to make rational or optimal decisions.

Cognitive biases impact every aspect of our lives, but, from an investor's perspective, there are several that are particularly pernicious. The first is *overconfidence*, which leads us to put more weight in our own judgment than is objectively warranted. For example, if we are given a test and after taking it asked to determine the number of questions that we got right, we tend to overrate how well we performed. This is not a matter of simply incorrectly guessing our performance on the test because the errors all tend to be in one direction—we reliably overestimate how well we perform. Further, the more difficult the questions, and the less familiar we are with the content, the *more* we tend overestimate how well we performed. The two pioneers of the field of behavioral finance, Daniel Kahneman and Amos Tversky, suggest that our overconfidence may stem from two other biases, *self-attribution bias* and *hindsight bias*.[34] Self-attribution bias refers to our propensity to ascribe our successes to our skill, while blaming our failures on bad luck, rather than a lack of skill. For example, the stocks we buy that go up show our great stock picking skills, while those we buy that go down do so because of some outside factor, like Congress changing the law or the Federal Reserve increasing interest rates. If we do it often enough, we are led to the conclusion that we are skillful, which is as pleasant as it is wrong. Hindsight bias is the propensity to believe, after an event has occurred, that we predicted it before it happened. If, after watching some unlikely event unfold, you've ever said, "I knew that would happen," when your reason for saying so was just some gut-feeling, you were subject to hindsight bias. The problem with hindsight bias is that if we think we predicted the past better than we actually did, we tend to believe that we can predict the future better than we actually can.

A related bias is *neglect of the base case*. The bias manifests when we try to answer probabilistic questions like, "What is the probability that object A originates from class B?" or "What is the probability that process A will generate outcome B?" The neglect-of-the-base-case bias is caused by a heuristic called *representativeness*. It is called the representativeness heuristic because we answer the questions by determining how much A represents—or resembles—B, rather than determining the likelihood of A given B.

Kahneman and Tversky give the classic example in their 1974 paper "Judgment under Uncertainty: Heuristics and Biases" [35]:

> *Steve is very shy and withdrawn, invariably helpful, with little interest in people, or in the world of reality. A meek and tidy soul, he has need for order and structure and a passion for detail. How do people assess the probability that Steve is engaged in a particular occupation from a list of possibilities (for example, farmer, salesman, airline pilot, librarian, or physician)?*

Kahneman and Tversky find that we guess that Steve is a librarian by assessing the degree to which the description of Steve is similar to the stereotype of a librarian. We should instead focus on the base rate. In Steve's case, the fact that there are many more farmers than librarians in the population should lead us to guess that Steve is a farmer. We evaluate probability by representativeness and we ignore base rates.

There are many other cognitive biases. For example, the *availability* bias leads us to weight more heavily information that can be easily brought to mind. We are influenced by vivid stories in the media about shark attacks and plane crashes when determining the likelihood of such an event's occurring to us, and so we overestimate the likelihood of a shark attack or a plane crash, when driving in a car is a more dangerous pastime. An example of the bias in the context of stock markets is the drop in airline stocks beyond any reasonable estimate of the ongoing risk following high-profile plane crashes. *Anchoring* and *adjustment* biases describe our tendency to rely too heavily, or "anchor," on one piece of information when making decisions. For example, if we buy a stock at a given price and it falls, we tend to anchor on the purchase price when determining the right price at which to sell. We want to "break even," and hold on to the stock hoping to do so, ignoring new information. Our starting point influences us too much, so we don't adjust sufficiently to account for new information, and as a result, our actions are biased toward the starting point.

We so regularly distort what we see, interpret illogically, and make poor judgments that our errors in reasoning become predictable. We are, as Dan Ariely puts it, "predictably irrational." [36] Systematic behavioral biases create opportunities for investors who can find a way to control their innate weaknesses. For example, many researchers have found that most investors avoid "value" stocks—stocks that trade at a discount to book value, and instead buy "glamour" or "growth" stocks—stocks that trade at a premium to their book value. Why? We like the vivid story of the glamour stock, hear stories about our friends getting rich after buying them, and ignore the base rate returns for stocks that trade at high P/B value multiples. We happily buy high-tech companies, and we lose money. We don't like boring stocks in label manufacturing businesses; our friends would laugh if we told them we owned them. Instead, we ignore the base rate returns for stocks with low P/B value multiples, even though those stocks tend to go up.

The reliance on heuristics and prevalence of biases is not restricted to laymen. Experts are also subject to the same biases when reasoning intuitively. In his book, *Expert Political Judgment,* [36] Philip Tetlock discusses his extensive study of people who make prediction their business—the experts. Tetlock's conclusion is that experts suffer from the same behavioral biases as the laymen. Tetlock's study fits within a much larger body of research that has consistently found that experts are as unreliable as the rest of us. A large number of studies have examined the records of experts against simple statistical model, and, in almost all cases, concluded that experts either underperform the models or can do no better. It's a compelling argument against human intuition and for the statistical approach, whether it's practiced by experts or nonexperts.

Even Experts Make Behavioral Errors

In many disciplines, simple quantitative models outperform the intuition of the best experts. The simple quantitative models continue to outperform the judgments of the best experts, *even when those experts are given the benefit of the outputs from the simple quantitative model.* James Montier, an expert in behavioral investing, discusses this phenomenon in his book, *Behavioral Investing: A Practitioners Guide to Applying Behavioral Finance.* [38] The first example he cites, which he describes as a classic in the field, and which succinctly demonstrates the two important elements of his thesis, is the diagnosis of patients as either neurotic or psychotic. The distinction is as follows: a psychotic patient "has lost touch with the external world," while a neurotic patient "is in touch with the external world but suffering from internal emotional distress, which may be immobilizing." According to Montier, the standard test to distinguish between neurosis and psychosis is the Minnesota Multiphasic Personality Inventory (MMPI).

In 1968, Lewis Goldberg, now a professor of psychology at the University of Oregon, analyzed more than 1,000 patients' MMPI test responses and final diagnoses as neurotic or psychotic. He used the data to develop a simple model to predict the final diagnosis based on the MMPI test response. Goldberg found that his model applied out-of-sample accurately predicted the final diagnosis approximately 70 percent of the time. He then gave MMPI scores to experienced and inexperienced clinical psychologists and asked them to diagnose the patient. Goldberg found that his simple model outperformed even the most experienced psychologists. He ran the study again, this time providing the clinical psychologists with the simple model's prediction. Goldberg was shocked. Even when the psychologists were provided with the results of the model, they continued to underperform the simple model. While the performance of the psychologists improved from their first attempt without the benefit of the model, they still didn't perform as well the model did by itself. Montier draws an interesting conclusion from the results of the study: "[As] much as we all like to think we can add something to the quant model output, the truth is that very often quant models represent a ceiling in performance (from which we detract) rather than a floor (to which we can add)."[39]

In his 2007 book *Super Crunchers*,[40] Ian Ayres discusses a myriad of other fields in which simple models prevail over experts, often in areas that would not appear to be friendly to a quantitative analysis. One such example is a statistical algorithm for predicting the outcome of Supreme Court decisions. The outcome of a Supreme Court hearing does not appear to be a subject matter that would be easy to reduce to a quantitative model because the language of law is language, and it's rarely plain. Ayres discusses a study by Andrew Martin and Kevin Quinn, "Competing Approaches to Predicting Supreme Court Decision Making," in which they found that just a few variables concerning the politics of a case predict how the U.S. Supreme Court justices will vote. Martin and Quinn analyzed data from 628 cases decided by the Supreme Court justices sitting at the time. Martin and Quinn considered six factors, including such unrelated matters as the circuit court of origin and the political ideology of the lower court's ruling, from which they developed simple models that predicted the votes of the individual justices. For example, the model predicted that if the lower court decision were "liberal," Justice Sandra Day O'Connor would vote to reverse it. If, however, the decision were "conservative" and came from the 2nd, 3rd, or Washington, D.C., circuit courts or the Federal circuit, she would vote to affirm.

Ayres writes that Ted Ruger, a law professor at the University of Pennsylvania, approached Martin and Quinn at a seminar and suggested that they test the accuracy of the simple model against a group of legal experts. The men decided to run a horse race. On one horse was Martin and Quinn's simple model, and on the other, 83 legal experts, law professors and legal practitioners, who would each assist in their own particular areas of expertise. The race was run over the Supreme Court's 2002 term. Who would most accurately predict the votes of the individual justices for every case that was argued? As you might expect by now, Martin and Quinn's simple model won, beating out the legal experts. The model predicted 75 percent of the court's decisions correctly, while the legal experts collectively could manage only 59 percent accuracy. Ayres writes that the model was most useful when predicting the crucial swing votes of Justices O'Connor and Kennedy. The model predicted O'Connor's vote correctly 70 percent of the time, while the experts' success rate was only 61 percent.[41] How can it be that simple models perform better than experienced clinical psychologists or renowned legal experts with access to detailed information about the cases? Are these results just flukes? No. In fact, the MMPI and Supreme Court decision examples are not even rare. There are an overwhelming number of studies and meta-analyses—studies of studies—that corroborate this phenomenon. In his book, Montier provides a diverse range of studies comparing statistical models and experts, ranging from the detection of brain damage, the interview process to admit students to university, the likelihood of a criminal to reoffend, the selection of "good" and "bad" vintages of Bordeaux wine, and the buying decisions of purchasing managers.

Value Investors Have Cognitive Biases, Too

Graham recognized early on that successful investing required emotional discipline. He wrote in the introduction to *The Intelligent Investor*[42]:

> *Our main objective will be to guide the reader against the areas of possible substantial error and to develop policies with which he will be comfortable. We shall say quite a bit about the psychology of investors. For indeed, the investor's chief problem—and even his worst enemy—is likely to be himself. ("The fault, dear investor, is not in our stars—and not in our stocks—but in ourselves. ...") This has proved the more true over recent decades as it has become more necessary for conservative investors to acquire common stocks and thus to expose themselves, willy-nilly, to the excitement and the temptations of the stock market. By arguments, examples, and exhortation, we hope to aid our readers to establish the proper mental and emotional attitudes toward their investment decisions. We have seen much more money made and kept by "ordinary people" who were temperamentally well suited for the investment process than by those who lacked this quality, even though they had an extensive knowledge of finance, accounting, and stockmarket lore.*

As we have seen in other disciplines, the problem is that simply exhorting investors to "establish the proper mental and emotional attitudes toward their investment decisions" is not enough. Graham seems to nod to this when he says that "'ordinary people'... temperamentally well suited for the investment process" will make more money than those who have "extensive knowledge of finance, accounting, and stockmarket lore." The problem is behavioral rather than rational. We can understand the issue on an intellectual level, and still fall victim to it because our emotions let us down. Seth Klarman acknowledged as much when he said[43]:

> *So if the entire country became securities analysts, memorized Benjamin Graham's Intelligent Investor and regularly attended Warren Buffett's annual shareholder meetings, most people would, nevertheless, find themselves irresistibly drawn to hot initial public offerings, momentum strategies and investment fads. People would still find it tempting to day-trade and perform technical analysis of stock charts. A country of security analysts would still overreact. In short, even the best-trained investors would make the same mistakes that investors have been making forever, and for the same immutable reason—that they cannot help it.*

If mere awareness that our judgments are biased does little to correct the errors we make, how then can we protect against these errors?

Nassim Taleb, author of *Fooled by Randomness*[44] and who calls himself a "literary essayist and mathematical trader," argues that we should not even attempt to correct our behavioral flaws, but should instead seek to "go around" our emotions:

> *We are faulty and there is no need to bother trying to correct our flaws. We are so defective and so mismatched to our environment that we can just work around these flaws. I am convinced of that after spending almost all my adult and professional years in a fierce fight between my brain (not Fooled by Randomness) and my emotions (completely Fooled by Randomness) in which the only success I've had is in going around my emotions rather than rationalizing them. Perhaps ridding ourselves of our humanity is not in the works; we need wily tricks, not some grandiose moralizing help. As an empiricist (actually a skeptical empiricist) I despise the moralizers beyond anything on this planet: I wonder why they blindly believe in ineffectual methods. Delivering advice assumes that our cognitive apparatus rather than our emotional machinery exerts some meaningful control over our actions. We will see how modern behavioral science shows this to be completely untrue.*

Research seems to support Taleb's method—tricking ourselves into doing the right thing—works better than simply trying to do the right thing (or flagellating ourselves if we don't).[45] Montier says, "Even once we are aware of our biases, we must recognize that knowledge does not equal behavior. The solution lies in designing and adopting an investment process that is at least partially robust to behavioral decision-making errors."[46] The advantage of the quantitative method is that it starts with the idea that most of us are temperamentally unsuited to investment, and then seeks to protect against those potential errors. If we acknowledge this flaw from the outset, we can build a process to force or trick us into exhibiting the correct behaviors. Given the diversity of fields in which quantitative models outperform experts, it would be remarkable if we did not observe the phenomenon in value investment. Yet within the world of value investing the quantitative approach continues to be uncommon. Where it does exist, says Montier, the practitioners tend to be "rocket scientist uber-geeks." Why isn't quantitative value investing more common? According to Montier, the most likely answer is that old cognitive bias overconfidence. We think we know better than simple models, which have a known error rate, but prefer our own judgment, which has an unknown error rate:

> The most common response to these findings is to argue that surely a fund manager should be able to use quant as an input, with the flexibility to override the model when required. However, as mentioned above, the evidence suggests that quant models tend to act as a ceiling rather than a floor for our behaviour. Additionally there is plenty of evidence to suggest that we tend to overweight our own opinions and experiences against statistical evidence.

Our cognitive biases are most pronounced when we reason intuitively, so the more we rely on statistical evidence and limit our discretion, the fewer errors we should make. This is a powerful argument for a quantitative approach to value investment. As Buffett says, "Paradoxically, when 'dumb' money acknowledges its limitations, it ceases to be dumb."[47]

THE POWER OF QUANTITATIVE VALUE INVESTING

Charlie Munger, vice chairman to Buffett's chairman of Berkshire Hathaway, Inc., says that playing poker in the Army and as a young lawyer made him a better investor. "What you have to learn is to fold early when the odds are against you," says Munger, "or if you have a big edge, back it heavily because you don't get a big edge often."[48] Good poker players know that exploiting their edge leads over time to a reliable return, which can be expressed as an hourly rate: "big blinds per hour" (the "big blind" is the minimum bet in a hand of poker. By calculating their edge in terms of big blinds, good poker players can calculate the likely hourly rate available to them in a game by multiplying their edge by the minimum bet). For poor poker players, the hourly rate is negative. It is amazing that in a game where luck plays such a huge role, the relative skill of a player can be quantified into an hourly rate. This not to say that good poker players expect to win every hand, every hour, or even every time they sit down to play. They know that over short periods of time luck is more important that skill. As David Einhorn, founder of Greenlight Capital and outstanding value investor, says[49]:

> *People ask me "Is poker luck?" and "Is investing luck?" The answer is, not at all. But sample sizes matter. On any given day a good investor or a good poker player can lose money. Any stock investment can turn out to be a loser no matter how large the edge appears. Same for a poker hand. One poker tournament isn't very different from a coin-flipping contest and neither is six months of investment results. On that basis luck plays a role. But over time—over thousands of hands against a variety of players and over hundreds of investments in a variety of market environments—skill wins out.*

The law of large numbers rears its head. As the number of hands played increases, skill wins out. Given a large enough sample size, a player's skill determines the player's return. Investing is no different. Investors who want to outperform the market need an edge, and a value investing philosophy provides that edge. The difficulty for many investors will be in exploiting it.

The power of quantitative investing is in its relentless exploitation of edges. The objective nature of the quantitative process acts both as a shield and a sword. As a shield, it serves to protect us from our own cognitive biases. We can also use it as a sword to exploit behavioral errors made by others. It can give us the confidence to sit down at the poker table and know we're not the patsy.

This book seeks to take the best aspects from quantitative investment and value investment and to apply them to stock selection and portfolio construction. Such an approach has several important advantages over pure quantitative investment, or pure value investment. We call our approach *Quantitative Value Investing*. This book describes our philosophy and sets out to describe the state-of-the-art in quantitative value investment techniques.

We seek to marry Ed Thorp's quantitative approach to Warren Buffett's value investment philosophy. We focus on the key to both investment styles, which is a valuation of the target security based on imperfect information, and the consistent exploitation of the differential between the valuation and the pricing available in the market. Buffett seeks to determine the value of an equity security through careful fundamental analysis, relying on his vast experience and superior intellect. Thorp also processed information to generate valuations, but focused on probability and statistical theory to dictate his decisions.

Our connection of the quantitative process with a value-investing philosophy is not without antecedents. The first is, of course, Graham, the man who stands astride the entire value-investing edifice. The second is Joel Greenblatt, Graham's heir in the application of systematic methods to value investment. Greenblatt has recently defined a quantitative value strategy he calls the *Magic Formula*. The Magic Formula follows the same broad principles as Graham's simple model, but diverges from Graham's strategy by exchanging for Graham's absolute price measures a ranking system that seeks those stocks with the best combination of price and quality more akin to Buffett's value investing philosophy. We examine the Magic Formula in detail in the next chapter.

We believe Greenblatt's Magic Formula is an elegant step in the right direction, but we want to take the study of quantitative value to its logical conclusion. For the remainder of this book, we apply the quantitative process to our strict value investment philosophy. We exhaustively examine the state-of-the-art in quantitative value investment techniques. Then we test the research to find the best metrics for uncovering value: the cheapest price, the highest quality, and those stocks signaling that they are likely to quickly close the gap between price and value. Finally, we combine those metrics into a single method for finding high-performance value investment opportunities.

NOTES

1. Benjamin Graham and David Dodd, *Security Analysis: The Classic 1934 Edition* (McGraw-Hill, 1996).
2. Edward O. Thorp, "A Mathematician on Wall Street: Bridge with Buffett." *Wilmott Magazine*, November 2005, pp. 34–36, *www.wilmott.com/pdfs/110329_thorp.pdf*.
3. Jonathan Davis, "Buffett on Bridge," *www.buffettcup.com/BuffettonBridge/tabid/69/language/en-GB/Default.aspx*.
4. Ibid.
5. Thorp.
6. William Poundstone, *Fortune's Formula: The Untold Story of the Scientific Betting System that Beat the Casinos and Wall Street* (New York: Hill and Wang, 2005).
7. Scott Patterson, *The Quants: How a New Breed of Math Whizzes Conquered Wall Street and Nearly Destroyed It* (New York: Crown Business, 2010).
8. Poundstone, p. 148.

9. Poundstone, p. 320.
10. Warren Buffett, "Shareholder Letter," Berkshire Hathaway, Inc. Annual Report, 1992.
11. Edward O. Thorp and Sheen T. Kassouf, *Beat the Market: A Scientific Stock Market System* (Random House, 1967).
12. Warren Buffett, "Shareholder Letter," Berkshire Hathaway, Inc. Annual Report, 1987.
13. Thorp and Kassouf, 1967.
14. Thorp, 2005.
15. Warren Buffett, "Shareholder Letter," Berkshire Hathaway, Inc. Annual Report, 1988.
16. Warren Buffett, "The Superinvestors of Graham-and-Doddsville," *Hermes*, Columbia Business School alumni magazine, 1984. Available at *www7.gsb.columbia.edu/alumni/news/hermes/print-archive/superinvestors*.
17. Benjamin Graham, "Should Rich but Losing Corporations Be Liquidated?" Reprinted on *Forbes.com*, December 27, 1999. Available at *http://www.forbes.com/forbes/1999/1227/6415410a.html*.
18. Justin Fox, *The Myth of the Rational Market: A History of Risk, Reward, and Delusion on Wall Street* (New York: HarperBusiness, 2009).
19. Ibid.
20. Benjamin Graham, *The Intelligent Investor: A Book of Practical Counsel*, 4th ed. (New York: Harper & Row, 1986).
21. Warren Buffett, "Shareholder Letter," Berkshire Hathaway, Inc. Annual Report, 2008.
22. Seth A. Klarman, *Margin of Safety: Risk-Averse Value Investing Strategies for the Thoughtful Investor* (New York: HarperCollins, 1991).
23. Ibid.
24. Ibid.
25. J. Lakonishok, A. Shleifer, and R. W. Vishny, "Contrarian Investments, Extrapolation, and Risk." *Journal of Finance* 49(5): 1541–1578, 1994.
26. Warren Buffett, "Shareholder Letter," Berkshire Hathaway, Inc. Annual Report, 1985.
27. Graham and Dodd.
28. Benjamin Graham, "A Conversation with Benjamin Graham." *Financial Analysts Journal* 32(5) (1976): 20–23. This article was first brought to our attention by Charles Mizrahi.
29. Janet Lowe, *The Rediscovered Benjamin Graham: Selected Writings of the Wall Street Legend* (New York: John Wiley & Sons, 1999).
30. Graham, 1976.
31. Amy Stone, "Homespun Wisdom from the 'Oracle of Omaha.'" *BusinessWeek* (June 25, 1999), *www.businessweek.com/1999/99_27/b3636006.htm*.
32. Eleanor Laise, "Best Stock Fund of the Decade: CGM Focus." *Wall Street Journal*, Fund Track (December 31, 2009), *http://online.wsj.com/article/SB10001424052748704876804574628561609012716.html*.
33. Jesse J. Prinz, *Gut Reactions: A Perceptual Theory of Emotion (Philosophy of Mind)* (Oxford: Oxford University Press, USA, 2004).

34. Nicholas Barberis and Richard Thaler, "A Survey of Behavioral Finance." NBER Working Paper No. 9222, September 2002, *www.nber.org/papers/w9222*.

35. Amos Tversky and Daniel Kahneman, "Judgment under Uncertainty: Heuristics and Biases." *Science, New Series* 185(4157) (September 27, 1974): 1124–1131; *www.jstor.org/pss/1738360*.

36. Dan Ariely, *Predictably Irrational: The Hidden Forces that Shape Our Decisions* (New York: HarperCollins, 2008).

37. Philip E. Tetlock. *Expert Political Judgment: How Good Is It? How Can We Know?* (Princeton University Press, 2005).

38. James Montier, *Behavioural Investing: A Practitioners Guide to Applying Behavioural Finance* (Hoboken, NJ: John Wiley & Sons, 2007).

39. Ibid.

40. Ian Ayres, *Super Crunchers: Why Thinking-by-Numbers Is the New Way to Be Smart* (New York: Bantam, 2007).

41. Ibid.

42. Graham.

43. Montier.

44. Nassim Nicholas Taleb, *Fooled by Randomness: The Hidden Role of Chance in Life and in the Markets* (Random House, 2008).

45. See, for example, Charles G. Lord, Elizabeth Preston, and Mark Lepper, "Considering the Opposite: A Corrective Strategy for Social Judgment." *Journal of Personality and Social Psychology* 47(6) (1984): 1231–1243; or Asher Koriat, Sarah Lichenstein, and Baruch Fischhoff, "Reasons for Confidence." *Journal of Experimental Psychology: Human Learning and Memory* 6(2) (1980): 107–118.

46. James Montier, *The Little Book of Behavioral Investing: How Not to Be Your Own Worst Enemy* (*Little Books, Big Profits* [UK]) (Hoboken, NJ: John Wiley & Sons, 2010).

47. Warren Buffett, "Shareholder Letter," Berkshire Hathaway, Inc. Annual Report, 1993.

48. Janet Lowe, *Damn Right! Behind the Scenes with Berkshire Hathaway Billionaire Charlie Munger* (New York: John Wiley & Sons, 2000).

49. David Einhorn, "Winning Poker Strategies from an Investor, or Financial Learnings for Make Benefit Glorious Wiseguys." *Value Investing Congress*, November 10, 2006.

CHAPTER 2

A Blueprint to a Better Quantitative Value Strategy

Investors should be skeptical of history-based models. Constructed by a nerdy-sounding priesthood using esoteric terms such as beta, gamma, sigma and the like, these models tend to look impressive. Too often, though, investors forget to examine the assumptions behind the symbols. Our advice: Beware of geeks bearing formulas.

—Warren Buffett, Shareholder Letter, 2000[1]

Before *The Little Book that Beats the Market*[2] propelled Joel Greenblatt to celebrity-investor status, he was regarded as one of the best "special situations" investors of his generation. Special situations are opportunities created by corporate events like spin-offs, mergers, restructurings, rights offerings, bankruptcies, liquidations, and asset sales. Greenblatt's firm, Gotham Capital, had an astonishing track record in special situations. Greenblatt and his cofounder, Robert Goldstein, compounded Gotham's Capital at a phenomenal 40 percent annually before fees for the 10 years from Gotham's formation in 1985 to its return of outside capital in 1995. After Gotham returned all outside capital, Greenblatt and Goldstein continued to invest their own capital in special situations. In 1999, Greenblatt described the special situation investment strategy responsible for Gotham's outstanding returns in *You Can Be a Stock Market Genius.*[3] The book was Greenblatt's first bestseller. It is now regarded as a classic in the field, and essential reading for any prospective special situations investor.

Greenblatt's second book, *The Little Book that Beats the Market*, was born of an experiment he conducted in 2002. Greenblatt wanted to know if Warren Buffett's investment strategy could be quantified. Greenblatt read Buffett's public pronouncements, most of which are contained in his investment vehicle Berkshire Hathaway, Inc.'s Chairman's Letters. Buffett has written to the shareholders of Berkshire Hathaway every year since 1978, after he first took control of the company, laying out his investment strategy in some detail. Those letters describe the rationale for Buffett's dictum, "It's far better to buy a wonderful company at a fair price than a fair company at a wonderful price." Greenblatt understood that Buffett's "wonderful-company-at-a-fair-price" strategy required Buffett's delicate qualitative judgment. Still, he wondered what would happen if he mechanically bought shares in good businesses available at bargain prices. Greenblatt discovered the answer after he tested the strategy: mechanical Buffett made a lot of money.

The results were so impressive that in 2006 Greenblatt named the quantitative Buffett strategy the Magic Formula and turned it into *The Little Book that Beats the Market*. He didn't stop there. He and Goldstein spent the next five years refining the strategy, and in 2010, Gotham abandoned the special situation strategy for the Magic Formula. When one of the best special situations investors of his generation abandons a strategy that has served him so well, we think it's worth examining the strategy in some detail. In this chapter, we put it under the microscope.

GREENBLATT'S MAGIC FORMULA

Greenblatt's Magic Formula is a quantitative translation of Warren Buffett's observation that it is "far better to buy a wonderful company at a fair price than a fair company at a wonderful price."[4] The Magic Formula takes the two key elements of Buffett's investment strategy—first, a wonderful company, and, second, a fair price—and reduces them to two simple quantitative factors: a good business and a bargain price. Greenblatt's challenge, as we will shortly see, was to quantitatively define "good business" and "bargain price." Buffett's Chairman's Letters provide some guidance in this regard, but Greenblatt's translation of those woolly words into useable algorithms is where the rubber meets the road.

A Wonderful Business

Greenblatt uses Buffett's definition of a wonderful business, which Buffett says is a business earning a high return on equity capital. In his 1977 Chairman's Letter, Buffett describes his rationale for using return on equity capital as the measure for a good business[5]:

> Most companies define "record" earnings as a new high in earn-
> ings per share. Since businesses customarily add from year to year
> to their equity base, we find nothing particularly noteworthy in a
> management performance combining, say, a 10% increase in equity
> capital and a 5% increase in earnings per share. After all, even a
> totally dormant savings account will produce steadily rising interest
> earnings each year because of compounding.
>
> Except for special cases (for example, companies with unusual
> debt-equity ratios or those with important assets carried at unreal-
> istic balance sheet values), we believe a more appropriate measure
> of managerial economic performance to be return on equity capital.

Greenblatt translates Buffett's definition into the following algorithm:

*Return on Capital (ROC) = Earnings before Interest and Taxes (EBIT) /
Capital*

Capital is formally defined as fixed assets + current assets – current
liabilities – cash.[6] For simplicity, Greenblatt defines capital as net property,
plant and equipment, plus net working capital (current assets – current liabilities). Greenblatt's ROC is defined as follows:

*Greenblatt ROC = EBIT / Net Property, Plant and Equipment + Net
Working Capital (Current Assets – Current Liabilities)*

ROC measures how efficiently management has used the capital employed in the business. The measure specifically excludes excess cash and
interest-bearing assets from this calculation to focus only on those assets actually used in the business to generate the return. The higher a stock's ROC,
the more money earned per dollar of capital employed in the business—a
capitalist's dream.

A Bargain Price

For the second factor—a bargain price—Greenblatt uses earnings yield,
which is similar to the inverse of the familiar price-to-earnings (P/E) ratio.
Rather than simply using earnings, which is influenced by the particular
capital structure adopted by the company, Greenblatt uses earnings before
interest and taxes (EBIT). Greenblatt compares each company's EBIT to
its total enterprise value (TEV). TEV is the cost a purchaser must pay to
buy the whole company. It includes all the equity, including the preferred
stock; the debt, which the purchaser must service; any minority interests;

and adjusts for excess cash, which a purchaser of the whole company may access. He calls EBIT/TEV the "earnings yield":

$$Earnings\ Yield = EBIT/TEV$$

where TEV is formally defined as market capitalization + total debt − excess cash + preferred stock + minority interests, and excess cash means cash + current assets − current liabilities.

By using EBIT/TEV, rather than earnings on market capitalization (another name for the common P/E ratio), Greenblatt's formula allows us to compare on a like-for-like basis stocks with different capital structures. A stock's market capitalization does not tell us anything about the stock's capital structure, or how it finances its operations. Stocks with a heavy debt load appear the same as stocks that are debt free, when, all else being equal, we would prefer a stock with little to no debt. Also, companies with preferred stock on issue are treated the same as companies without, where again, all else being equal, we would prefer no preferred stock because it stands in front of the common equity for dividends and in a liquidation. The earnings yield employed by Greenblatt takes capital structure into account and allows us to compare the value of the entire company with its earnings adjusted for interest and tax. EBIT/TEV enables an apples-to-apples comparison of stocks with different capital structures.

Greenblatt's Findings

Equipped with algorithms to describe a good business and a bargain price, Greenblatt was ready to test his Magic Formula. He started with a list of the largest 3,500 stocks trading on the major U.S. stock exchanges. He then assigned to each stock a rank from 1 to 3,500 based on its Greenblatt ROC. The stock with the highest ROC received a rank of 1, and the company with the lowest ROC was ranked 3,500. Greenblatt repeated the process with the earnings yield factor, EBIT/TEV. The stock with the highest EBIT/TEV would be assigned a rank of 1, and the stock with the lowest EBIT/TEV would be assigned a rank of 3,500. Greenblatt combined the rankings to find the stock with the best combined return on capital and earnings yield. To do this, he summed each stock's rank for ROC with its rank for EBIT/TEV. So, for example, a stock ranked 12 for ROC and 587 for EBIT/TEV received a combined ranking of 599 (12 + 587), while a stock ranked 2,068 for ROC and 439 for EBIT/TEV received a combined ranking of 2,507 (2,068 + 439). Greenblatt reranked the stocks based on the combined ranking of each. The lower the combined ranking, the better the stock. So in the example above, the stock with the combined rank of 599 is more attractive than the stock with the combined rank of 2,507. Using historical data, Greenblatt studied the performance of a theoretical investor purchasing a portfolio comprising 30 stocks with the lowest combined rankings, holding the portfolio for one year before selling the stocks, and then repeating the process. The results were outstanding.

Greenblatt found that owning a portfolio of the 30 stocks that had the best combination of a high ROC and a high EBIT/TEV would have returned approximately 30.8 percent per year over the period 1988 to 2004. To put this in some context, investing at 30.8 percent per year for 17 years would have turned $10,000 into over $960,000. Over the same period, the market returned 12.3 percent year, which would have turned the same $10,000 into just $71,000. Further, Greenblatt found that the Magic Formula generated those returns while taking much less risk than the overall market. If this is the case, the Magic Formula is truly magic.

Our Examination of the Magic Formula

We have conducted our own independent study of the Magic Formula. Greenblatt does not discuss in granular detail his method of studying the performance of the Magic Formula, so we base our simulations on what we can glean from his public statements and the description of his strategy outlined in *The Little Book that Beats the Market*. Even with a great deal of data torture, we have not been able to replicate Greenblatt's extraordinary results. However, we can confirm that the Magic Formula performs well and has generated substantially better performance than the Standard & Poor's (S&P) 500.[7]

Next, we present the results of our study into the Magic Formula strategy for the period from 1964 to 2011. Figure 2.1 shows the cumulative performance of Greenblatt's Magic Formula strategy plotted against the performance of the S&P 500 TR (total return) and the total return for the 10-year Treasury bond for the period 1964 to 2011. We draw our Magic Formula stocks from a universe comparable to the S&P 500 in terms of size, and we weight the stocks in the portfolios by market capitalization for fair comparison to the benchmark.[8]

Table 2.1 sets out the summary annual performance statistics of the Magic Formula. "MF" represents a portfolio of stocks from the best decile of stocks ranked according to the Magic Formula. Greenblatt's strategy turns $100 invested on January 1, 1964, into $32,313 by December 31, 2011, which represents a compound annual growth rate of 12.79 percent. This return underperforms Greenblatt's results, which found 30.8 percent per year, because we require our stocks to have a larger market capitalization than Greenblatt.[9] We also weight the stocks in the portfolio by market

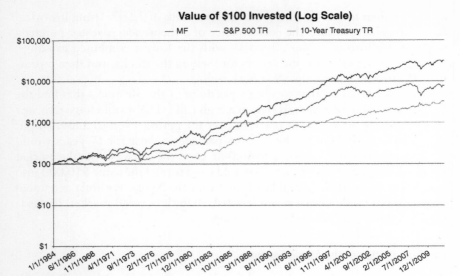

FIGURE 2.1 Greenblatt's Magic Formula Strategy Performance Chart (1964 to 2011)

TABLE 2.1 Performance Statistics for the Magic Formula Strategy (1964 to 2011)

	MF	S&P 500 TR	Ten-Year Treasury TR
CAGR	12.79%	9.52%	7.52%
Standard Deviation	16.54%	15.19%	10.39%
Downside Deviation	11.28%	10.66%	6.23%
Sharpe Ratio	0.50	0.33	0.25
Sortino Ratio (MAR = 5%)	0.75	0.50	0.45
Worst Drawdown	−37.97%	−50.21%	−20.97%
Worst Month Return	−23.90%	−21.58%	−11.24%
Best Month Return	14.91%	16.81%	15.23%
Profitable Months	61.28%	60.94%	59.20%
Rolling 5-Year Win	—	84.72%	78.92%
Rolling 10-Year Win	—	97.37%	96.06%

capitalization to make the returns comparable to the market capitalization–weighted S&P 500, while Greenblatt equally weights the stocks in his portfolios (we discuss our back-test procedures in detail in Chapter 11). Importantly, the Magic Formula's performance does compare favorably with the performance of the S&P 500 over the same period, which would have turned $100 invested on January 1, 1964, into $7,871 by December 31, 2011, an average yearly compound rate of return of 9.52 percent. Table 2.1 confirms that Greenblatt's Magic Formula was a better risk-adjusted bet: Sharpe, Sortino, and drawdowns are all better than the S&P 500.

Figures 2.2(a) and 2.2(b) show the rolling 1-year and 10-year returns for the Magic Formula for the period 1964 to 2011. As Figure 2.2 illustrates, Greenblatt's Magic Formula strategy has underperformed in many single-year periods; however, over longer periods of time, it has proven to perform exceptionally well.

Figure 2.3 shows the performance of each decile ranked according to the Magic Formula for the period 1964 to 2011.

Table 2.2 shows the summary performance statistics for a portfolio formed from each decile ranked according to the Magic Formula for the period 1964 to 2011. "Value" represents the portfolio formed from highest ranked decile, "MF (5)" represents the portfolio formed from the middle decile, and "Glamour" is the portfolio formed from the lowest ranked decile. Figure 2.2 and Table 2.2 demonstrate that the Magic Formula does quite well ranking the stocks. The first and best decile according to the Magic Formula outperforms the worst and last decile. The better deciles also tend to outperform with lower volatility, measured by standard and downside deviation, which leads to better risk-adjusted returns, represented by higher Sharpe and Sortino ratios.

As the figures and tables demonstrate, Greenblatt's Magic Formula has consistently outperformed the market, and with lower relative risk than the market. The nature of compounding means that, over long periods of time, small edges can result in big differences in returns. The small edge generated by the Magic Formula will make an investor very rich relative to the passive S&P 500 investor over the long term. An edge, some patience, and the magic of compounding translate into serious profits.

Our study of the Magic Formula shows that analyzing stocks according to some proxy for price (e.g., a "bargain" or a "fair" price), and some proxy for quality (e.g., a "good" business or a "wonderful" company) can help us to identify value, and provide us with an edge, that can lead to outperformance and excellent risk-adjusted returns. Naturally, we wondered if we could improve on the outstanding performance delivered by the Magic Formula. Are there other simple, logical strategies that can do better?

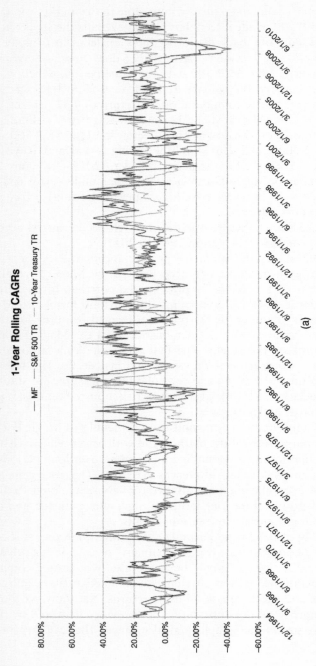

FIGURE 2.2(a) One-Year Rolling Period Performance Statistics: Magic Formula Strategy (1964 to 2011)

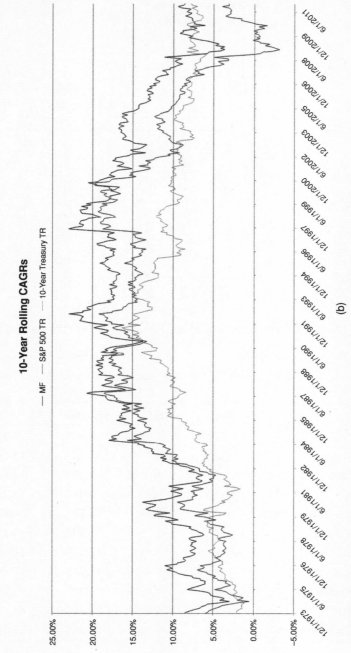

FIGURE 2.2(b) Ten-Year Rolling Period Performance Statistics: Magic Formula Strategy (1964 to 2011)

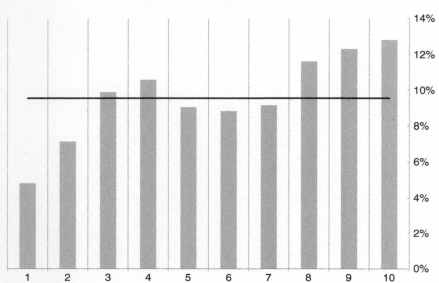

FIGURE 2.3 Decile Performance Chart: Magic Formula Strategy (1964 to 2011)

TABLE 2.2 Glamour, Middle, and Value Decile Performance Statistics: Magic Formula Strategy (1964 to 2011)

	Value	MF(5)	Glamour	S&P 500 TR
CAGR	12.79%	9.03%	4.83%	9.52%
Standard Deviation	16.54%	16.41%	20.96%	15.19%
Downside Deviation	11.28%	11.05%	15.28%	10.66%
Sharpe Ratio	0.50	0.29	0.08	0.33
Sortino Ratio (MAR = 5%)	0.75	0.45	0.13	0.50
Worst Drawdown	−37.97%	−51.03%	−75.80%	−50.21%
Worst Month Return	−23.90%	−19.98%	−27.04%	−21.58%
Best Month Return	14.91%	16.49%	22.36%	16.81%
Profitable Months	61.28%	59.90%	57.99%	60.94%
Rolling 5-Year Win	—	74.08%	95.16%	84.72%
Rolling 10-Year Win	—	85.78%	99.56%	97.37%

IT'S ALL ACADEMIC: IMPROVING QUALITY AND PRICE

We have created a generic, academic alternative to the Magic Formula that we call "Quality and Price." Quality and Price is the *academic* alternative to the Magic Formula because it draws its inspiration from academic research papers. We found the idea for the quality metric in an academic paper by Robert Novy-Marx called "The Other Side of Value: Good Growth and the Gross Profitability Premium."[10] The price ratio is drawn from the early research into value investment by Eugene Fama and Ken French. The Quality and Price strategy, like the Magic Formula, seeks to differentiate between stocks on the basis of ... wait for it ... quality and price. The difference, however, is that Quality and Price uses academically based measures for price and quality that seek to improve on the Magic Formula's factors, which might provide better performance.

Finding Quality, Academically

Recall that the Magic Formula uses Greenblatt's version of return on capital (ROC) as a proxy for a stock's relative quality. The higher the ROC, the higher the stock's quality and the higher the ranking received by the stock. Quality and Price substitutes for ROC a quality measure we call gross profitability to total assets (GPA). GPA is defined as follows:

$$GPA = (Revenue - Cost\ of\ Goods\ Sold)\ /\ Total\ Assets$$

In Quality and Price, the higher a stock's GPA, the higher the quality of the stock.

The rationale for using gross profitability, rather than any other measure of profitability like earnings or EBIT, is simple. Gross profitability is the "cleanest" measure of true economic profitability. According to Novy-Marx[11]:

The farther down the income statement one goes, the more polluted profitability measures become, and the less related they are to true economic profitability. For example, a firm that has both lower production costs and higher sales than its competitors is unambiguously more profitable. Even so, it can easily have lower earnings than its competitors. If the firm is quickly increasing its sales though aggressive advertising, or commissions to its sales force, these actions can, even if optimal, reduce its bottom line income below that of its less profitable competitors. Similarly, if the firm spends on research and development to further increase its production advantage, or invests in organizational capital that will help it maintain its com-petitive advantage, these actions result in lower current earnings. Moreover, capital expenditures that directly increase the scale of the firm's operations further reduce its free cash flows relative to its competitors. These facts suggest constructing the empirical proxy for productivity using gross profits.

A simple example can illustrate Novy-Marx's point. Consider stock A, which generates $100 million in revenues annually, of which $50 million must go to paying the cost of goods sold. In total, stock A has gross profits of $50 million. If stock A invests $30 million in highly productive advertising, stock A's earnings will be $20 million. Next, consider stock B, which generates $100 million in revenue annually, has $80 million in cost of goods sold, but spends nothing on advertising. Stock A's earnings are $20 million and stock B's earnings are $20 million; however, stock A is unambiguously more economically profitable. As this example demonstrates, gross profit is a measure of economic profitability independent of management's immediate operational decisions and is therefore a cleaner measure of the stock's true economic profitability.

Novy-Marx uses total assets as the denominator. He chose total assets because gross profitability is independent of the capital structure adopted by management (interest payments and dividends are accounted for further down the income statement). If the numerator is independent of the capital structure, it makes sense that the denominator should also be independent of the capital structure. Book value is not appropriate here because it's affected by the stock's capital structure (book value equals assets minus liabilities. If we hold assets constant, and increase the liabilities, we reduce book value). Total assets tells us the value of all the assets owned by the firm, and it is not affected by the manner in which they are financed. For this reason, it fits logically with gross profitability. Using GPA gives us the ability to compare the true economic profitability of stocks on a like-for-like basis, independent of the stocks' capital structure, and immediate operational decisions.

GPA has some logical appeal as a measure of quality, but its utility is most obvious empirically. Novy-Marx demonstrates in his paper that gross profits is a better measure of true economic profitability than earnings or free cash flows. It is a better measure because it better predicts future stock returns, and also long-run growth in earnings and free cash flows. He also considers profitability measures constructed using earnings (because "the popular media is preoccupied with earnings, the variable on which Wall Street analysts' forecasts focus") and free cash flows, the measure favored by financial economists. Novy-Marx finds that gross profits-to-total assets is the best measure[12]:

> *In a horse race between these three measures of productivity [net income, free cash flow, and gross profits all divided by total assets], [GPA] is the clear winner. [GPA] has roughly the same power predicting the cross-section of expected returns as book-to-market. It completely subsumes the earnings based measure, and has significantly more power than the measure based on free cash flows ... [GPA] also predicts long run growth in earnings and free cash flow, which may help explain why it is useful in forecasting returns.*

We have also found that GPA is also more predictive on a stand-alone basis than the Magic Formula measure of quality, ROC. Figure 2.4 shows the cumulative performance of the three measures of quality suggested by Novy-Marx (earnings to total assets, or E/TA), free cash flow to total assets (FCF/TA), and GPA, and Greenblatt's ROC measure (MF ROC) plotted against the performance of the S&P 500 for the period 1964 to 2011.

Figure 2.4 demonstrates that GPA is the best-performing measure of quality, outperforming the others considered by Novy-Marx, and the ROC measure favored by Greenblatt in the Magic Formula. In Table 2.3, we explore the performance of various quality measures.

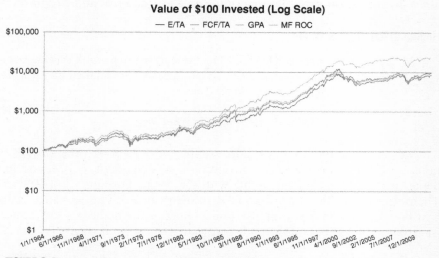

FIGURE 2.4　Quality Measures Cumulative Performance Chart (1964 to 2011)

TABLE 2.3 Performance Statistics for Common Quality Measures (1964 to 2011)

	E/TA	FCF/TA	GPA	MF ROC	S&P 500 TR
CAGR	9.65%	10.02%	12.06%	9.93%	9.52%
Standard Deviation	16.94%	16.88%	16.32%	16.27%	15.19%
Downside Deviation	10.79%	11.45%	11.00%	10.90%	10.66%
Sharpe Ratio	0.32	0.34	0.46	0.34	0.33
Sortino Ratio (MAR = 5%)	0.53	0.53	0.71	0.54	0.50
Worst Drawdown	−51.11%	−56.02%	−49.81%	−49.61%	−50.21%
Worst Month Return	−20.64%	−21.07%	−20.68%	−22.76%	−21.58%
Best Month Return	18.99%	19.82%	21.58%	19.27%	16.81%
Profitable Months	60.07%	60.94%	59.55%	60.42%	60.94%

Table 2.3 shows that most simple quality measures do not provide any differentiation from the market. The compound annual growth rate (CAGR) is indistinguishable from the S&P 500, and the risk-adjusted measures are almost identical. GPA is the only quality metric that adds value as a stand-alone investment strategy, outperforming on a raw and risk-adjusted basis.

Finding Price, Academically

The Magic Formula uses EBIT/TEV as its price measure to rank stocks. For Quality and Price, we substitute the classic measure in finance literature: book value-to-market capitalization (BM):

$$BM = Book\ Value\ /\ Market\ Price$$

We use BM rather than the more familiar price-to-book value or (P/B) notation because the academic convention is to describe it as BM, and it makes it more directly comparable with the Magic Formula's EBIT/TEV. The rationale for BM capitalization is straightforward. Eugene Fama and Ken French consider BM capitalization a superior metric because it varies less from period to period than other measures based on income[13]:

> We always emphasize that different price ratios are just different ways to scale a stock's price with a fundamental, to extract the

information in the cross-section of stock prices about expected returns. One fundamental (book value, earnings, or cashflow) is pretty much as good as another for this job, and the average return spreads produced by different ratios are similar to and, in statistical terms, indistinguishable from one another. We like [book-to-market capitalization] because the book value in the numerator is more stable over time than earnings or cashflow, which is important for keeping turnover down in a value portfolio.

Even so, it's worth noting that Fama and French acknowledge some problems with BM capitalization, as there are with all accounting variables. Sorting stocks on the price-to-earnings or other price ratios produces better returns than BM capitalization over the past 38 years, which we examine in some detail in Chapter 7.

Book Smarts or Street Smarts?

Here, we compare the Magic Formula to our Quality and Price strategy. Quality and Price adheres to the same intellectual framework as the Magic Formula in that, like the Magic Formula, it seeks to identify the best combination of high quality and low price. The difference is that Quality and Price substitutes different measures for the quality and price factors. There are reasonable arguments for adopting the measures used in Quality and Price over those used in the Magic Formula, but it's not an unambiguously more logical approach than the Magic Formula. Whether one combination of measures is better than any other ultimately depends here on their relative performance. So how does Quality and Price stack up against the Magic Formula?

Here, we present the results of our study comparing the Magic Formula and Quality and Price strategies for the period from 1964 to 2011. Figure 2.5 shows the cumulative performance of the Magic Formula and the Quality and Price strategies for the period 1964 to 2011.

Table 2.4 sets out the summary annual performance statistics for Quality and Price. Quality and Price handily outpaces the Magic Formula, turning $100 invested on January 1, 1964, into $93,135 by December 31, 2011, which represents an average yearly compound rate of return of 15.31 percent. Recall that the Magic Formula turned $100 invested on January 1, 1964, into $32,313 by December 31, 2011, which represents a CAGR of 12.79 percent. As you can see in Table 2.4, while much improved, Quality and Price is not a perfect strategy: the better returns are attended by higher volatility and worse drawdowns. Even so, on a risk-adjusted basis, Quality and Price is the winner.

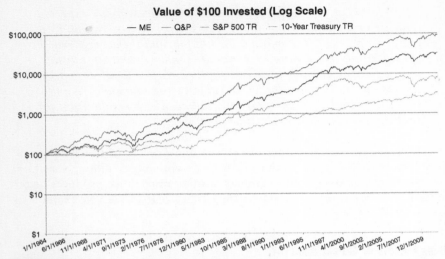

Value of $100 Invested (Log Scale)

— ME — Q&P — S&P 500 TR ⋯ 10-Year Treasury TR

FIGURE 2.5 Magic Formula and Quality and Price Strategies Comparative Performance Chart (1964 to 2011)

Figures 2.6(a) and (b) show the rolling 1- and 10-year returns for Quality and Price for the period 1964 to 2011. Figures 2.6(a) and (b) illustrate that the strategy underperformed in many single-year periods; however, over longer periods of time, Quality and Price stands out.

TABLE 2.4 Summary Annual Performance Statistics: Quality and Price (1964 to 2011)

	MF	Q&P	S&P 500 TR	Ten-Year Treasury TR
CAGR	12.79%	15.31%	9.52%	7.52%
Standard Deviation	16.54%	17.94%	15.19%	10.39%
Downside Deviation	11.28%	12.32%	10.66%	6.23%
Sharpe Ratio	0.50	0.60	0.33	0.25
Sortino Ratio (MAR = 5%)	0.75	0.89	0.50	0.45
Worst Drawdown	−37.97%	−46.50%	−50.21%	−20.97%
Worst Month Return	−23.90%	−23.48%	−21.58%	−11.24%
Best Month Return	14.91%	26.28%	16.81%	15.23%
Profitable Months	61.28%	62.85%	60.94%	59.20%

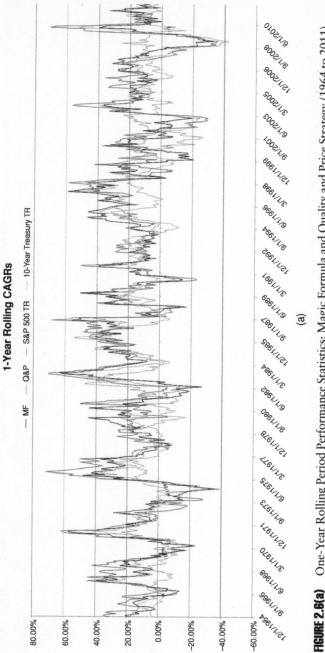

FIGURE 2.6(a)   One-Year Rolling Period Performance Statistics: Magic Formula and Quality and Price Strategy (1964 to 2011)

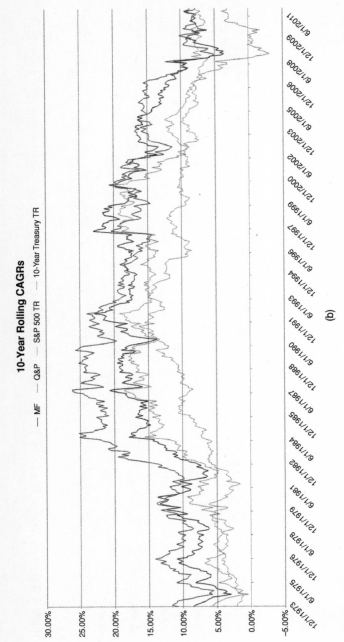

FIGURE 2.6(b)   Ten-Year Rolling Period Performance Statistics: Magic Formula and Quality and Price Strategy (1964 to 2011)

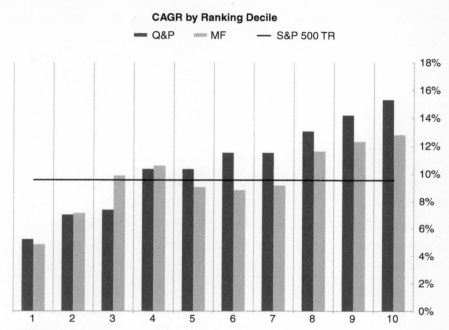

FIGURE 2.7 Decile Performance Chart: Magic Formula and Quality and Price Strategy (1964 to 2011)

Figure 2.7 shows the performance of each decile ranked according to the Magic Formula and Quality and Price for the period 1964 to 2011. Both strategies do a respectable job identifying market-beating stocks.

Table 2.5 shows the summary performance statistics of the value and glamour deciles according to the Magic Formula and Quality and Price for the period 1964 to 2011 period. Table 2.5 demonstrates that Quality and Price does well ranking stocks. The value decile performs well; the glamour decile performs poorly like a portfolio of Internet stocks in March 2000.

Our brief examination of the Magic Formula and its generic academic brother Quality and Price, shows that analyzing stocks along price and quality contours can produce market-beating results. This is not to say that our Quality and Price strategy is the best strategy. Far from it. Even in Quality and Price, the techniques used to identify price and quality are crude. More sophisticated measures exist. At heart, we are value investors, and there are a multitude of metrics used by value investors to find low prices and high quality. We want to know whether there are other, more predictive price and quality metrics than those used by Magic Formula and Quality and Price.

TABLE 2.5 Top and Bottom Decile Performance Statistics: Magic Formula and Quality and Price Strategy (1964 to 2011)

	MF (Value)	MF (Glamour)	Q&P (Value)	Q&P (Glamour)
CAGR	12.79%	4.83%	15.31%	5.18%
Standard Deviation	16.54%	20.96%	17.94%	19.66%
Downside Deviation	11.28%	15.28%	12.32%	14.36%
Sharpe Ratio	0.50	0.08	0.60	0.09
Sortino Ratio (MAR = 5%)	0.75	0.13	0.89	0.14
Worst Drawdown	−37.97%	−75.80%	−46.50%	−67.61%
Worst Month Return	−23.90%	−27.04%	−23.48%	−26.35%
Best Month Return	14.91%	22.36%	26.28%	28.26%
Profitable Months	61.28%	57.99%	62.85%	58.51%

Our study of the Magic Formula and Quality and Price demonstrates the utility of a quantitative approach to investing. Relentlessly pursuing a small edge over a long period of time, through booms and busts, good economies and bad, can lead to outstanding investment results. Like the simple Graham strategy in the first chapter, these strategies have concrete rules that have been applied consistently in our study. The very consistency of the application of the strategy is an important reason for its success: our results are best when we stick closely to the model. If we allow ourselves to be overwhelmed by our nature and deviate from the model, our returns rapidly regress to the market or slightly below, as the next story demonstrates.

STRATEGY IMPLEMENTATION: INVESTORS BEHAVING BADLY

In 2012, Greenblatt conducted a study into the performance of retail investors using the Magic Formula over the period May 1, 2009, to April 30, 2011.[14] Greenblatt's firm offers two choices for retail investors wishing to use the Magic Formula, a "self-managed" account, and a "professionally managed" account. The self-managed account allows clients to choose which stocks to buy and sell from a list of approved Magic Formula stocks. Investors were given guidelines for when to trade the stocks, but were ultimately able to decide when to make those trades. Investors selecting the professionally managed accounts had their trades automated. The firm bought and sold Magic Formula stocks at fixed, preset intervals. During the two-year period in Greenblatt's study, both types of account were able to select only from the approved list of Magic Formula stocks.

What happened? The self-managed accounts, where clients could choose their own stocks from the preapproved list and then exercise discretion about the timing of the trades, slightly underperformed the market. An aggregation of all self-managed accounts for the two-year period showed a cumulative return of 59.4 percent after all expenses, against the 62.7 percent performance of the S&P 500 over the same period. The aggregated professionally managed accounts returned 84.1 percent after all expenses over the same two years, beating the self-managed accounts by almost 25 percent (and the S&P by well over 20 percent). For a two-year period, that's a huge difference. It's especially so since both the self-managed accounts and the professionally managed accounts chose investments from the same list of stocks and followed the same basic game plan. People who self-managed their accounts took a winning system and used their judgment to eliminate all the outperformance and then some. Greenblatt has a few suggestions about what caused the underperformance, and they are related to behavioral biases.

First, self-managed investors didn't buy many of the biggest winners. Instead, they exercised their discretion to avoid them, probably because they looked scary at the time of purchase. This is not a case of randomized errors in the selection of stocks. The investors *reliably* and *systematically* avoided the best performers. Greenblatt says that stocks are often depressed for reasons that are well known. If you watch CNBC, you know why they're cheap. That's part of the reason they're cheap in the first place. They look scary for one reason or another. This is a great example of the representativeness heuristic at work. We know the base case: Buying value stocks—stocks that are cheap relative to trailing measures of cash flow or other measures—generally leads to outperformance. But we neglect the base case because we're fooled by the representativeness heuristic. We can't help it. Stocks only get cheap because they are scary or out of favor. We focus on the scary, near-term issues and ignore the base case. Many self-managed investors eliminated stocks from the preapproved Magic Formula list that are scary because CNBC told them so. And many of these stocks turn out to be the biggest future winners.

Second, the self-managed investors tended to sell after periods of bad performance—either the strategy underperformed for a period of time, or the portfolio simply declined (regardless of whether the self-managed strategy was outperforming or underperforming the declining market)—and they tended to buy after periods of good performance. Greenblatt found that many self-managed investors got discouraged after the Magic Formula strategy underperformed the market or the portfolio declined and simply sold stocks without replacing them, held more cash, or stopped updating the strategy on a periodic basis. To compound the error, they then bought stocks after good periods of performance. Investors tend to sell right after bad performance and buy right after good performance, which, says Greenblatt, is a great way to lower long-term investment returns.

Perhaps Greenblatt's most interesting data point comes from the best-performing self-managed account. It didn't do anything. After the initial account was opened, the client bought stocks from the list and didn't trade again for the entire two-year period. It seems that even doing nothing outperformed all the other active self-managed accounts.

This is, of course, the result that we would expect. We already know that even experts will underperform simple models. We also know that we will continue to underperform when provided with the model's output because we prefer our own judgment—even when we're wrong. These are errors not made out of ignorance (the model presents us with the correct choice), but rather out of incompetence (we simply fail to follow the model). We are incompetent because of cognitive flaws that manifest when we make decisions under uncertainty. We become overwhelmed. We panic. We make the wrong decision. Our detailed analysis of Quality and Price is more complex than the simple two-variable strategies we've encountered so far. We increase the complexity in an effort to generate better results, but increased complexity is a double-edged sword. More steps in the model means more opportunities to make a mistake. How can we create a more complex investment process and expect to maintain discipline when investors have a hard time sticking to a simple strategy like the Magic Formula? We next introduce the concept of a checklist, which is a simple way to break a necessarily complicated process into manageable pieces that can be repeated without errors and with a high success ratio.

The Case for a Checklist

Atul Gawande, a surgeon and professor of surgery at Harvard Medical School, wrote an article in 2007 for *The New Yorker* magazine called "The Checklist,"[15] in which he described the manner in which intensivists successfully manage the incredibly complex range of tasks required to keep alive a patient in intensive care. Gawande's thesis is that modern intensive care medicine has advanced to a degree of complexity that renders it beyond the ability of clinicians to effectively administer without technical help. Intensivists now know how to save people from conditions that were once uniformly fatal—"crushing, burning, bombing, a burst blood vessel in the brain, a ruptured colon, a massive heart attack, rampaging infection"—but the methods involved are so complex that they routinely make simple, preventable mistakes.

Gawande likens modern intensive care's problem to that encountered by B-17 pilots in World War II. A B-17 model crashed spectacularly in test flight, not due to a mechanical fault, investigators concluded, but due to "pilot error." The problem was that the planes had become so advanced that they were, as one newspaper put it, "too much airplane for one man to fly." The solution was the pilot's checklist, a step-by-step guide for take-off, flight, landing, and taxiing. The checklist worked. B-17 pilots flew 1.8 million miles without a single accident, and the Allies ruled the air. Observing that ICU life support is now "too much medicine for one person to fly," Gawande wondered whether checklists might work there, too.

He found an early adopter of the practice in Peter Pronovost, a critical-care specialist at Johns Hopkins Hospital. Pronovost introduced a simple checklist in 2001 to tackle the problem of "line infections": infections that result from the insertion of a central line catheter. Pronovost outlined the five steps to take in order to avoid infections when inserting a line: (1) wash hands with soap; (2) clean the patient's skin with antiseptic; (3) put sterile drapes over the patient; (4) wear a sterile mask, hat, gown, and gloves; and (5) put a sterile dressing over the catheter site once the line is inserted. Pronovost had the nurses in the ICU observe the doctors for a month as they put lines into patients, and record how often they completed each step. He found that in more than a third of patients, the doctors forgot to complete at least one.

Pronovost next had the nurses prompt the doctors if they skipped a step on the checklist, and monitored the results over the following year. The improvement was dramatic: over the first 12 months, the infection rate dropped from 11 percent to zero. Over the next 15 months, only two line infections occurred. Pronovost estimated that the checklist prevented 43 infections and 8 deaths, and saved $2 million in costs. Gawande reports that a broader study in Michigan, published in the *New England Journal of Medicine*, found that the implementation of a checklist protocol reduced the infection rate in Michigan's ICUs by 66 percent. The typical ICU cut its infection rate to zero. Michigan's infection rates fell so low that its average ICU outperformed 90 percent of ICUs nationwide. In the first 18 months of the study, the hospitals saved an estimated $175 million in costs and more than 1,500 lives. The successes have been sustained for almost four years—all, writes Gawande, because of "a stupid little checklist." The implications are clear: intensivists need checklists to walk them step-by-step through the complex ICU processes.

Gawande eventually turned his article into the best-selling book, *The Checklist Manifesto: How to Get Things Right*,[16] which argues for a

THE QUANTITATIVE VALUE CHECKLIST

We have created a quantitative value checklist based on our research. We divide our quantitative value checklist into four parts: risk of permanent impairment of capital, price, quality, and signals. The broad outline of our checklist looks like this:

Step 1: Avoid Stocks that Can Cause a Permanent Loss of Capital (See Part 2)

Check for stocks with high risk of permanent loss of capital caused by:

1. Financial statement manipulation (Chapter 3)
2. Fraud (Chapter 3)
3. Financial distress or bankruptcy (Chapter 4)

Step 2: Find Stocks with the Cheapest Quality (See Part 3)

Check for *franchise power* (Chapter 5):

1. Long-term returns on assets
2. Long-term returns on capital
3. Long-term free cash flow on assets
4. Long-term gross margin growth
5. Long-term gross margin stability

Check for *financial strength* (Chapter 6)

1. Current profitability
2. Liquidity and leverage
3. Recent operational improvements

Step 3: Find Stocks with the Cheapest Prices (See Part 4)

Check *current* (Chapter 7) and *long-term* and *composite* (Chapter 8) pricing ratios.

Step 4: Find Stocks with Corroborative Signals (See Part 5)

Check for catalysts (Chapter 9):

1. Buyback announcements
2. Insider buying
3. Institutional buying, both passive and activist
4. Short interest

The beauty of quantitative value investing is that we can test the performance of our checklist using historical data. Parts Two, Three, and Four of the checklist are the heart of our quantitative value model. Over the next nine chapters we describe the rationale for each check on our list, including the research behind it, and the returns to each fragment of the strategy. We then describe in Part Six the investment simulation methods we use to ensure that the back-test results we find are robust, and, finally, examine the structure and performance of the strategy, its risk profile, and its return.

broader implementation of checklists. Gawande believes that in many fields, the problem is not a lack of knowledge but in making sure we apply the knowledge we do have consistently and correctly. He includes examples of successes in fields as diverse as weather prediction, skyscraper construction, and, yes, even investment.

NOTES

1. Warren Buffett, "Shareholder Letter," Berkshire Hathaway, Inc. Annual Report, 2008.
2. Joel Greenblatt, *The Little Book that Beats the Market* (Hoboken, NJ: John Wiley & Sons, 2005).
3. Joel Greenblatt, *You Can Be a Stock Market Genius: Uncover the Secret Hiding Places of Stock Market Profits* (New York: Touchstone, 1999).
4. Warren Buffett, "Chairman's Letter," Berkshire Hathaway, Inc. Annual Report, 1989.
5. Warren Buffett, "Shareholder Letter," Berkshire Hathaway, Inc. Annual Report, 1977
6. Aswath Damodaran, "Return on Capital, Return on Invested Capital (ROIC), and Return on Equity (ROE): Measurement and Implications." Accessed

July   2007,   from   *http://pages.stern.nyu.edu/~adamodar/pdfiles/papers/ returnmeasures.pdf.*

7. Unless we explicitly state otherwise, the simulation assumptions and methodology we use to conduct all the studies in this book, including our examination of the Magic Formula and Graham's Simple Value Strategy in Chapter 1, are described in detail in Chapter 11.

8. We perform all our analyses on an equal-weight basis and find similar conclusions for all analyses in the book.

9. We have tried multiple waiting systems, rebalance periods, and portfolio constructions (i.e., we mined the data) and were unable to generate returns over the 1988 to 2004 period that were close to 30.8 percent a year.

10. Robert Novy-Marx, "The Other Side of Value: Good Growth and the Gross Profitability Premium" (April 2010). NBER Working Paper No. w15940. Available at *http://ssrn.com/abstract=1598056.*

11. Ibid.

12. Ibid.

13. Eugene Fama and Kenneth French, "Q&A: Why Use Book Value to Sort Stocks?" Fama/French Forum, June 27, 2011; *www.dimensional.com/ famafrench/2011/06/qa-why-use-book-value-to-sort-stocks.html.*

14. Joel Greenblatt, "Adding Your Two Cents May Cost a Lot Over the Long Term." *Perspectives, Morningstar,* January 16, 2012; *http://news.morningstar. com/articlenet/SubmissionsArticle.aspx?submissionid=134195.xml&part=2.*

15. Atul Gawande, "The Checklist." *The New Yorker,* Annals of Medicine (December 10, 2007); *www.newyorker.com/reporting/2007/12/10/071210fa_fact_ gawande?currentPage=2.*

16. Atul Gawande, *The Checklist Manifesto: How to Get Things Right* (New York: Metropolitan Books, 2009).

Two

Margin of Safety—How to Avoid a Permanent Loss of Capital

In Part Two, we describe the first step in our checklist: how to avoid stocks at risk of a permanent loss of capital. The potential for a total loss manifests in three ways: financial statement manipulation, fraud, and financial distress and bankruptcy. All are three different risks, but are closely related and frequently found together. For example, management may manipulate a stock's financial statements to create the illusion of better performance than exists in reality. They may justify it on the basis that these are "white lies" amounting to something less than fraud. Where manipulation exists we can't trust our valuation or management. Where there's financial statement manipulation, it's likely that there are other cockroaches in the kitchen, and it's a short step to outright fraud.

Outright fraud is a high-risk situation for investors. Not only are the financial statements incorrect, but management is stealing from the company. The fraud can go on only for a limited period of time, and the dénouement is often financial distress and bankruptcy for the stock. It's also possible that the cause and effect is reversed, and the financial distress leads a panicked management to manipulate the financial statements to stave off creditors. The end is rarely pretty for the common stockholder, who ranks last in the pecking order behind all other stakeholders.

Firms subject to financial statement manipulation, fraud, or financial risk have the potential to cause a total and permanent destruction of capital. There is no price at which we would be comfortable buying them. For this reason, we wish to avoid them completely, and we do so by removing them from our investable universe. We discuss the first two problem areas—financial statement manipulation and outright fraud—in Chapter 3, and the third—financial distress and bankruptcy risk—in Chapter 4.

Hornswoggled! Eliminating Earnings Manipulators and Outright Frauds

"[Accounting] shenanigans have a way of snowballing: Once a company moves earnings from one period to another, operating shortfalls that occur thereafter require it to engage in further accounting maneuvers that must be even more "heroic." These can turn fudging into fraud. (More money, it has been noted, has been stolen with the point of a pen than at the point of a gun.)"
—Warren Buffett, Shareholder Letter, 2000

In *The Great Crash of 1929*,[1] John Kenneth Galbraith referred to embezzlement as "the most interesting of crimes":

Alone among the various forms of larceny it has a time parameter. Weeks, months, or even years may elapse between the commission of the crime and its discovery. (This is a period, incidentally, when the embezzler has his gain and the man who has been embezzled, oddly enough, feels no loss. There is a net increase in psychic wealth.) At any given time there exists an inventory of undiscovered embezzlement in—or more precisely, not in—the country's businesses and banks. This inventory—it should perhaps be called the bezzle—amounts at any moment to many millions of dollars. It also varies in size with the business cycle.

The "bezzle" is the sum of all undiscovered swindles, hornswoggles, chisels, and flimflammery perpetrated on the economy. According to Galbraith, it swells in good times, when money is plentiful, and shrinks in the depression as audits become more penetrating and meticulous. It is by definition hidden, and a potential foil to our best-laid quantitative plans. Why so? Well, our quantitative analysis can only be as accurate as the underlying data. For example, several of our quality measures rely on some form of earnings to determine the stock's return on capital or assets employed. To the extent that the numbers reported in the financial statements are fraudulent or manipulated, the output will be plain wrong, as this well-known proof shows:

$$GI \times (1 + e^{-i\omega t})^{\sum_1^n \sin x} = GO \times (1 + e^{-i\omega t})^{\sum_1^n \sin x} GI$$

which simplifies to
$$GI = GO,$$

where   GI = garbage in
        GO = garbage out
        QED.

All is not lost. There are ways to tease out of the data some of the tricks that the fraudsters and manipulators use, from fudging to outright fraud.

We propose three measures to shrink the bezzle. The first is scaled total accruals (STA), which uncovers early-stage earnings manipulations. The second is scaled net operating assets (SNOA) which captures a management's historical attempts at earnings manipulation. The final weapon in our arsenal is the probability of manipulation, or PROBM, a comprehensive predictive tool that identifies stocks with a high probability of fraud or manipulation. First, we examine the gentle art of earnings manipulation, and then we use the probability of manipulation tool to examine the enormous Enron fraud. Could we have found Enron in advance of its eventual demise?

ACCRUALS AND THE ART OF EARNINGS MANIPULATION

In his 2002 Chairman's Letter, Warren Buffett suggested that investors be wary of companies displaying what he described as "weak accounting"[2]:

> *When managements take the low road in aspects that are visible, it is likely they are following a similar path behind the scenes. There is seldom just one cockroach in the kitchen.*

Buffett describes earnings manipulation—the "smoothing" of earnings and "big bath" accounting—as "'white lie' techniques employed by otherwise upright managements" who view GAAP "not as a standard to be met, but as an obstacle to overcome."[3] Earnings manipulation may be a more benign form of deceit, but it still contributes to the bezzle, and that's a tax we don't want to pay.

In order to manipulate earnings, managers need some discretion over the income statement. Accounting standards provide this discretion because they must accommodate a wide variety of businesses. The crowd favorite for frauds and manipulations is the humble accrual. To accrue means to accumulate, collect, grow, or increase. Accruals apply to all kinds of accounting items, but let's take a simple accrual example to demonstrate how accruals work and how they can create valuation anomalies (see Table 3.1).

Let's say we have two boys, Bernie and Warren, who mow lawns every spring.[4] During April, May, and June, each mows 10 lawns, and then sends out an invoice to each customer that says, "Pay $10 for mowing services rendered." (Incidentally, if you know any kids who will mow lawns for $10, please call us.) The two budding capitalists slowly receive payments, and, by the end of September, everyone who is going to pay has gotten around to paying her or his bill. Now let's say that every year the same thing happens to each kid: two of the neighbors just won't pay (generally accepted accounting principles has some detailed approaches to this situation, but we're going to skip the gory details for now).

At the end of June, Bernie's simplified income statement shows $100 in net income, and his balance sheet shows $100 in accounts receivable. By September, something terrible has become apparent: two customers haven't paid. Bernie's income statement still shows net income of $100 for the six months, but now he has accounts receivable of $20, and his cash flow is only $80. Over the summer Bernie's net income exceeded his cash flow by $20. Unless he can somehow get the two deadbeats to pay up, which he can't, he is eventually going to have to take a charge to his income statement to get rid of those bad debts and clean up his balance sheet. Bernie would rather postpone the bad news.

Now let's say Warren has more business and accounting savvy. You ask him at the end of June how he is doing. Since he is more realistic about what he hopes to make, he tells you that his net income is only $80 (having anticipated and now expensed the bad debt). Meanwhile, his balance sheet shows $80 in accounts receivable (net of the bad debt). At the end of September, he has already taken his medicine (expensed the bad debt), collected his $80, and has a clean balance sheet with no receivables on it. Now Warren shows net income of $80 and cash flow of $80. Warren's net income equals his cash flow. The $80 in net income represents what Warren's business has made over the summer.

TABLE 3.1   Bernie's and Warren's Simplified Financial Statements

	Bernie	Warren
Income Statement		
Revenue	$100	$100
Bad Debts	0	($20)
Net Income	$100	$80
Cash Flow Statement		
Cash from Ops	$80	$80
Balance Sheet		
Accounts Receivable	$20	$0

Now let's say you have the chance to buy a 10 percent interest in either business. Each boy tells you he wants an earnings multiple of 5 on his business. So you can buy either half of Bernie's business for $250 (net income of $100 × 5 = $500 × 50 percent = $250) or half of Warren's business for $200 (net income of $80 × 5 = $400 × 50 percent = $200). Which deal do you prefer? Warren's deal is obviously better. First, it's cheaper. We know that both businesses are the same. Both businesses therefore have the same intrinsic value, but Warren's deal is 20 percent cheaper than Bernie's. The low quality of Bernie's earnings means that his net income is overstated, and so is the value of his business. Second, Warren is the better manager. His figures more accurately describe the underlying economics of his business, and he looks to be the more honest and realistic of the two, at least in this regard. Of course, there are many ways to manipulate earnings. Bernie's bad debt expense trick is just one. Interestingly, simply measuring net income against cash flow captures many of the earnings manipulations, and, as it turns out, is predictive of future returns.

There is a vast literature on the relationship between accruals, manipulation, and stock returns. In "Earnings Management and the Long-Run Market Performance of IPOs,"[5] authors Teoh, Welch, and Wong found evidence that issuers with unusually high accruals in the initial public offering (IPO) year experience poor stock return performance in the three years after IPO. Some IPO stocks report unusually high earnings by adopting discretionary accounting accrual adjustments that raise reported earnings relative to actual cash flows. If buyers are guided by earnings but are unaware that earnings are inflated by the generous use of accruals, they may overpay. As further information about the stock is revealed over time by the media, analysts' reports, and subsequent financial statements, investors recognize that earnings are not keeping up with the early promise and may lose their optimism. All else being equal, the greater the earnings management at the time of offering, the larger the ultimate price correction.

DuCharme, Malatesta, and Sefcik show in "Earnings Management, Stock Issues, and Shareholder Lawsuits"[6] that stock offers are accompanied by unusual accounting accruals, and many of the most egregious offers subsequently attract lawsuits. Some stocks opportunistically manipulate earnings upward before stock issues rendering themselves vulnerable to litigation. Chou, Gombola, and Liu, in "Earnings Management and Stock Performance of Reverse Leveraged Buyouts,"[7] provide further evidence of earnings manipulation around security offerings. The authors found significant discretionary current accruals corresponding with offerings of reverse leveraged buyouts (LBOs). Issuers in the most "aggressive" quartile of earnings management—those that make the largest adjustments—have a one-year aftermarket return that is between 15 percent and 25 percent less than the most "conservative" quartile—those that make the least adjustments. With so much evidence that management use accruals to manipulate earnings, value investors are well paid to focus on the topic. One reason why manipulation may have gone largely undetected by the investment community is the dearth of manipulation detection tools. The next section outlines several approaches to detect accrual earnings manipulation.

How to Detect Earnings Manipulation

The most well-known article on accruals is from Richard Sloan, who famously left academia for a position at Barclays Global Investors after identifying the "accrual anomaly" in his article "Do Stock Prices Fully Reflect Information in Accruals and Cash Flows about Future Earnings?"[8] Professor Sloan's paper investigates whether stock prices reflect information about future earnings contained in the accrual and cash flow components of current earnings. Sloan finds that stock prices act as if investors "fixate" on earnings or, in other words, whether they think Warren and Bernie's business are different, when we've shown that they are the same. The returns to a portfolio that buys stocks with low-scaled total accruals and shorts stocks with high-scaled total accruals are exceptional. Sloan uses a complicated measure to identify scaled total accruals (STA). Sloan calculates STA using information from the balance sheet and income statement, as follows:

$$STA = (CA - CL - DEP) \, / \, Total \; Assets$$

where CA = change in current assets – change in cash and equivalents
  CL = change in current liabilities – change in LT debt included in
      current liabilities – change in income taxes payable
  DEP = depreciation and amortization expense

Sloan's method is useful for researchers running investment simulations on accrual-based strategies. Compustat has data only for the variable "cash flow from operations" from 1987, which leaves a limited time in which to study stock returns.

For current investments, one can use a simplified scaled total accruals variable because cash flow statement data is readily available in real time. The simple accrual measure can be calculated in the following manner:

STA = (Net Income – Cash Flow from Operations) / Total Assets

Authors Hirshleifer, Hou, Teoh, and Zhang developed another accrual-related metric that they discuss in their paper, "Do Investors Overvalue Firms with Bloated Balance Sheets?"[9] The authors observe that when the growth in cumulative accruals (net operating income) outstrips the growth in cumulative free cash flow, the balance sheet becomes "bloated," and firms find it increasingly difficult to sustain earnings growth. During the 1964 to 2002 sample period, the authors find that net operating assets scaled by total assets is a strong predictor of poor long-term stock returns. Papanastasopoulos, Thomakos, and Wang took the analysis a step further in "Information in Balance Sheets for Future Stock Returns: Evidence from Net Operating Assets,"[10] demonstrating that the relationship between scaled net operating assets and stock returns is negative (i.e., the higher the net operating assets, the lower the stock returns) due to a combination of opportunistic earnings manipulation and over investment.

We create a variable based on the work of Hirshleifer et al. called scaled net operating assets, or SNOA:

SNOA = (Operating Assets – Operating Liabilities) / Total Assets

where   OA = total assets – cash and equivalents
        OL = total assets – ST debt – LT debt – minority interest –
             preferred stock – book common equity

The SNOA strategy buys stocks with low SNOA and shorts stocks with high SNOA. Figure 3.1 shows the long/short SNOA strategy over the period 1965 to 2002 for equal-weight and market-weight portfolios.

We examined the long/short STA and SNOA strategies described above in our universe of stocks. For our analysis, we created long/short monthly return data by subtracting the return on the portfolio of top-decile firms and subtracting the return on a portfolio of companies in the lowest-decile portfolio. The results are set out in Figures 3.2 and 3.3.

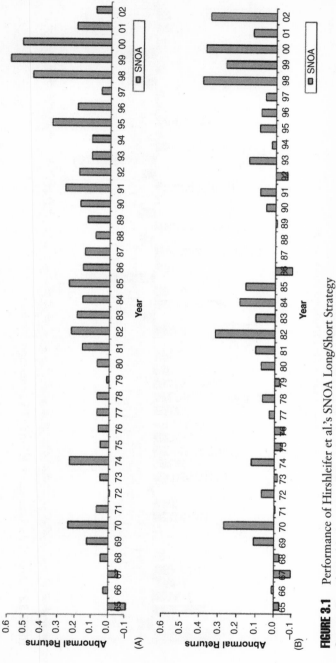

FIGURE 3.1 Performance of Hirshleifer et al.'s SNOA Long/Short Strategy

Source: David Hirshleifer, Kewei Hou, Siew Hong Teoh, and Yinglei Zhang, 2004, "Do Stock Prices Fully Reflect Information in Accruals and Cash Flows about Future Earnings?" *Journal of Accounting and Economics* 38: 297–331.

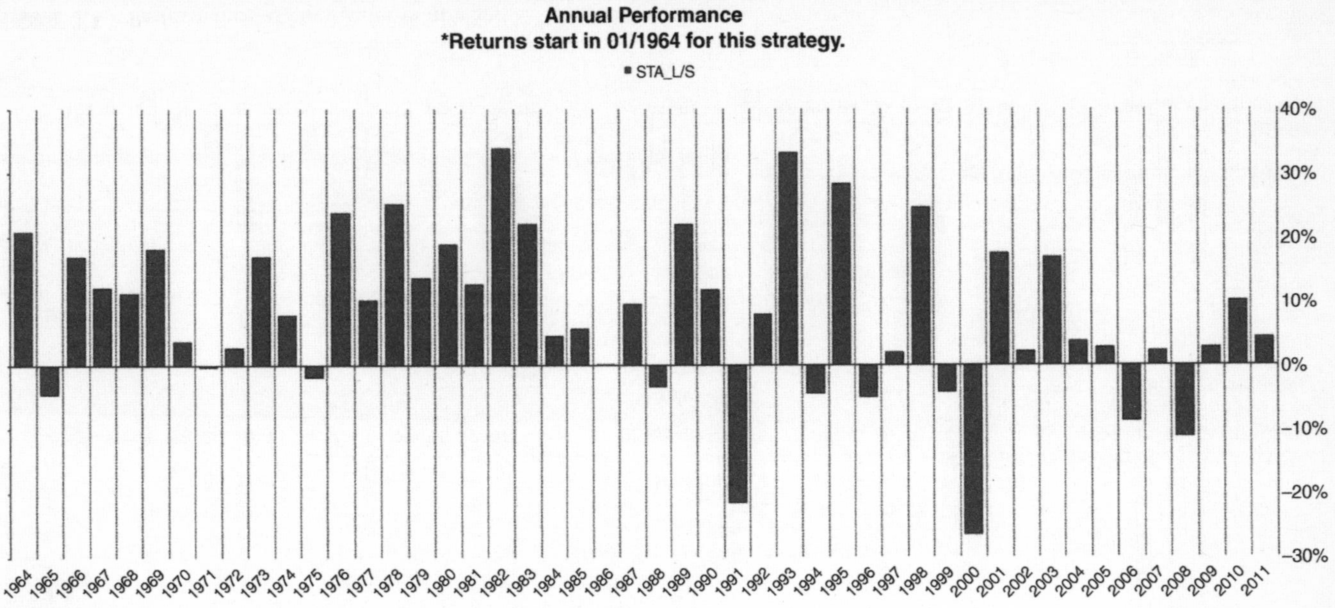

Annual Performance
*Returns start in 01/1964 for this strategy.

● STA_L/S

FIGURE 3.2 Annual Performance of Sloan's STA Long/Short Strategy

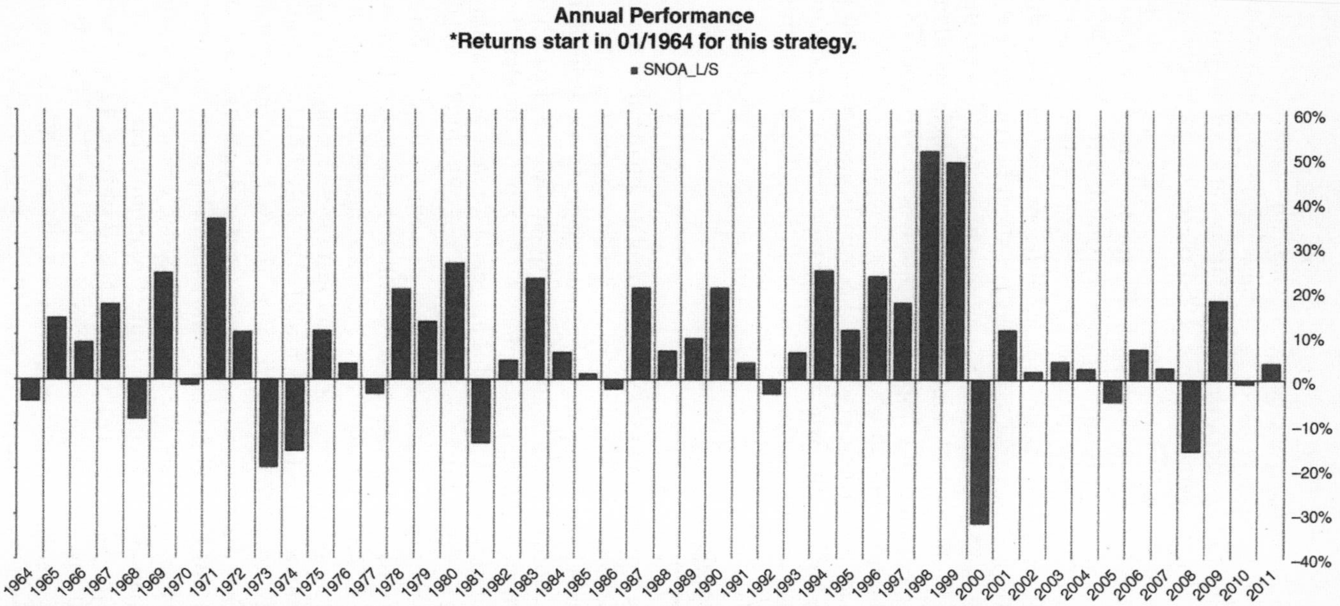

Annual Performance

*Returns start in 01/1964 for this strategy.

■ SNOA_L/S

FIGURE 3.3 Annual Performance of Hirshleifer's SNOA Long/Short Strategy (1964 to 2011) replication

71

Figure 3.2 shows what happens when an academic takes an idea to Wall Street—the effect vanishes or diminishes. From 1964 to 1996 (when Sloan published his paper), the STA strategy on a liquid universe had an exceptional run. Nonetheless, after 1996 there is a decidedly worse run of performance from the STA strategy.

The SNOA long/short strategy in Figure 3.3 shows a similar pattern as STA: SNOA long/short returns effectively vanish after 2000. While the two accrual metrics have degraded over time with respect to their investment performance, the measures do capture different aspects of accruals that we find useful. In the case of STA, the measure identifies the current flow of accruals, whereas SNOA captures the growth of accruals over time.

We use both the STA and SNOA metrics to help us identify stocks manipulating earnings. It's important to note that STA and SNOA are not measures of quality like those analyzed in Chapters 5 and 6. Instead, STA and SNOA act as gatekeepers. They keep us from investing in stocks that appear to be high quality, when in fact the numbers are heavily manipulated by management to create that illusion, and the reality is something less.

PREDICTING PROBMs

Accruals are not the only way to manipulate financial statements. For a more holistic view on manipulation, we need to dig deeper into the academic literature. Dr. Messod Beneish, an accounting professor at Indiana University's Kelley School of Business, outlined a quantitative approach to detecting financial statement manipulation in his 1999 paper "The Detection of Earnings Manipulation."[11] He based his model on forensic accounting principles, calling it the "probability of manipulation," or "PROBM" model.

Despite the sophisticated statistical procedures used by Beneish, his research is easy to understand. First, he collated a sample of known earnings manipulators. Then he identified their distinguishing characteristics and used those characteristics to create a model for detecting manipulation. Simple. The result was the PROBM model. The PROBM model includes variables that are designed to capture either the effects of manipulation or preconditions that may incentivize management to engage in such activity. The resulting PROBM model predicts future financial statement manipulators.

In out-of-sample tests, the PROBM model identifies approximately half of the companies involved in earnings manipulation prior to public discovery. The model correctly identified, ahead of time, 12 of the 17 highest-profile fraud cases in the period 1998 to 2002.[12] The PROBM model also consistently predicted stock returns over 1993 to 2007. Between 1993 and 2007, a 15-year period after the model's data, stocks that were flagged as potential earnings manipulators by the model returned 9.7 percent lower returns each year than stocks that were not flagged. While relatively few management teams are actually indicted for accounting fraud, the probability of manipulation generated by the model may well be indicative of the stock's prospects. Stocks that share common attributes with known earnings manipulators, also have other problems (either lower earnings quality or more challenging economic conditions) that are not yet fully transparent to the market. So while the accounting games they engage in might not result in indictments, on average these stocks tend to earn lower returns.

The PROBM model is made up of the following components:

- *DSRI* = **days' sales in receivables index.** Measured as the ratio of days' sales in receivables in year t to year $t - 1$. Large increases could indicate attempts by management to inflate revenues
- *GMI* = **gross margin index.** Measured as the ratio of gross margin in year $t - 1$ to gross margin in year t. Gross margin has deteriorated when this index is above 1. All else being equal, a firm with poor prospects is more likely to engage in manipulation.
- *AQI* = **asset quality index.** Asset quality is measured as the ratio of non-current assets other than plant, property and equipment to total assets. AQI measures the proportion of total assets where future benefits are more opaque and the assets are considered intangible. The measure may indicate attempts at cost deferrals in the form of intangible assets on the balance sheet.
- *SGI* = **sales growth index.** Ratio of sales in year t to sales in year $t - 1$. Sales growth does not indicate manipulation; however, high sales growth does create certain expectations for management—many of which are unsustainable. Managers who face decelerating fundamentals and who currently manage high-expected-growth firms have high incentive to manipulate earnings.
- *DEPI* = **depreciation index.** Measured as the ratio of the rate of depreciation in year $t - 1$ to the corresponding rate in year t. DEPI greater than 1 indicates that assets are being depreciated at a slower rate. Managers may be adjusting depreciation methods to temporarily inflate earnings.
- *SGAI* = **sales, general and administrative expenses index.** The ratio of SGA expenses in year t relative to year $t - 1$. Firms with growing SGA may indicate managers who are capturing firm value via higher salaries.
- *LVGI* = **leverage index.** The ratio of total debt to total assets in year t relative to year $t - 1$. An LVGI greater than 1 indicates an increase in leverage, which may increase the probability that a firm will breach a debt covenant. All else being equal, the probability of manipulation is higher in the face of a potential covenant breach.

- *TATA* = **total accruals to total assets.** Total accruals calculated as the change in working capital accounts other than cash less depreciation. High accruals indicate a higher likelihood of earnings manipulation.

The eight variables from PROBM are then weighted together according to the following:

$$PROBM = -4.84 + 0.92 \times DSRI + 0.528 \times GMI + 0.4.404 \times AQI + 0.892 \times SGI + 0.115 \times DEPI - 0.172 \times SGAI + 4.679 \times TATA - 0.327 \times LVGI$$

In order to use the PROBM model as a practical investment tool, we calculate a PROBM for every single stock in our investable universe. We have to transform the PROBM measure (which is referred to as a "probit") into a value that can be interpreted as the probability of manipulation (PMAN). The transformation equation is as follows $PMAN = CDF(PROBM)$, where CDF is the cumulative density function for a normal $(0,1)$ variable.[13] You don't have to understand the calculation to understand PMAN. It's easy to interpret. PMAN is simply the chance of manipulation. A PMAN value of zero would imply no chance of manipulation, while a PMAN value of one indicates that manipulation is certain.

Enron's PROBMs

Before its bankruptcy on December 2, 2001, Enron Corporation was a highly regarded American energy, commodities, and services company based in Houston, Texas. It employed approximately 20,000 staff and was one of the world's leading electricity, natural gas, communications, and pulp and paper companies. It was touted by Wall Street for its stellar revenue growth (666 percent over the decade from 1990), massive revenues (nearly $101 billion in 2000), huge net income of $1.4 billion, and a market capitalization of $61.4 billion (at which it sported a price-to-earnings ratio of 44). Table 3.2 sets out some of Enron's financials.

Enron was perceived to be a company of the highest quality, run by the "smartest guys in the room," as Bethany McLean described them in her book of the same name.[14] *Fortune* magazine named it "America's Most Innovative Company" for six consecutive years. The stock followed suit, as the chart in Figure 3.4 demonstrates.

In March 2001, McLean wrote an article for *Fortune* magazine called "Is Enron Overpriced?"[15] in which she pointed out that Enron's financial statements were impenetrable to "even quantitatively minded Wall Streeters." She quoted one analyst who said, "Enron is a big black box." In the

TABLE 3.2   Enron Select Financials (1990 through 2000)

Year Ending	Revenues ($ million)	NI ($ million)	EBIT ($ million)
1990	$ 13,165.36	$ 431.26	$202.18
1991	$ 5,562.67	$ 498.00	$241.78
1992	$ 6,324.75	$ 620.10	$306.19
1993	$ 7,972.48	$ 617.48	$332.52
1994	$ 8,983.72	$ 715.77	$453.41
1995	$ 9,189.00	$ 618.00	$519.69
1996	$ 13,289.00	$ 690.00	$584.00
1997	$ 20,273.00	$ 790.00	$105.00
1998	$ 31,260.00	$1,439.00	$703.00
1999	$ 40,112.00	$1,243.00	$893.00
2000	$100,789.00	$1,953.00	$979.00
Total Growth	666%	353%	384%

FIGURE 3.4   Value of $100 Invested in Enron

TABLE 3.3   Enron's PROBM Results (1994 to 2000)

	DSRI	GMI	AQI	SGI	DEPI	SGAI[16]	LVGI	TATA	PROBM	PMAN
1994	0.761	1.048	1.155	1.127	1.038	1.000	0.919	−0.088	−2.509	0.6%
1995	1.645	1.127	0.992	1.023	1.039	1.000	0.974	−0.028	−1.802	3.6%
1996	0.989	1.304	1.136	1.446	0.946	1.000	1.053	−0.033	−1.915	2.8%
1997	0.625	1.278	1.308	1.526	1.017	1.000	1.041	−0.022	−2.107	1.8%
1998	0.872	0.946	1.063	1.542	0.853	1.000	1.007	−0.038	−2.154	1.6%
1999	0.956	1.376	1.064	1.283	0.956	1.000	0.908	−0.020	−2.028	2.1%
2000	1.376	1.891	0.771	2.513	1.110	1.000	1.354	−0.004	−0.511	30.5%

article, McLean noted that she had not been able to find anyone who could satisfactorily answer the simple question, "How exactly does Enron make its money?"

By October 2001, when Enron collapsed into bankruptcy, it was clear that the most innovative group at Enron was its accounting department. Its financial statements were impressive, but they were more fiction than fact. Is it possible that a quantitatively minded analyst could in fact have penetrated Enron's black box? Let's examine the PROBM model's ability to predict the largest corporate fraud in history.

In Table 3.3, we set out the historical PROBM model estimates for Enron. It shows the year-by-year PROBM and PMAN results leading up to the Enron scandal revealed in October 2001.

The results aren't particularly interesting for the period 1994 through 1999. The PMAN (probability of manipulation) floats between 1 percent in 1994, peaks at 5.2 percent the next year and then drifts down for the next few year. Even 5.2 percent is weak signal, suggesting little manipulation or fraud. The results get much more interesting in 2000, approximately a year before unveiling of the fraud.

Here is a detailed breakdown of the calculations for 2000. The "mean index" shows the average score in each variable for manipulators—"Mean Index (Manipulators)"—and nonmanipulators—"Mean Index (Nonmanipulators)—alike.[17] The closer Enron's variable is to the Mean Index (Manipulators), the more likely it is to be manipulating its financial statements:

- DSRI = 1.376 (Red Flag)
  - Mean Index (Nonmanipulators) = 1.031
  - Mean Index (Manipulators) = 1.465

- GMI = 2.162 (Red Flag)
  - Mean Index (Nonmanipulators) = 1.014
  - Mean Index (Manipulators) = 1.193
- AQI = 0.771
  - Mean Index (Nonmanipulators) = 1.039
  - Mean Index (Manipulators) = 1.254
- SGI = 2.513 (Red Flag)
  - Mean Index (Nonmanipulators) = 1.134
  - Mean Index (Manipulators) = 1.607
- DEPI = 1.11 (Red Flag)
  - Mean Index (Nonmanipulators) = 1.001
  - Mean Index (Manipulators) = 1.077
- SGAI = 1.0
  - Mean Index (Nonmanipulators) = 1.054
  - Mean Index (Manipulators) = 1.041
- LVGI = 1.354 (Red Flag)
  - Mean Index (Nonmanipulators) = 1.037
  - Mean Index (Manipulators) = 1.111
- TATA = 0.014
  - Mean Index (Nonmanipulators) = 0.018
  - Mean Index (Manipulators) = 0.031

PROBM = −0.511, which implies PMAN = CDF (−0.551) = 30.5 percent.

Enron's 2000 PMAN score sent a very strong signal that something fishy was occurring. A 30.5 percent chance of earnings manipulation is a clear indication that Enron's financial statements were being manipulated. In Beneish's 1999 study, a typical stock actually engaging in manipulation had a PMAN score of 39.86 percent prior to the exposure of shenanigans. Moreover, five of the model's signals—DSRI, GMI, SGI, DEPI, and LVGI—received red flags, indicating potential manipulation. The PROBM model appears to be effective at detecting accounting fraud in one of the most famous cases in recent years.

But did anyone actually use the model to detect Enron's financial chicanery? It seems someone did. A group of MBA students at Cornell University posted the earliest warning about Enron's accounting manipulation score using the PROBM model a year before the first analyst reports. Greg Morris recounts the story in "Enron 101."[18] In May 2000, Cornell MBA students enrolled in Professor Charles M. C. Lee's course in financial statement analysis selected Enron as the subject of their term project. At the time, Enron was trading around $90, and, as we have seen, was well regarded by Wall Street. To the students' own surprise, the team returned a "sell" recommendation based on the strict application of the PROBM model, noting that it indicated likely earnings manipulation. By October 2000, the students noticed further weakening on Enron's PROBM model scores, increasing the chances of earnings manipulation. The students knew that Enron was a highly admired company and were not convinced that it was a fraud. They did, however, recommend selling Enron. How did a team of business school students see plainly what professional analysts, asset managers, and regulators missed? They applied the PROBM model.

In an ideal world, financial statements would convey a faithful portrait of the stock's financial affairs. It is not an ideal world. As long as investors— including supposedly sophisticated ones—place rosy valuations on reported earnings that march steadily upward, some managers and promoters will exploit accounting standards to paint that picture.[19] Investors need to be alert to the bezzle. Fortunately, there are several methods that allow us to look deeper into financial statements to extract some truth about a stock's underlying quality.

We have proposed three measures to identify financial statement manipulation. The first was scaled total accruals or STA, which sought to uncover earnings manipulations. It does so by comparing net income to cash flow from operations and then scaling the resulting accrual to total assets. The greater the scaled total accrual, the more likely earnings are being manipulated. The utility of the STA measure as a predictive method has diminished over time.

When the growth in cumulative accruals (net operating income) outstrips the growth in cumulative free cash flow, the balance sheet becomes "bloated." Stocks with balance sheets bloated in this way find it increasingly difficult to sustain earnings growth. This "bloated balance sheet" phenomenon is measured by our second metric, scaled net operating assets, or SNOA. SNOA detects management's historical attempts at earnings manipulation, and continues to be a strong predictor of poor long-term stock returns.

The final weapon in our arsenal is PROBM, a comprehensive predictive tool that identifies stocks with a high probability of fraud or manipulation. The PROBM tool detected Enron's financial statement manipulations at least 12 months ahead of its bankruptcy. In the narrow view, the Enron example demonstrates the power of a tool like PROBM, but it also has a broader lesson. It was heresy in 2000 to declare Enron a fraud. The conventional wisdom on Wall Street was that Enron was America's most innovative company run by the smartest guys in the room. PROBM showed that the emperor had no clothes. This is the power of pure, quantitative analysis: it is free from bias. In the next chapter, we examine another objective quantitative tool for uncovering financial distress and calculating financial distress risk.

NOTES

1. Galbraith, John Kenneth. *The Great Crash of 1929* (New York: Mariner Books, 1997).
2. Warren Buffett, "Chairman's Letter," Berkshire Hathaway, Inc. Annual Report, 2002.
3. Warren Buffett, "Chairman's Letter," Berkshire Hathaway, Inc. Annual Report, 1988.
4. This story was first described to us by David P. Foulke as a way to describe accrual shenanigans in a simple way.
5. Siew Hong Teoh, Ivo Welch, and T. J. Wong, "Earnings Management and the Long-Run Market Performance of Initial Public Offerings." *Journal of Finance* 53(6) (December 1998); *www.jstor.org/stable/i300839.*
6. L. L. DuCharme, P. H. Malatesta, and S. E. Sefcik, "Earnings Management, Stock Issues, and Shareholder Lawsuits." *Journal of Financial Economics* 71 (January 2004): 27–40.
7. De-Wai Chou, Michael Gombola, and Feng-Ying Liu, "Earnings Management and Stock Performance of Reverse Leveraged Buyouts." *Journal of Financial and Quantitative Analysis*, forthcoming. Available at *http://ssrn.com/abstract=684426.*
8. Richard Sloan, "Do Stock Prices Fully Reflect Information in Accruals and Cash Flows about Future Earnings?" *Accounting Review* 71 (1996): 289–315.
9. David Hirshleifer, Kewei Hou, Siew Hong Teoh, and Yinglei Zhang, "Do Stock Prices Fully Reflect Information in Accruals and Cash Flows about Future Earnings?" *Journal of Accounting and Economics* 38 (2004): 297–331.
10. George A. Papanastasopoulos, Dimitrios D. Thomakos, and Tao Wang, "Information in Balance Sheets for Future Stock Returns: Evidence from Net Operating Assets (June 20, 2011)." *International Review of Financial Analysis* 20 (2011): 269–282. Available at *http://ssrn.com/abstract=937361.*
11. M. D. Beneish, "The Detection of Earnings Manipulation." *Financial Analysts Journal* (September/October 1999): 24–36.
12. Messod Daniel Beneish, Craig Nichols, and Charles M. C. Lee, "To Catch a Thief: Can Forensic Accounting Help Predict Stock Returns? (July 27, 2011)." Available at *http://ssrn.com/abstract=1903593 or http://dx.doi.org/10.2139/ssrn.1903593.*
13. The NORMDIST function in Excel can be used to perform the transformation of a PROBM score into a more interpretable PMAN, or probability of manipulation score.
14. Bethany McLean and Peter Elkind, *Smartest Guys in the Room: The Amazing Rise and Scandalous Fall of Enron* (Mountain View, CA: Portfolio Hardcover, 2003).
15. Bethany McLean, "Is Enron Overpriced?" *Fortune* (March 5, 2001).
16. Data for SGAI are unavailable, so we assume a value of 1 in the regression.
17. All mean figures for manipulators and nonmanipulators are taken from Beneish, Table 2.
18. G. D. L. Morris, "Enron 101: How a Group of Business Students Sold Enron a Year before the Collapse." *Financial History* (Spring/Summer 2009): 12–15.
19. Buffett, 1988.

CHAPTER 4

Measuring the Risk of Financial Distress: How to Avoid the Sick Men of the Stock Market

[The] corpse is supposed to file the death certificate. Under this "honor system" of mortality, the corpse sometimes gives itself the benefit of the doubt.
— Warren Buffett, "Shareholder Letter," 1984

From its inception in 1983 as LDDS Communications to its 1999 peak, WorldCom's stock rose from pennies per share to over $60. The WorldCom story is emblematic of the investing public's infatuation with telecommunications stocks in the dot com era. At its pinnacle, WorldCom was the United States' largest handler of Internet data,[1] and a darling of Wall Street, worth almost $150 billon. In July 2002, WorldCom collapsed into bankruptcy under the ignominy of an accounting scandal. At the time, the bankruptcy filing was the largest in U.S. history, and it still remains the largest nonbank filing ever. What caused WorldCom's spectacular fall from grace, and how can we avoid stocks at risk of sustaining a permanent loss of capital?

In the aftermath of the bankruptcy filing, numerous accounting irregularities came to light, among them an improper accounting of operating expenses as capital expenses. After a torturous financial audit of the company, utilizing an army of over 500 WorldCom employees, over 200 employees of the company's outside auditor, KPMG, and a supplemental workforce of almost 600 people from Deloitte & Touche, at a total cost $365 million, WorldCom was required to make a staggering $79.5 billion adjustment for the period from 1999 through the first quarter of 2002. Misplacing $79.5 billion takes some serious talent. The "skilled performers" were the CEO, Bernie Ebbers, and CFO, Scott Sullivan, who were eventually convicted of securities fraud.[2]

WorldCom loosely interpreted accounting rules to create the illusion of steadily increasing profits. For example, management would in one quarter write down millions of dollars in assets it acquired, also including expenses not yet incurred. The result was bigger losses in that quarter but smaller ones in future quarters, which gave the impression that profits were improving. In 1998, Buffett described this phenomenon as "big bath" accounting, writing in his Chairman's Letter that "[in] this bit of legerdemain, a large chunk of costs that should properly be attributed to a number of years is dumped into a single quarter, typically one already fated to disappoint investors. In some cases, the purpose of the charge is to clean up earnings misrepresentations of the past, and in others it is to prepare the ground for future misrepresentations."[3]

The postbankruptcy audit found two additional accounting treatments that increased the size of the fraud at WorldCom. WorldCom overvalued acquisitions by about $5.8 billion. In addition, WorldCom reported a pretax profit for 2000 of $7.6 billion, when in reality it lost $48.9 billion (including a $47 billion write-down of impaired assets). The effect was to turn a combined $10 billion profit for the years 2000 and 2001 into a combined loss for the years 2000 through 2002 of $73.7 billion. If the $5.8 billion of overvalued assets is added to this figure, the total fraud at WorldCom amounted to $79.5 billion.[4]

WorldCom's auditors were not the only ones deceived by Ebbers and his accounting. Jack Grubman, Salomon Smith Barney's infamous telecommunications analyst, maintained his ardor for WorldCom until just before its grisly end. Grubman was no slouch. *Institutional Investing* magazine ranked him as a top analyst in 1999, and *Business Week* called him "one of the most powerful players on Wall Street." He also knew WorldCom well. He started following it in the early 1990s when it was still called LDDS Communications. Grubman persisted with his highest rating on WorldCom until March 18, 2002, when he finally raised its risk rating. By that time, the stock had fallen almost 90 percent from its high two years before, and it was only months away from its bankruptcy filing. On December 19, 2002, Grubman was fined $15 million and banned from securities industry for life by the Securities and Exchange Commission (SEC).

Is it possible that investors could have divined WorldCom's troubles before it was too late? Despite the fact that its own auditors and respected analysts were unable to see them, were there signs of WorldCom's financial ill health visible from the outside? This chapter considers whether we can predict financial distress or bankruptcy.[5] When we examine a firm's probability of financial distress, we are stepping into the realm of the lender or actuary. We conduct a financial statement analysis that any value investor would recognize, but we take it a step further and examine market-based indicators that signal the possibility of financial distress on the horizon.

A BRIEF HISTORY OF BANKRUPTCY PREDICTION

Financial and accounting researchers have expended considerable energy endeavoring to predict which stocks will go bankrupt. Early attempts sought to find the single best predictor. Recall from Chapter 2 that Benjamin Graham's simple quantitative value strategy required that stocks "own at least twice what they owe," meaning they should have a debt-to-equity ratio of no more than 50 percent. Another early study concluded that the cash flow-to-debt ratio was the single best predictor of financial health.[6] Later research abandoned the hunt for a single predictor, focusing instead on finding a combination of measures that might forecast bankruptcy.

In 1968, Edward I. Altman,[7] now a professor of finance at New York University's Stern School of Business, led the charge to find a comprehensive model. He collated a sample of 33 publicly listed manufacturing stocks that filed for bankruptcy from 1945 to 1965. Altman then examined the small universe using 22 intuitive predictors of bankruptcy. After each examination, he excluded the measure that contributed least to the explanatory power of the model, winnowing the original 22 measures down to just 5. The original Altman model was as follows:

$$Z = 0.012\ X_1 + 0.014\ X_2 + 0.033\ X_3 + 0.006\ X_4 + 0.999\ X_5$$

where X_1 = working capital/total assets
X_2 = retained earnings/total assets
X_3 = earnings before interest and taxes/ / total assets
X_4 = market value of equity/book value of total liabilities
X_5 = sales / total assets

Altman suggested a cutoff for the "Z-score" of 2.675. If the Z-score was below 2.675, Altman classified the stock as *bankrupt*, if above 2.675, Altman regarded the stock as *not bankrupt* (or heading that way). He subsequently lowered the cutoff Z-score to 1.81 after conducting three later tests (86 bankrupt stocks between 1969 and 1975, 110 between 1976 and 1995, and 120 between 1997 and 1999).

Altman's Z-score performed well forecasting bankruptcy one year ahead. The score correctly classified 94 percent of the bankrupt stocks and 97 percent of the nonbankrupt stocks one year prior to filing for bankruptcy. It still performed well when the forecast was pushed out to two years in advance, accurately predicting of 72 percent of bankrupt stocks and 94 percent of the nonbankrupt stocks.

Altman intended that his original Z-score be used only for publicly traded manufacturing stocks, but it is no surprise that Wall Street applied the metric to any and all situations. Perhaps it has something to do with the fact that the score performs reasonably well, even for nonmanufacturing stocks. Researchers Nikolai Chuvakhin and L. Wayne Gertmenia applied the model after the WorldCom bankruptcy. They computed Z-scores for WorldCom for fiscal years ending December 31, 1999, 2000, and 2001, based on its annual 10-K reports filed with the SEC. Using the accounting data made available prior to later restatements, they found WorldCom's Z-score to be 2.697 in 1999, 1.274 in 2000, and 0.798 in 2001.

There are several observations that jump out from WorldCom's Z-scores over the three years prior to its bankruptcy filing. The first is that World-Com's Z-score deteriorated precipitously between 1999 and 2001, dropping from 2.697 to 0.798. Its 1999 Z-score is nonbankrupt, being over both Altman's later, lower 1.81 cutoff, and his original, stricter 2.675 cutoff. By 2000, WorldCom's Z-score had dropped off to 1.274, well below Altman's later 1.81 cut off, indicating that WorldCom was heading to bankruptcy, and giving investors plenty of time to exit the stock. If investors had not done so in 2000, WorldCom's 2001 Z-score was a flashing neon warning light to get out of the stock. At 0.798. WorldCom's Z-score was less than half the Z-score cutoff. At this point WorldCom could be said to be un-equivocally in trouble, and probably heading to bankruptcy absent some *deus ex machina* like a substantial capital raising.

It is interesting—given that we now know Bernie Ebbers cooked World-Com's books—that the Z-score was still able to predict WorldCom's bank-ruptcy, indicating that it is robust to certain types of accounting irregulari-ties. Even though management improperly recorded billions of dollars as capital expenditures instead of operating expenses, the Z-score determined the stock was heading into bankruptcy. Chuvakhin and Gertmenia note that the improper accounting for capital expenditures would have a twofold im-pact on WorldCom's financial statements. First, it overstates earnings, and, second, it overstates assets. Overstated earnings increase the X_3 ratio in the Z-score, while overstated assets decrease three ratios, X_1, X_2, and X_5 (all three of which are calculated with total assets in the denominator). The overall impact of management's accounting improprieties on the World-Com's Z-score, therefore, was *downward*, which make it appear *more* likely to enter bankruptcy. The Z-score seems to work.

While Altman's Z-score performed remarkably well in the WorldCom example, there are more robust metrics for examining the financial stability of a stock. The results of this single stock study should be taken with a grain of salt. There are two issues with the Z-score. First, Altman designed the Z-score for manufacturing companies. Clearly there is sufficient overlap be-tween manufacturing companies and telecommunication companies for the Z-score to be useful, but there's a little more luck here than meets the eye.[8]

The other problem is that accounting impropriety can affect the Z-score. Again, in the WorldCom example, the Z-score performed well. Ebbers's accounting shenanigans only served to lower WorldCom's Z-score, but other accounting maneuvers may have increased it. Never fear: Academics have been hard at work since Altman published his 1968 paper and have improved financial distress and bankruptcy prediction technology over the past 40 years. Let's now examine more comprehensive and empirically robust methods to predict financial distress and/or bankruptcy.

IMPROVING BANKRUPTCY PREDICTION

While Altman's Z-score did predict WorldCom's bankruptcy after the fact, researchers have identified several issues with it. In 1980, James Ohlson,[9] then an associate professor at the University of California, Berkeley, found a problem with Altman's data. Ohlson concluded that the Z-score back-test had used financial data not available to investors in real time. This is known as *look-ahead bias,* and we discuss it in some detail in Chapter 10. Look-ahead bias is caused by the use of a database that does not record the date information becomes available to investors. For example, financial statements for the period to December 31, 2011, are often not made available until mid-January or February, but the database will assume the information was available on December 31, 2011. Ohlson concluded that the error rate in predicting bankruptcy was much higher than Altman thought, which meant that the Altman Z-score was less accurate than reported by Altman. Researchers now use a "point-in-time" database to correct for this error. Using such a point-in-time database, Ohlson created the "O-score," which focused on four primary factors to determine the probability of a stock's failure: the size of the stock, its financial structure, its financial performance, and its liquidity.

Tyler Shumway, professor of finance at the University of Michigan's Ross School of Business, explored the use of a multiperiod "hazard" model to forecast bankruptcy in a 1999 paper, "Forecasting Bankruptcy More Accurately: A Simple Hazard Model."[10] Shumway's model used accounting variables, but also incorporated equity market variables like the standard deviation of a stock's returns or its past excess stock returns. Shumway found that his bankruptcy prediction model outperformed both the Altman Z-score and Ohlson's O-score. Shumway concluded that half of the variables proposed by Altman's Z-score were no longer predictive of bankruptcy.

In 2004, Sudheer Chava and Robert Jarrow took Shumway's model one step further, concluding that Shumway's results were robust and agreeing that Altman's Z-score no longer reliably forecasted bankruptcy. They argued that when forecasting bankruptcy, we must take into account the stock's industry. Intuitively, this makes sense for two reasons. Stocks in different industries will face differing levels of competition, and have different accounting conventions. It makes sense that stocks with otherwise identical balance sheets, but in different industries with different competition and accounting conventions, will face different risks of bankruptcy. Chava and Jarrow show that adjusting for these industry effects enhances Shumway's model's predictive capability.

HOW WE CALCULATE THE RISK OF FINANCIAL DISTRESS

In a 2008 paper called "In Search of Distress Risk,"[11] John Campbell, Jens Hilscher, and Jan Szilagyi comprehensively explore the determinants of corporate failure. Examining U.S. data over the period 1963 to 2003, they find that stocks with higher leverage, lower profitability, lower market capitalizations, lower past stock returns, more volatile past stock returns, lower

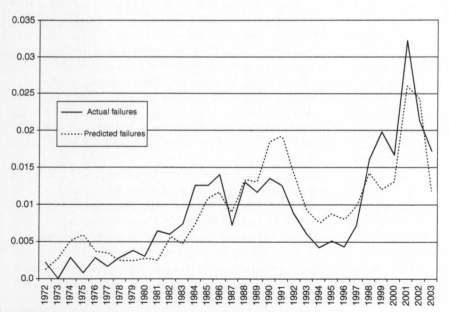

FIGURE 4.1   Campbell et al. Model's Prediction Capability
Source: John Campbell, Jens Hilscher, and Jan Szilagyi, "In Search of Distress Risk," *Journal of Finance* 63 (2008): 2899–2939.

cash holdings, lower price-to-book value ratios, and lower prices per share are more likely to file for bankruptcy, be delisted, or receive a "D" rating. Noting that earlier papers on bankruptcy had concentrated on predicting bankruptcy in the very short term, Campbell et al. argue that short-horizon predictions are as useful as predicting a heart attack by observing a person dropping to the floor clutching his chest. They then attempt to lengthen the horizon at which they can predict failure, finding that the most persistent stock characteristics—market capitalization, the price-to-book value ratio, and equity volatility—are the most significant at long horizons. Campbell et al.'s resulting model improves the forecast accuracy of Shumway's prediction model (see Figure 4.1).

Campbell et al. take a similar approach to Shumway, including in their financial distress model both accounting and equity market variables. They use the following inputs:

- NIMTA = weighted average (quarter's net income / MTA)
  - MTA = market value of total assets = book value of liabilities + market cap
- TLMTA = total liabilities / MTA
- CASHMTA = cash and equivalents/ / MTA
- EXRET = weighted average (log(1 + stock's return) − log(1 + S&P 500 return)
- SIGMA = annualized stock's standard deviation over the previous 3 months
- RSIZE = log(stock market cap / S&P 500 total market value)
- MB = MTA / adjusted book value, where adjusted book value = book value + .1 × (market cap-book value)
  PRICE = log(recent stock price), capped at $15, so a stock with a stock price of $20, would be given a value of log(15) instead of log(20)

The authors use a statistical technique called "logistic regression," sometimes called a "logit model." Logistic regression is used where the outcome of an event is binary (for example, "one or zero," "yes or no"). A stock is either financially distressed or not, so the logit model is appropriate. The inputs to the logit model are the independent variables listed earlier (NIMTA, TLMTA, CASHMTA, etc.). In the final model, the NIMTA and EXRET variables have been transformed into NIMTAAVG and EXRETAVG. These new variables are weighted averages of four quarters of data from the original NIMTA and EXRET variables, calculated as follows:

$$XAVG = .5333 \times t + .2666 \times t - 1 + .1333 \times t - 2 + .0666 \times t - 3$$

The logit model generates a binary dependent variable or logit value, "logit probability of financial distress" or LPFD, calculated as follows:

$$LPFD = -20.26 \times NIMTAAVG + 1.42 \times TLMTA - 7.13 \times EXRETAVG$$
$$+ 1.41 \times SIGMA - 0.045 \times RSIZE - 2.13 \times CASHMTA + 0.075 \times MB -$$
$$0.058 \times PRICE - 9.16$$

The variables in the LPFD model may appear daunting, but they are all intuitive to value investors. For example, NIMTAVG, EXRETAVG, RSIZE, CASHMTA, and PRICE all have negative signs. This suggests that, all else being equal, having more income to assets (NIMTAVG), better recent relative performance (EXRETAVG), a bigger market capitalization (RSIZE), more cash relative to assets (CASHMTA), and a higher price (PRICE) all tend to reduce the probability of financial distress over the next 12 months. In contrast, TLMTA, SIGMA, and MB have a positive sign. The positive signs imply that, all else equal, stocks with higher leverage to assets (TLMTA), more volatility (SIGMA), and higher market price-to-book values (MB) are more likely to run into financial distress.

The LPFD value is not interpretable in the logit form. A further step must be undertaken to transform the logit value into a probability. First, we calculate a LPFD for every stock in our investable universe. Next, we transform the LPFD value into a probability measure that we can interpret, the "probability of financial distress" (PFD). The equation to transform the logit value into a useable probability is as follows:

$$PFD = \frac{1}{1 + e^{-LPFD}}$$

The probability of financial distress ranges between zero and 100 percent. Zero implies no probability of financial distress in the next 12 months, while 100 percent suggests certain financial distress. Let's return to the WorldCom example and see how the PFD performs alongside our fraud and manipulation variables from the previous chapter.

Table 4.1 sets out our three financial statement manipulation/fraud models and our financial distress risk models for WorldCom leading up to the bankruptcy. STA is scaled accruals to total assets, SNOA is scaled net operating assets to total assets, PMAN is the probability of manipulation,

TABLE 4.1 WorldCom Distress Model Warning Signals

	STA	SNOA	PMAN	PFD
Universe Percentile	84%	98%	77%	93%

and PFD is the probability of financial distress. All values are percentile ranks relative to the entire universe of firms. Relative to the universe of firms, WorldCom was a pig with red lipstick. The SNOA and PFD variables are shouting, "Please don't invest in me," while STA and PMAN quietly suggested you look elsewhere. Any way we cut it, the group of warning signals we examine, collectively, indicated trouble for WorldCom.

As the WorldCom example demonstrates, our distress model helps us to avoid "falling knives": falling stocks with deteriorating fundamentals, destined for the bankruptcy courts. We use the PFD measure when we wish to assess the probability that a stock will find itself in financial distress in the next 12 months. While the construction of Campbell et al.'s distress model might appear intimidating, its implications should be familiar to value investors: stocks with higher leverage, lower profitability, lower market capitalization, lower past stock returns, more volatile past stock returns, lower cash holdings, lower price-to-book ratios, and lower prices per share are more likely to file for bankruptcy, be delisted, or receive a "D" rating. The PFD measure is a better measure of future financial distress than earlier models of financial distress like the Altman Z-score or Ohlson's O-score. It's also more useful because it was designed to predict failure at longer time horizons (we use the 12-month variation of the estimated model). Investors should be aware that stocks with a high risk of failure tend to deliver particularly poor returns, and at heightened risk. The PFD can help investors avoid stocks at risk of sustaining a permanent loss of capital.

SCRUBBING THE UNIVERSE

One question remains: Do the fraud, manipulation, and distress risk models improve the performance of our universe? Table 4.2 shows the results of our examination of two portfolios: Universe and "Cleaned" Universe. Universe is the entire universe of firms under examination. "Cleaned" Universe is the same portfolio excluding the 5 percent of stocks with the highest combined risk of fraud, manipulation, and financial distress risk.

Table 4.2 shows that we can improve the performance of the universe by eliminating those stocks at the highest risk of sustaining a total loss of capital. The growth rate is marginally improved, but, most important, risk is also slightly lower, meaning that risk-adjusted statistics such as the Sharpe and Sortino ratios are increased. The improvements are small but significant considering that we eliminated only a small portion of the universe. These models are intended primarily to shift the distribution of returns further into positive territory and away from large negative losses. Figure 4.2 graphically shows this improvement by comparing the distribution of the historical one-year returns for the universe and the "cleaned" universe.

TABLE 4.2   Improvements to Our Stock Universe through the Elimination of Frauds, Manipulators, and Distressed Firms (1964 to 2011)

	Universe	"Cleaned" Universe
CAGR	10.80%	11.04%
Standard Deviation	15.49%	15.31%
Downside Deviation	11.01%	10.85%
Sharpe Ratio	0.40	0.42
Sortino Ratio (MAR = 5%)	0.59	0.62
Worst Drawdown	−44.38%	−43.48%
Worst Month Return	−21.55%	−21.37%
Best Month Return	17.66%	17.73%
Profitable Months	61.84%	61.62%

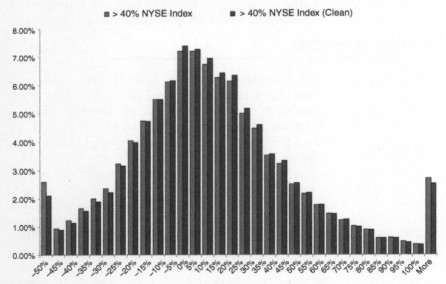

FIGURE 4.2   Histogram Comparing Distribution of One-Year Returns for the Universe and the "Cleaned" Universe (1974 to 2011)

The shift in the distribution of returns in the "cleaned" universe indicates that the models eliminated the subset of stocks that permanently destroy capital. This simple analysis suggests that we have identified a tool that can help us define a universe in which we can further assess quality and price.

In this chapter, we have considered a key element of investing: avoiding stocks at high risk of financial distress. We examined the research on the prediction of financial distress. We identified a model that can help value investors quantify a stock's risk of financial distress, bankruptcy, or insolvency: the PFD model. We have demonstrated that it would have been possible for investors to have divined WorldCom's troubles before it was too late, even using earlier bankruptcy prediction models like Altman's Z-score. Using the modern PFD model, we can clearly see that WorldCom was in trouble as early as 1999.

Part Two examined a variety of ways to avoid stocks at risk of permanent impairment of capital. In Chapter 3, we discussed the indicia of earnings manipulation and fraud, and in this chapter we checked for the risk of financial distress. Both the manipulation and distress measures are used to winnow from the investable universe the stocks with the lowest margin of safety—those at the highest risk of sustaining permanent and total impairments. In Part Three, we're looking for stocks of the highest quality—those with franchises and financial strength. The next chapter, Chapter 5, examines the key characteristics of franchises: high long-term returns on capital and high, stable profit margins.

NOTES

1. Simon Romero and Riva D. Atlas, "WorldCom's Collapse: The Overview; WorldCom Files for Bankruptcy; Largest U.S. Case." *New York Times*, July 22, 2002. *www.nytimes.com/2002/07/22/us/worldcom-s-collapse-the-overview-worldcom-files-for-bankruptcy-largest-us-case.html.*

2. Dennis, Moberg and Edward J. Romar, "WorldCom," 2003; *www.scu.edu/ethics/dialogue/candc/cases/worldcom.html.*

3. Warren Buffett, "Shareholder Letter," Berkshire Hathaway, Inc. Annual Report, 1992.

4. Edward J. Romar and Martin Calkins, "WorldCom Case Study Update 2006," *www.scu.edu/ethics/dialogue/candc/cases/worldcom-update.html.*

5. While we use the term *bankruptcy* to illustrate what we mean by "financial distress," there are key differences between the two terms. Filing for bankruptcy is the most vivid outcome for a stock in financial distress, but there are other options, including delisting, receiving a D rating, and highly dilutive capital raisings, all of which are bad for stock holders. Suffice it to say that the empirical

evidence is that stocks with a high risk of financial distress earn particularly poor returns, and at heightened risk.

6. N. Chuvakhin, and L. Gertmenian, "Predicting Bankruptcy in the WorldCom Age," 2003, *http://gbr.pepperdine.edu/031/bankruptcy.html.*
7. Edward I. Altman, "Financial Ratios, Discriminant Analysis and the Prediction of Corporate Bankruptcy." *Journal of Finance* 23(1968): 589–609.
8. Luck might not be the complete story. In a 2000 paper Altman wrote that, according to his 1999 review of U.S. industrial stocks in the Compustat database, some 20 percent had Z-scores below 1.81, foretelling the unusually high incidence of bankruptcies in 2001 and 2002.
9. James A. Ohlson, "Financial Ratios and the Probabilistic Prediction of Bankruptcy." *Journal of Accounting Research* 18(1) (Spring 1980): 109–131.
10. Tyler Shumway, "Forecasting Bankruptcy More Accurately: A Simple Hazard Model" (July 16, 1999). Available at *http://ssrn.com/abstract=171436 or http://dx.doi.org/10.2139/ssrn.171436.*
11. John Campbell, Jens Hilscher, and Jan Szilagyi, "Do Stock Prices Fully Reflect Information in Accruals and Cash Flows about Future Earnings? In Search of Distress Risk." *Journal of Finance* 63 (2008): 2899–2939.

Three

Quality—How to Find a Wonderful Business

In Part Two of this book we described how we seek a margin of safety by avoiding stocks at risk of a permanent loss of capital. Part Three of this book is about finding high-quality stocks. A quality firm has a business with an economic franchise and superior financial strength. In Chapter 5, we explain why an economic franchise is valuable and examine in some detail the characteristics of franchises: exceptional long-term returns on capital and pricing power manifesting as a high, stable gross margin. A franchise provides a margin of safety by protecting a firm's return against competitors.

In Chapter 6, we examine financial strength. Financial strength is related to the measures we use to identify firms in serious financial distress, but in the financial strength chapter we have a different goal. Our manipulation and financial distress models are meant to eliminate firms at high risk of financial distress. In contrast, we use our financial strength measures to find companies in rude financial health, able to withstand shocks from the business cycle and competitors.

CHAPTER 5

Franchises—The Archetype of High Quality

An economic franchise arises from a product or service that: (1) is needed or desired; (2) is thought by its customers to have no close substitute and; (3) is not subject to price regulation. The existence of all three conditions will be demonstrated by a company's ability to regularly price its product or service aggressively and thereby to earn high rates of return on capital.
—Warren Buffett, Shareholder Letter, 1991[1]

Warren Buffett likes to buy "franchises," which are businesses earning high returns on capital with a sustainable competitive advantage. Buffett's ability to identify such high-quality businesses at a discount to their intrinsic value has made him one of the wealthiest men in the world. For Buffett, the prototypical franchise is See's Candies, a U.S. West Coast manufacturer and retailer of boxed chocolates. See's results are so good that Buffett credits his acquisition of See's as teaching him about the importance of franchises and marked a significant departure from his previous investment style. It was an acquisition he almost did not make.

Buffett had previously employed his mentor Benjamin Graham's "cigar butt" approach to investing, so-called because "a cigar butt found on the street that has only one puff left in it may not offer much of a smoke, but the 'bargain purchase' will make that puff all profit." Under the influence of his partner, Charlie Munger, and Phil Fisher's *Common Stocks and Uncommon Profits*,[2] Buffett started to appreciate that it was, as he described it, better to buy a "wonderful company at a fair price than a fair company at a wonderful price." Between 1965 and 1972, Buffett started buying stocks with franchises: businesses with sustainable high returns. This is not to suggest that Graham was unaware of the value of higher-quality businesses. He recommended in *Security Analysis*[3] that any quantitative analysis be supplemented by qualitative considerations:

> *An important principle of security analysis is: Quantitative data are useful only to the extent that they are supported by a qualitative survey of the enterprise.*
>
> *In order for a company's business to be regarded as reasonably stable, it does not suffice that the past record should show stability. The nature of the undertaking, considered apart from any figures, must be such as to indicate an inherent permanence of earning power.*

We're not going to undertake a qualitative analysis in the way Graham intended. We propose to undertake the qualitative analysis quantitatively. When Graham says, "The nature of the undertaking, considered apart from any figures, must be such as to indicate an inherent permanence of earning power," we believe he's referring to an analysis of the business's competitive advantages, or its "franchise." In this chapter, we consider the academic research on sustainable high returns, and examine some simple metrics that help to identify firms with franchises.

THE CHAIRMAN'S SECRET RECIPE

One of the bedrocks of modern corporate finance theory is that the value of any security is the present value of its future cash flows. This simple principle was first described in 1934 by John Burr Williams in his *Theory of Investment Value*.[4] Williams's principle gives us the discounted cash flow (DCF) analysis, which allows us to calculate intrinsic value by taking a series of growing future cash flows and discounting them back to the present at a rate of return that takes into account the time value of money and the particular risk of the business analyzed.

More recently, academics and practitioners alike have come to recognize the significance of Buffett's observation that the value of a business depends on its ability to generate returns on invested capital in excess of its cost of capital.[5] Businesses expected to produce returns on invested capital in excess of market rates of return are worth more than the capital invested in them, and the market price of the stock should in time exceed its asset value. Businesses expected to produce returns on invested capital lower than market rates of return are worth less than the capital invested in them, and the market price of the stock should eventually fall below its asset value. The market value of a stock therefore depends on the return on invested capital in excess of its cost of capital: the higher the return on invested capital over its cost of capital, the more valuable the business.

The importance of high returns on capital is fully revealed when we think about reinvestment and business growth. Businesses must constantly reinvest capital to maintain existing production capability. If the business's return on invested capital is lower than the rate of return otherwise available in the market, the reinvestment of capital into the business destroys value. Each dollar reinvested at a rate of return on invested capital below market rates of return translates into less than a dollar of market value. Let's return to the example of See's Candies, and examine it in the light of returns on invested capital.

Buffett bought See's Candies in 1972 for $25 million. Its annual sales at the time of purchase were $30 million, and pretax earnings were less than $5 million. See's Candies required just $8 million in invested capital to generate those earnings. This equates to a return on invested capital of 60 percent, which is an extraordinarily high return. We can assume that Buffett believed the returns were sustainable, which must have indicated to Buffett that See's possessed a franchise. If the prevailing market return at the time was around 11 percent, Buffett may have estimated the intrinsic value of See's at approximately 5.45 times (60 percent / 11 percent = 5.45) its invested capital of $8 million, or approximately $45 million (5.45 × $8 million = $45 million). At a purchase price of $25 million, Buffett paid only slightly more than 3 times ($25 million / $8 million = 3.125) invested capital, or about 56 percent of See's Candies' intrinsic value ($25 million / $45 million = 55.56 percent). Viewed in this light, See's Candies was a steal at $25 million. Buffett, however, not yet fully appreciating the value of a franchise, was ready to walk away if the vendors would not accept $25 million. The vendor was asking $30 million, but Buffett was adamant about not going above $25 million. Fortunately for Buffett, the vendor caved.

In his 1983 Shareholder Letter, Buffett undertook the following thought experiment: Consider a hypothetical ordinary business that, like See's Candies, also earned $5 million pretax, but required $45 million in invested capital, rather than See's Candies' $8 million. An ordinary business earning only 11 percent on invested capital would be unlikely to possess a franchise. A low-return business might be worth the value of its invested capital, or $45 million, which is the same value as See's Candies. However, See's Candies is the better business to own.

The value of its high returns on invested capital is best understood if we consider what happens if both businesses maintain the same unit sales in a world of persistent inflation. Imagine the effect that inflation has on the two businesses. A relatively low inflation rate of 2 percent steals half of our purchasing power over 35 years. Both businesses must double earnings to $10 million to keep up with this inflation. How can they achieve this? Given that unit volume remains flat, they must double the price of the product. Assuming profit margins remain unchanged, if we double the price, profits will also double.

Each business is also subject to input higher prices, and this will result in both businesses doubling their assets, since that is the economic burden imposed on business by inflation. A doubling of dollar sales means a proportionate increase in working capital, and fixed assets. This inflation-induced investment produces no improvement in rate of return. The motivation for this investment is maintenance, not growth. Remember, however, that See's had invested capital of only $8 million, so it need only commit an additional $8 million to finance the capital expenditure imposed by inflation. The hypothetical ordinary business has a burden over five times as large—and therefore needs $45 million of additional capital.

Thirty-five years later, the ordinary business, now earning $10 million annually, is probably still worth the value of its tangible assets, or $90 million. This means that its owners have gained only a dollar of nominal value for every new dollar invested. See's Candies, also earning $10 million, might also be worth $90 million if valued on the same basis as it was at the time of Buffett's purchase. So it would have gained $45 million in intrinsic value while the owners reinvested only $8 million in additional capital, which equates to over $5 of nominal value gained for each $1 invested.

What actually happened to See's Candies? Thirty-five years after it was purchased, See's Candies' pretax profits were $82 million. By 2007, the capital required to run the business was just $40 million. This means Buffett had to reinvest only $32 million over 35 years to fund the growth of the business. In the intervening period, pretax earnings totaled $1.35 billion. All of those earnings, excluding the $32 million reinvested in the business, were sent back to Buffett, which he was able to use to buy other businesses and grow Berkshire Hathaway. More than 97 percent of See's Candies' return was paid out to Buffett, yet the business grew at more than 7.5 percent a year for 35 years (and to think that the acquisition nearly fell over for want of $5 million). If the vendor had stuck to his guns and demanded $30 million, Buffett might have balked, and that $1.35 billion would have gone to somebody else.

As the See's Candies example demonstrates, high returns provide managers with opportunity. They can pay out capital to owners without affecting the stock's ability to grow, or they can compound the capital of the business by reinvesting it year after year after year. See's Candies is extraordinary because it has been able to grow over the long term with so little additional capital. Buffett extracted most of its excess capital to invest in other Berkshire Hathaway businesses, and it has still been able to grow at a high compound rate for four decades and counting. If you own a sustainable, high-return business like See's, you don't need to get too many other investments right. The sheer volume of capital thrown off every year means you can buy a lot of other losers and still get ahead. Of course, See's Candies' capital compounded in Berkshire Hathaway at the direction of Buffett, the world's greatest capital allocator. Buffett used See's Candies' distributed capital to buy other high-return businesses like See's Candies. The result is that Buffett has compounded Berkshire Hathaway's capital at a high rate. It's good to own a franchise.

HOW TO FIND A FRANCHISE

Let's take a look at some well-known measures that quantitatively capture the hallmark characteristics of franchises. For a stock to be a franchise it must possess some sustainable competitive advantage, which enables it to generate excess returns on capital and pricing power for its product. The goal of the quantitative techniques outlined in this chapter is to find those stocks likely to maintain excess returns on capital and possess pricing power.

Economic Moats and Excess Returns

Managers invest capital in assets expecting to generate future cash flows from those assets. When the cash flows from the assets exceed the cost of capital used to finance those assets, the investment creates value. The extent to which the excess returns can be maintained may indicate the presence or absence of a competitive advantage or economic moat.[6] How do we calculate the return generated by a firm's assets? There are many methods. The first is a simple and direct assessment called return on assets (ROA):

$$ROA = Net\ Income\ before\ Extraordinary\ Items\ /\ Total\ Assets$$

Buffett's favored measure is return on equity (ROE):

$$ROE = Net\ Income\ /\ Book\ Value\ of\ Equity$$

When Buffett discusses ROE, he adds the following qualifier: "[except] for special cases (for example, companies with unusual debt-equity ratios or those with important assets carried at unrealistic balance sheet values). ... " We can adjust straight ROE to include both net debt and equity, giving us one version of return on capital (ROC):

$$ROC = EBIT(1 - Tax\ Rate) / (Book\ Value\ of\ Debt$$
$$+ Book\ Value\ of\ Equity - Cash)$$

ROC is the theoretically more appealing measure because it uses earnings before interest and taxes (EBIT, which is almost equivalent to operating income) in the numerator instead of net income. EBIT represents the earnings to all forms of capital, not just equity. Net income is the "bottom line" number on the income statement. As many value investors have learned the hard way, the further down the income statement an accounting number appears, the less reliable the number becomes. We calculate gross profits on total assets (GPA), which we discussed in Chapter 2, for the same reason. The advantage of the gross profits measure is that it appears higher on the income statement than EBIT, and is therefore less easily manipulated:

$$GPA = (Revenue - Cost\ of\ Goods\ Sold) / Total\ Assets$$

Greenblatt's return on capital (ROC) measure seeks See's Candies–type businesses:

$$ROC = EBIT / Capital$$

Recall from Chapter 2 that capital is fixed assets + current assets – current liabilities – cash, which, for simplicity, Greenblatt substitutes net property, plant and equipment plus net working capital as a close approximation. Buffett seeks "businesses earning good returns on equity while employing little or no debt." By undertaking additional calculations, the use of ROC instead of ROE is attempting to identify businesses that earn high returns on only the capital *required* to operate the business, or only the stock's productive assets. Such a firm could theoretically distribute excess capital and continue to grow like See's Candies.

The utility of any given measure is not in its ability to identify historical excess returns, but in its ability to predict excess returns in the future. At this stage we're not concerned with the subsequent stock price performance of high-return businesses. We want instead to measure the stock's underlying business performance independent of its stock price performance. Next, we look at the research examining whether high-return stocks maintain their high returns.

Excess Returns Revert to the Mean

It might seem that franchise investing is a simple strategy: find a stock earning high returns, buy it, and never sell it. The reality is quite different. The problem is that stocks can't seem to sustain excess returns over long periods of time, tending instead to mean revert toward their cost of capital. Stocks may start out earning excess returns, but those returns diminish over the stocks' economic life cycle.[7] This means that when we identify stocks earning excess returns, those excess returns tend to erode in subsequent periods.

There are two reasons for the apparent erosion of excess return. The first is a problem of sampling. Any sample of high-return stocks will contain a few stocks with genuine franchises but consist mostly of stocks at the peak of their business cycle. Michael Mauboussin, chief investment strategist of Legg Mason Capital Management and an adjunct professor of finance at the Columbia Business School, suggests that any system that combines skill and luck will mean revert over time because the influence of luck diminishes. Mauboussin says that apparently excellent performance combines strong skill and good luck, while apparently poor performance reflects weak skill and bad luck. The influence of luck diminishes over time such that the results more closely reflect the underlying skill. Without the influence of luck, strong skill and weak skill appear closer to the average. Teasing out the relative contributions of skill and luck is no easy task, but sample size is crucial because skill only surfaces with a large number of observations.

The second reason for the diminution in excess returns is economic. It is an iron law of microeconomics that businesses earning excess returns attract competition. The competition then competes for return until the average business earns only its cost of capital. Further, Fama and French find that this mean reversion is faster when it is further from its mean.[8] This suggests that identifying franchises can be a dangerous exercise if we simply extrapolate past results into the future.

As we seek franchise stocks, these two phenomena—luck and competition—present a difficult challenge. Any sample of high-return stocks will contain some with genuine franchises (strong skill, good luck), and some at the peak of the business cycle (weak skill, good luck). Even if we are able to tease out the genuine franchises from the rest, some of the genuine franchises will lose their franchise to the competition. Luck and competition act to push excess returns to the cost of capital. There are, however, a number of stocks that do seem to maintain persistently high returns on capital over time. What if, rather than simply seeking high returns on capital, we look for those stocks with persistently high returns on capital?

Finding Persistence

By definition, stocks possessing a franchise earn sustainable high returns on capital. If we seek stocks possessing a franchise, we would do well to look for stocks that have already sustained high returns over a business cycle. This might indicate that they can withstand competitive pressures and consistently earn excess returns in the future. Such stocks have already proved themselves on the capitalist battlefield.

To this end, we focus our quantitative metrics on long-term averages for a set of simple measures. We have chosen eight years as our "long term" for two reasons: First, eight years likely captures a boom-and-bust cycle for the typical stock, and, second, there are sufficient stocks with eight years of historical data that we can identify a sufficiently large universe of stocks.[9] We analyze three long-term, high-return operating performance metrics and rank these variables against the entire universe of stocks: long-term free cash flow on assets, long-term geometric return on assets, and long-term geometric return on capital, discussed next.

The first measure is long-term free cash flow on assets (CFOA), defined as the sum of eight years of free cash flow divided by total assets. The measure can be expressed more formally as follows:

$$CFOA = Sum\ (Eight\ Years\ Free\ Cash\ Flow)\ /\ Total\ Assets$$

We define free cash flow as net income + depreciation and amortization – changes in working capital – capital expenditures. The CFOA measure seeks to capture how much cash a stock has generated in excess of capital expenditures over an eight-year cycle. In any single year, a stock might invest in assets to generate future cash flows. Such a stock is unduly penalized by a single-year examination of its free cash flow. By examining a longer eight-year period, we seek to capture the stock's ability to generate cash on its investments over a business cycle. If we use the CFOA measure to screen for stocks as of December 31, 2011, we identify many well-known names. Some top performers on the CFOA measure are household names that we would commonly expect to possess a franchise, including Coca-Cola (KO), Google (GOOG), Microsoft (MSFT), Apple (AAPL), Wal-Mart (WMT), and Procter & Gamble (PG).

In Table 5.1, we examine these stocks and their CFOA performance relative to the entire universe of U.S. exchange-traded stocks with a market capitalization greater than $250 million.

TABLE 5.1 CFOA Performance (as of December 31, 2011)

Name	CFOA Value	Percentile
KO	56.1%	82.1%
GOOG	54.5%	81.2%
MSFT	128.8%	98.4%
AAPL	66.9%	87.5%
WMT	31.1%	59.4%
PG	59.0%	83.9%
Average	**66.1%**	**82.1%**

These well-known franchise stocks perform exceptionally well on the CFOA metric. The one exception is Wal-Mart, which performs admirably relative to the universe but does not break into the top 20 percent. The Wal-Mart result highlights the reason why we use multiple measures when quantitatively determining if a stock has an economic franchise.

The second metric employed is long-term geometric ROA (8yr_ROA), the eight-year geometric return on assets, which is formally described as follows:

$$8yr\_ROA_i = \left[\prod_{t=1}^{8}[1+ROA_{it}]\right]^{1/8} - 1$$

where   ROA = return on assets
  t = years
  i = an individual firm

The third measure is long-term geometric ROC, the eight-year geometric return on capital, which is more formally described as follows:

$$8yr\_ROC_i = \left[\prod_{t=1}^{8}[1+ROC_{it}]\right]^{1/8} - 1,$$

where   ROC = return on capital
  t = years
  i = an individual firm

For robustness, we examine both ROA and ROC. Generally speaking, a firm with a franchise will score high on both of these metrics, whereas data errors or complicated capital structure might cause a firm to score high on one metric but poorly on the other. We use the geometric mean rather than the arithmetic mean because the geometric mean penalizes volatility. Volatility in long-term ROA or ROC is a red flag, indicating that a stock does not have a strong economic moat. For example, consider the following two streams of cash flows, one from Moody's Corp. and the other from a fictitious company ("Fake Co."). Fake Co.'s fate is completely driven by a boom-bust commodity cycle. Fake Co. has no pricing power or sustainable competitive advantage. Table 5.2 sets out Moody's ROA each year against Fake Co.'s ROA:

While Moody's and Fake Co. have the same eight-year arithmetic mean, 8yr_ROA tells a completely different story. A quick glance at the year-by-year numbers demonstrates that Moody's earns consistent returns on assets with relatively little variation. Meanwhile, Fake Co. is completely beholden to market forces. Sometimes Fake Co. wins big, other times it loses big. Fake Co.'s arithmetic mean is the same as Moody's, but it is half Moody's 8yr_ROA.

Table 5.3 sets out a list of well-known stocks and each stock's 8yr_ROA and 8yr_ROC measures as of December 31, 2011. As we found with the CFOA measure, many of the stocks we would anecdotally expect to possess a franchise perform very well on the 8yr_ROA and 8YR_ROC metric. The average percentile rank of 8yr_ROA and 8YR_ROC is 91.3 percent and 90.6 percent, respectively.

TABLE 5.2 Comparison of Moody's and Fake Co.'s ROA

Year End	Moody's ROA	Fake Co. ROA
2011	20.2%	100.0%
2010	20.0%	−25.0%
2009	25.8%	−10.0%
2008	40.1%	84.0%
2007	50.3%	125.0%
2006	38.4%	−35.0%
2005	30.9%	−50.0%
2004	38.7%	75.4%
Eight-Year Geometric Mean	**32.8%**	**15.6%**
Eight-Year Arithmetic Mean	**33.1%**	**33.1%**

TABLE 5.3 Franchise Stocks' 8yr_ROA, 8yr_ROC Performance

Name	8yr_ROA	Percentile	8yr_ROC	Percentile
KO	14.8%	95.4%	21.4%	96.3%
GOOG	14.6%	95.2%	16.2%	91.3%
MSFT	20.8%	98.2%	29.5%	98.3%
APPL	13.8%	94.1%	19.9%	95.4%
WMT	8.0%	82.7%	12.1%	82.7%
PG	9.2%	82.3%	10.9%	79.3%
Average	**13.5%**	**91.3%**	**18.3%**	**90.6%**

Finding genuine franchises is a difficult task. For most stocks, returns on capital are highly mean reverting. A sample of stocks with high returns will contain few with a genuine franchise, and many at the peak of the business cycle. Luck and competition will act to drive the high returns on capital to the cost of capital. Teasing out the genuine franchises from the peaking businesses is no easy task. Stocks that cannot maintain high returns over the business cycle do not possess a franchise. We can make an argument that stocks that have maintained high returns over the long term may possess a franchise. Stocks with high, stable returns maintained over the business cycle have demonstrable persistence, and are therefore good candidates for franchises. We use long-term, geometric measures to separate out those stocks with high, stable returns on capital. When we run a screen using these long-term, geometric measures, we identify stocks we would commonly expect to possess a franchise. Next, we examine firms with pricing power.

Pricing Power and Big, Stable Margins

> *"The single most important decision in evaluating a business is pricing power. If you've got the power to raise prices without losing business to a competitor, you've got a very good business. And if you have to have a prayer session before raising the price by 10 percent, then you've got a terrible business."*
> —Warren Buffett, testimony before the Financial Crisis Inquiry Commission, 2011

When Buffett bought control of See's Candies, the vendors asked for a nominal $40 million, which, after deducting $10 million of excess cash, equated to a true offering price of $30 million. Buffett, not yet fully apprehending the value of an economic franchise, looked at the business's mere $7 million of tangible net worth and said $25 million was as much as he would pay. After the acquisition, sales grew rapidly, but profits grew even faster. In his See's Candies purchase, Buffett has said that he had one important insight: He saw that the business had untapped pricing power.[10] The key to the astonishing growth in profits was See's Candies' ability to raise prices faster than inflation.

When he bought See's Candies in 1972, the business sold 16 million pounds of candy each year. In 2007, See's Candies had increased its sales by just 15 million pounds to 31 million pounds, which represents an unimpressive average annual growth rate in sales of just 2 percent. The boxed-chocolates industry in which it operates is unexciting: per-capita consumption in the United States is extremely low and doesn't grow. Yet See's Candies' franchise—a reputation for quality that enables it to charge more for its candy—has led to extraordinary investment results for Buffett. Over the same period that unit volume increased only 2 percent per year, sales increased at more than 7.5 percent per year, from $30 million in 1972 to $383 million in 2007. See's Candies achieved this outstanding result simply by increasing prices, but it was able to consistently increase prices only because See's Candies sells a uniquely desirable product preferred by an enormous margin to that of any competitor. Buffett believes that most lovers of chocolate prefer See's Candies to candy costing two or three times as much, joking in his 1983 letter that "[in] candy, as in stocks, price and value can differ; price is what you give, value is what you get."

Sustainable, high profit margins indicate a franchise. See's Candies' franchise manifests in its pricing power, which enables it to maintain and increase its profit margins. Profit margins are a function of price and cost, so a stock can maintain high margins without pricing power if it can control its costs. The low-cost producer in an industry will maintain high margins, and so this is also an indication that it may possess a franchise.

Profit Margin Growth

There are two broad measures of profit margin strength. The first, margin growth (MG), measures the long-term geometric growth in a stock's profit margins. The higher the MG, the better the stock. MG is formally defined as follows:

$$MG_i = \left[\prod_{t=1}^{8} \left[1 + \frac{GM_{i,t+1}}{GM_{i,t}} \right] \right]^{1/8} - 1,$$

where   GM = gross margin
$\quad\quad\quad t$ = years
$\quad\quad\quad i$ = an individual firm

TABLE 5.4 Apple Inc. Margin Growth Analysis

Year End	Profit Margin	Margin Growth
2011	42.4%	9.28%
2010	38.8%	1.84%
2009	38.1%	11.08%
2008	34.3%	–2.00%
2007	35.0%	15.89%
2006	30.2%	5.96%
2005	28.5%	2.15%
2004	27.9%	N/A
Eight-year geometric annual growth rate		5.4%

MG is simply a stock's eight-year compound annual growth rate in profit margins. We use the geometric mean instead of the arithmetic mean to penalize stocks with erratic profit margin growth, and reward stocks that consistently increase profit margins over time. Consistent growth in profit margins, as measured by MG, may indicate a franchise.

Apple Inc. (AAPL) is an example of a stock with high margin growth. In Table 5.4, we examine AAPL's MG.

Over the past eight years AAPL's profit margin has grown at a compound rate of 5.4 percent a year, which is a very high rate of growth. As of December 31, 2011, AAPL's margin growth score of 5.4 percent puts it in the 93rd percentile of US exchange-traded stocks with a market capitalization over $250 million. Anyone with an *iPhone*, an *iPod*, an *iPad*, and access to *iTunes* well understands why AAPL has been able to increase margins year over year: unparalleled pricing power.

Profit Margin Stability

As businesses mature, profit margin growth will slow. To capture the mature franchise, we use another measure of profit margin strength. Margin stability (MS) measures the extent to which a stock can maintain its profit margin over a business cycle. Margin stability is formally calculated as follows:

$$MS_i = \frac{\frac{1}{t}\sum_{t=1}^{8}[GM_{it}]}{\sqrt{\frac{1}{t-1}\sum_{t=1}^{8}[GM_{it} - \overline{GM}_{it}]^2}} = \frac{\text{Average(GM)}}{\text{STD(GM)}}$$

where   GM = gross margin
         t = years
         i = an individual firm
    STD = sample standard deviation

Let's examine Procter & Gamble (P&G): the stock has been profitably selling razors, cleaning supplies, and toothpaste for a long time. P&G's profit margins are high, but they have not grown for many years. Table 5.5 sets out P&G's margin growth (MG) score.

The margin growth metric does not work in the context of P&G. Nonetheless, although P&G's profit margins have not grown, P&G does possess a franchise. P&G has maintained profit margins of around 50 percent for many years. A consistently high, stable profit margin indicates the presence of a franchise. How does margin stability increase our ability to identify a franchise that is no longer growing margins?

Here we set out an example demonstrating how margin stability treats three stocks with the following characteristics:

- Stock A has high profit margins, but they are extremely variable and depend on the market cycle. Stock A has the highest average profit margin among Stocks A, B, and C.
- Stock B is in a low-margin business, but their margins are extremely stable and reliable. Stock B has the lowest average profit margin, but the same volatility as Stock C.

TABLE 5.5   Procter & Gamble Profit Margin Analysis

Year	Profit Margin	Margin Growth*
2011	50.0%	−3.47%
2010	51.8%	1.17%
2009	51.2%	0.99%
2008	50.7%	−2.69%
2007	52.1%	0.58%
2006	51.8%	1.77%
2005	50.9%	−0.78%
2004	51.3%	N/A
Eight-year compound annual growth rate		−0.32%

*May not sum due to rounding.

■ Stock C is Procter & Gamble, which has high profit margins that are very stable. P&G has an average profit margin that is less than firm A, but greater than Stock B. In addition, P&G has the same volatility of profit margin as Stock B.

Even without performing a single calculation, we know intuitively from the description of the stocks that the stock with the best economics is P&G. P&G maintains high profit margins and the margins are stable. If we look simply at the calculation of average profit margins, Stock A looks the best. If we look at volatility, Stocks B and C are a toss-up. Without a quantitative tool we are lost. Our margin stability measure, however, identifies the stock we intuitively believe is most likely to possess a franchise based on common sense. We can see in Table 5.6 that our margin stability measure correctly identifies P&G as the best firm and Stock B as the second best, and puts Stock A in last place. Margin stability points us to those stocks with high, stable profit margins, which, intuitively, we believe should possess a franchise.

Max Margin

Our two measures of profit margin strength—margin growth and margin stability—each assess a different aspect of profit margin performance. Margin growth measures growth and margin stability measures stability.

TABLE 5.6   Example of Margin Stability Calculation

Year End	Stock A	Stock B	P&G
2011	70.0%	25.0%	50.0%
2010	65.0%	23.0%	51.0%
2009	40.0%	25.0%	50.0%
2008	75.0%	24.0%	49.0%
2007	36.0%	24.0%	47.5%
2006	19.0%	26.0%	49.5%
2005	75.0%	27.0%	49.0%
2004	50.0%	23.0%	52.0%
Average	53.8%	22.0%	49.8%
Standard deviation	20.8%	1.4%	1.4%
Margin stability	2.59	15.63	36.51

TABLE 5.7 Comparison of Apple's and Procter & Gamble's Profit Margins

Year End	Procter & Gamble	Apple
2011	50.00%	42.40%
2010	51.80%	38.80%
2009	51.20%	38.10%
2008	50.70%	34.30%
2007	52.10%	35.00%
2006	51.80%	30.20%
2005	50.90%	28.50%
2004	51.30%	27.90%
Margin Growth	−0.3%	5.4%
Margin Stability	74.4	6.6

There is an obvious conflict between the two. Stocks that perform well on margin growth will by definition perform poorly on margin stability, and vice versa. Table 5.7 sets out a comparison of our two example stocks, Procter & Gamble and Apple.

Apple's margin growth value of 5.4 percent puts it above 93 percent of all stocks. Its margin stability value, however, ranks *below* 80 percent of all stocks. In contrast, Procter & Gamble's margin growth value of −0.3 percent ranks in the bottom 20 percent of all stocks, but its margin stability value of 74.4 ranks above 97 percent of all stocks. Which do we believe? Does Apple possess a franchise? Does Procter & Gamble possess a franchise? Perhaps both possess a franchise? Perhaps neither does. We are confronted with a problem. It is clear we have two stocks with exceptional economic characteristics. One has very high profit margin growth, while the other has very stable profit margins. How can we compare the two?

We do so by creating a new variable called maximum margin (MM), which combines both measures of profit margin strength (growth and stability). Maximum margin is calculated in the following way:

$$MM = Max\ [Percentile\ (MS),\ Percentile\ (MG)]$$

where percentile is simply the performance of the stock according to each variable expressed as its percentile in the universe of stocks.

Maximum margin takes each stock's best-performing profit margin metric and awards this rank to the stock. For example, a stock that scores

50 on the margin growth, and 64 on the margin stability, is awarded a maximum margin rank of 64 because this is the stock's best-performing metric. MM allows each stock to put its best foot forward. It ensures that stocks with high profit margin growth get recognized for the growth, and are not penalized for the lack of stability. Similarly, maximum margin credits stocks for stable profit margins, but does not penalize them for the lack of growth. Stocks with low margins, low growth, and low stability are placed on the bottom of the pile. By calculating percentile ranks for margin stability and margin growth, we can compare maximum margin across all stocks. Using our example above, Apple Inc.'s maximum margin would be 93 percent versus Procter & Gamble's maximum margin of 97 percent, giving a slight edge to Procter & Gamble, the consumer staples king.

Buffett owes much of his investment success to his early recognition of the value of economic franchises. A franchise enables a stock to aggressively price its product, which in turn leads to high profit margins and high returns on capital. The indicia of franchises then are sustainable high returns on capital, and high, stable profit margins. See's Candies is the prototypical franchise. Its reputation for quality allows it to charge more for its candy, which gives it pricing power. The pricing power has led to high and growing profit margins and extraordinarily high returns on capital. See's Candies–like businesses are few and far between. Most businesses cannot maintain high profit margins or high rates of return on assets. If we take a sample of high-return businesses, the sample will contain few genuine franchises and many businesses at the peak of the cycle. Even if we can identify a franchise, competitors will attempt to push returns down. For this reason, return on capital is highly mean reverting.

We propose several methods to deal with the high rate of mean reversion in return on capital. First, we seek stocks with a franchise proven over a business cycle. Our CFOA measure seeks to identify stocks that generate masses of cash after capital investments over an average business cycle. The eight-year geometric mean of ROA and ROC measures seek stocks that earn consistently high returns on capital over the business cycle. These metrics are intuitive and identify stocks that we would commonly assume to possess a franchise.

Firms possessing a franchise will also maintain growing, or high, stable profit margins. We propose measures that capture these two elements of profit margin strength. Margin growth identifies a stock's profit margin growth. Margin stability identifies a stock's profit margin stability. These measures seek stocks that have *increased* profit margins over a business cycle or stocks that have *maintained* high profit margins over a business cycle. A stock cannot simultaneously perform well along both measures, so we use maximum margin, a measure that awards to a stock its highest ranking in margin growth or margin stability. Stocks with high maximum margin rankings possess either the highest growth in margins, or the most stable margins, both of which may indicate the presence of a franchise.

Finding a genuine franchise is as worthwhile as it is difficult. As the See's Candies example demonstrates, franchises are valuable because they can pay out capital to owners without affecting their ability to grow, or they can compound the capital of the business by reinvesting it year after year after year. Sustainable, high-return businesses like See's Candies are forgiving investments. They throw off a great deal of capital every year, which means we can buy a lot of other losers and still get ahead. It's good to own a franchise.

There is another element of quality not captured by a stock's return on capital or its profit margins: its financial strength. Financial strength is an accounting-based fundamental measure of a stock's financial health. It involves a holistic analysis of financial statements that any Graham-and-Dodd investor will recognize, including an assessment of a stock's current business quality, balance sheet strength, and liquidity. In the next chapter, we discuss how we calculate financial strength.

NOTES

1. Warren Buffett, "Shareholder Letter," Berkshire Hathaway, Inc. Annual Report, 1991.
2. Philip A. Fisher, *Common Stocks and Uncommon Profits and Other Writings* (Wiley Investment Classics) (New York: John Wiley & Sons, 1996).
3. Benjamin Graham and David Dodd, *Security Analysis: The Classic 1934 Edition* (New York: McGraw-Hill, 1996).
4. John Burr Williams, *The Theory of Investment Value* (Contrary Opinion Library) (Flint Hill, VA: Fraser, 1997).
5. Aswath Damodaran, "Return on Capital (ROC), Return on Invested Capital (ROIC) and Return on Equity (ROE): Measurement and Implications," July 2007. Available at *http://ssrn.com/abstract=1105499 or http://dx.doi.org/10.2139/ssrn.1105499*.
6. Ibid.
7. Michael J. Mauboussin, "Common Errors in DCF Models: Do You Use Economically Sound and Transparent Models?" Mauboussin on Strategy, Legg Mason Capital Management, March 16, 2006.
8. Eugene F. Fama and Kenneth R. French, "Forecasting Profitability and Earnings," February 1999. CRSP Working Paper No. 456. Available at *http://ssrn.com/abstract=40660 or http://dx.doi.org/10.2139/ssrn.40660*.
9. We do not mine the data to get our choice of eight years. The results are robust to periods both a few years longer and shorter.
10. Buffett.

CHAPTER 6

Financial Strength: Foundations Built on Rock

Huge debt, we were told, would cause operating managers to focus their efforts as never before, much as a dagger mounted on the steering wheel of a car could be expected to make its driver proceed with intensified care. We'll acknowledge that such an attention-getter would produce a very alert driver. But another certain consequence would be a deadly—and unnecessary—accident if the car hit even the tiniest pothole or sliver of ice. The roads of business are riddled with potholes; a plan that requires dodging them all is a plan for disaster.
— Warren Buffett, Shareholder Letter, 1990[1]

Buffett prizes stocks with unusual financial strength maintained through thick and thin. His frequent discussions of financial strength typically occur in the context of Berkshire's insurance operations. Buffett believes that more than simply providing protection, Berkshire's "towering" financial strength provides it with a competitive advantage. He writes that Berkshire's "premier financial strength" makes "a real difference in the competitive position of [Berkshire's] insurance operation."[2] It's so important that Buffett says, "[at] Berkshire, financial strength that is unquestionable takes precedence over all else."[3]

Buffett credits Graham with teaching him the value of financial strength. Graham's view was that financial strength and the margin of safety were inextricably intertwined[4]:

Analysts may place primary emphasis upon the presence of a large margin of safety for the security to absorb whatever adverse developments are reasonably likely to occur. In such cases, the analyst will be prepared to see unsatisfactory earnings for the issue during recession periods, but will expect that the company's financial strength will carry it unharmed through such a setback. ..."

[Emphasis Graham's]

We determine financial strength through a comprehensive assessment of financial health, assembled from a penetrating fundamental analysis of several periods of financial statements and business performance. Our financial strength measure is related to the risk of financial distress we discussed in Chapter 3. It differs, however, in that, rather than seeking to avoid stocks highly likely to permanently impair capital, the financial strength analysis seeks stocks positioned to protect capital. A stock's financial strength contributes to its margin of safety. The greater the financial strength, the more likely the stock is able to absorb the shocks of the business cycle and assaults by competitors. Below we discuss the Piotroski Fundamental Score, or F_SCORE, a quantitative method of conducting accounting-based fundamental analysis.

THE PIOTROSKI FUNDAMENTAL SCORE (F_SCORE)

In a 2002 study, "Value Investing: The Use of Historical Financial Statement Information to Separate Winners from Losers,"[5] Joseph Piotroski examined whether an investor could improve her or his investment returns by using a simple accounting-based fundamental analysis. Piotroski is an associate professor of accounting at Stanford University's Graduate School of Business. His research focuses on how capital market participants use financial accounting information for valuation and risk assessment purposes, and on the economic impact of different financial reporting and governance practices around the world.

Working on the theory established in 1992 by Fama and French that cheap stocks tend to beat the market—but only because they are more financially distressed, and therefore fundamentally riskier, than the average stock—Piotroski set out to find some way that investors could sort financially healthy stocks that are cheap from cheap stocks that are in financial distress. Piotroski settled on nine financial measures that best indicated the underlying financial health of a stock. These nine financial measures are grouped into three key areas: profitability, financial leverage or liquidity, and operating efficiency. Piotroski calls his measure the F_SCORE.

Through his F_SCORE, Piotroski sought cheap stocks that were also financially strong. For Piotroski, a cheap stock, or "value stock," is defined as a stock with a high book value relative to its market price (in other words, a low price-to-book value). One of his most interesting findings is that, despite the strong performance of low price-to-book value portfolios, a majority of the stocks (approximately 57 percent) underperform the market over one- and two-year stretches. Piotroski concluded that any strategy that could eliminate the left tail of the return distribution (i.e., the stocks that underperform the market) could greatly improve the portfolio's performance. Piotroski found that by identifying financially strong value stocks according to his F_SCORE, he could improve the return of a low price-to-book value portfolio by at least 7.5 percent per year, which is an astonishing outperformance. In addition, he found that an investment strategy that buys expected winners and shorts expected losers generated a 23 percent annual return between 1976 and 1996. The strategy of applying fundamental analysis seems to be robust over time: Graham and Dodd were promoting the use of the same techniques in their classic 1934 text *Security Analysis*.

Assuming that the "average [value stock] is financially distressed," Piotroski chose nine fundamental signals to measure three areas of the stock's financial health: profitability, financial leverage/liquidity, and operating efficiency. He sought to classify each stock's fundamental signal as either "good" or "bad," depending on the signal's implication for the stock's future prices and profitability. Each fundamental analyzed is given a binary outcome. In other words, if the fundamental analyzed is good, the signal is a one, if the fundamental analyzed is bad, the signal is marked zero. The aggregate of the signals is the F_SCORE, which represent the sum of the nine binary signals. The aggregate signal is designed to measure the overall quality, or strength, of the stock's financial health, and the decision to include the stock in a portfolio is ultimately based on the strength of the aggregate signal.

Analyzing the F_SCORE

Here we examine each of Piotroski's nine fundamental signals in the three areas of financial health: profitability; leverage, liquidity, and source of funds; and operating efficiency.

Profitability

Piotroski uses four variables to measure a stock's current profitability and cash flow realizations to glean information about the stock's ability to generate funds internally. These performance-related variables are: return on assets (ROA), cash flow from operations (CFO), the change in return on assets (ΔROA), and accruals (ACCRUAL). (Note that "Δ" is called *delta* and means "change in" or "difference," so ΔROA means "change in ROA").

- ROA and CFO are net income before extraordinary items and cash flow from operations, respectively, divided by beginning-of-the-year total assets. If the stock's ROA or CFO is positive, Piotroski defines the variable F_ROA or F_CFO as one, and zero if otherwise.
- He defines ΔROA as the current year's ROA less the prior year's ROA. If ΔROA is greater than 0, the variable F_ΔROA is marked one, and zero otherwise.
- Piotroski defines the variable ACCRUAL as the stock's current year's net income before extraordinary items less cash flow from operations, scaled by beginning of the year total assets. The variable F_ ACCRUAL is marked one if CFO is greater than ROA, and zero if otherwise.

Leverage, Liquidity, and Source of Funds

Piotroski's F_SCORE assumes that an increase in leverage, a deterioration in liquidity, or the use of external financing is a bad signal about financial health. Three of the nine financial signals are therefore designed to measure changes in capital structure and the stock's ability to meet future debt service obligations: ΔLEVER, ΔLIQUID, and EQ_OFFER.

- ΔLEVER seeks to capture changes in the stock's long-term debt levels. Piotroski measures ΔLEVER as the historical change in the ratio of total long-term debt to average total assets, and view an increase in financial leverage as a negative signal, and vice versa. By raising external capital, a financially distressed stock is signaling its inability to generate sufficient internal funds. In addition, an increase in long-term debt is likely to place additional constraints on the stock's financial flexibility. Piotroski defines the variable F_LEVER as one if the stock's leverage ratio fell in the preceding year, and zero if otherwise.
- ΔLIQUID seeks to measure the historical change in the stock's current ratio between the current and prior year, where Piotroski defines the current ratio as the ratio of current assets to current liabilities at fiscal year-end. He assumes that an improvement in liquidity is a good signal about the stock's ability to service current debt obligations. The variable F_ΔLIQUID is one if the stock's liquidity improved, and zero if otherwise.
- Piotroski argues that financially distressed stocks raising external capital could be signaling their inability to generate sufficient internal

funds to service future obligations. The fact that these stocks are willing to issue equity when their stock prices are depressed highlights their poor financial health. EQ_OFFER captures whether a stock has issued equity in the year preceding portfolio formation. It is set to one if the stock did not issue common equity in the preceding year, and zero if otherwise.

Operating Efficiency

Piotroski's two remaining signals—ΔMARGIN and ΔTURN—seek to measure changes in the efficiency of the stock's operations. Piotroski believes these ratios are important because they reflect two key parts of the return on assets.

- Piotroski defines ΔMARGIN as the stock's current gross margin ratio (gross margin divided by total sales) less the prior year's gross margin ratio. Piotroski believes that an improvement in margins signifies a potential improvement in costs, a reduction in inventory costs, or a rise in the price of the stock's product, all of which are positive for the stock. The indicator variable F_ΔMARGIN equals one if ΔMARGIN is positive, and zero if otherwise.
- Piotroski defines ΔTURN as the stock's current year asset turnover ratio (total sales scaled by beginning of the year total assets) less the prior year's asset turnover ratio. He says that an improvement in asset turnover signifies greater productivity from the asset base. Such an improvement can arise from more efficient operations (fewer assets generating the same levels of sales) or an increase in sales (which could also signify improved market conditions for the stock's products). The indicator variable F_ΔTURN equals one if ΔTURN is positive, and zero if otherwise.

Now that we've defined all of the signals in the F_SCORE, let's see how Piotroski combined them to find the F_SCORE, and then learn how to interpret the output.

F_SCORE Formula and Interpretation

Piotroski calculates his F_SCORE by summing the individual binary signals, or, more formally:

$$F\_SCORE = F\_ROA + F\_\Delta ROA + F\_CFO + F\_ ACCRUAL +$$
$$F\_\Delta MARGIN + F\_\Delta TURN + F\_\Delta LEVER + F\_\Delta LIQUID + EQ\_OFFER$$

An F_SCORE ranges from a low of zero to a high of nine, where a low F_SCORE represents a stock with very few good signals, and a high score indicates a stock with many good signals. To the extent current fundamentals predict future fundamentals, the F_SCORE should indicate future stock returns. Piotroski's investment strategy is simply to select value stocks with high F_SCORE signals.

Piotroski tested his F_SCORE using data for the 21 years between 1976 and 1996. He divided the universe into quintiles (i.e., fifths) based on price-to-book value, and then measured the quintile portfolio returns over one and two years after each formation. Piotroski provides statistics about the financial characteristics of the value quintile portfolio of stocks, as well as evidence on the long-run returns from such a portfolio. The median stock in the value quintile of all stocks has a median price-to-book value ratio of 0.58, which is cheap, but an end-of-year market capitalization of just $14.4 million dollars, which is tiny, and probably uninvestable even for very small investors. The value portfolio is made up of poorly performing stocks; the median ROA is just 1.28 percent, and the median stock saw declines in both ROA and gross margin over the preceding year. Finally, the average value stock saw an increase in leverage and a decrease in liquidity over the prior year.

Piotroski finds that the value portfolio earns market-beating returns in the one-year and two-year periods following portfolio formation. This is old news. Piotroski's insightful observation, however, is that despite the strong overall performance of the value portfolio, a majority of the stocks (approximately 57 percent) actually underperform the market. Piotroski concludes that any strategy that can eliminate the left tail of the return distribution (i.e., the underperforming stocks) will greatly improve the portfolio's overall performance.

Piotroski uses his F_SCORE to further classify the value portfolio according to the financial health of the stocks in it (the higher the F_SCORE, the financially healthier the stock). He finds that high F_SCORE value stocks beat the market by 13.4 percent per year versus 5.9 percent for the entire value quintile. This means that the high F_SCORE value stocks beat the average value stock by 7.5 percent per year (13.4 percent less 5.9 percent). The high F_SCORE value portfolio also contains a higher proportion of winners than the average portfolio. The high F_SCORE value portfolio picks winners 50 percent of the time. Clearly the F_SCORE discriminates between eventual winners and losers.

One criticism of the F_SCORE is that the best-performing stocks—the high F_SCORE value stocks—tend to be very small, with a median end-of-year market capitalization of just $14.4 million dollars (the average market capitalization is a little larger at $188.5 million). Piotroski deals with this issue by examining the returns in higher market capitalizations. He divides the universe into three portfolios based on market capitalization. The vast majority (almost 60 percent) of value stocks are in the small market capitalization portfolio. Around 28 percent of value stocks are in the medium-sized portfolio, and just 13 percent of value firms are in the top market capitalization portfolio. Piotroski finds that the above-market returns earned by value stocks are concentrated in the smaller companies. Applying the F_SCORE within each size grouping, he also finds the strongest benefit from financial statement analysis in the small stock portfolio. Piotroski finds some benefit from the application of the F_SCORE in the medium size portfolio, with high-score stocks earning approximately 7 percent more than the average medium-size firms and 17.3 percent more than the low F_SCORE firms. Disappointingly, the F_SCORE does not differentiate much between the largest stocks. The improvement in returns from the application of the F_SCORE is isolated to stocks in the bottom two-thirds of market capitalization. This makes sense. Larger stocks are more widely followed by analysts and so are less likely to suffer from chronic undervaluation that can be easily identified by reading financial statements.

Piotroski's F_SCORE is clearly a useful, and intuitive metric for value investors. His key insight is that quantitatively analyzing financial statements can improve performance. The F_SCORE is designed to eliminate underperforming stocks. It succeeds in doing so by classifying the stocks according to their financial health. The resulting returns to cheap, financially strong stocks are outstanding, albeit limited to small and medium market capitalization. In the next section, we discuss some small improvements to the F_SCORE that we use to enhance the ability of financial statement analysis to separate the winners and losers.

OUR FINANCIAL STRENGTH SCORE (FS_SCORE)

Using the F_SCORE as a foundation, we have created a new financial strength score (FS_SCORE), which we divide into the following three categories:

- Current profitability
- Stability
- Recent operational improvements

Like the F_SCORE, the FS_SCORE seeks to find the financially strongest stocks. We have modified the F_SCORE to tweak three variables and moved the variables into slightly more intuitive categories. The variables in our FS_SCORE are set out in the following manner:

Current Profitability

We use three variables to measure a stock's current profitability and cash flow realization:

- ROA and FCFTA are net income before extraordinary items and free cash flow, respectively, divided by most recent total assets. If the stock's ROA or FCFTA is positive, we define the variable FS_ROA or FS_FCFTA as one, and zero if otherwise.
- ACCRUAL is the stock's current year's net income before extraordinary items less cash flow from operations, scaled by beginning of the year total assets. The variable F_ ACCRUAL is marked one if CFO is greater than ROA, and zero if otherwise.

Our current profitability variables are similar to Piotroski's profitability variables, except that we replace the CFO variable with free cash flow divided by total assets (FCFTA). We make this change to take into account the impact of capital expenditures on the stocks' cash flows. We also exclude the variables ΔROA and ΔFCFTA from this category, and move each to our "recent operational improvements" category because we believe it is a more intuitive category for these variables.

Stability

Like Piotroski, we assume that an increase in leverage, a deterioration in liquidity, or the use of external financing is a bad signal about financial health. Our stability signals measure changes in capital structure and the stock's ability to meet future debt service obligations:

- ΔLEVER is the historical change in the ratio of total long-term debt to total assets. FS_LEVER is one if the stock's leverage ratio fell in the preceding year, and zero if otherwise.
- ΔLIQUID is defined as the year-over-year change in the ratio of current assets to current liabilities. The variable FS_ΔLIQUID is one if the stock's liquidity improved, and zero if otherwise.
- NEQISS is equity repurchases minus equity issuance, or net equity issuance. FS_NEQISS is set to one if repurchases exceed equity issuance, and zero otherwise.

Our stability category differs from Piotroski's in one important way: We replace the F_SCORE's equity issuance variable, EQ_OFFER, with *net* equity issuance, or NEQISS, which is defined as repurchases minus issuances. (We use the same technique found in Boudoukh, Michaely, Richardson, and Roberts's 2007 article, "On the Importance of Measuring Payout

Yield: Implications for Asset Pricing."[6]) We make this small, but important, change because we believe Piotroski's EQ_OFFER can be a misleading metric. For example, many firms issue shares for a variety of reasons unrelated to financial health, including management or employee incentive programs. A company may issue a small number of shares to compensate a CEO, but simultaneously initiate a substantial repurchase program that dwarfs the number of shares issued to the CEO. EQ_OFFER would penalize this stock because of the small equity issuance, while NEQISS would consider the relative size of both the buyback and the issuance and score accordingly. Each metric would be scored in the following way: EQ_OFFER would be zero and have no effect on F_SCORE; NEQISS would increase by one and increase FS_SCORE.

Recent Operational Improvements

We introduce a new section for the FS_SCORE: recent operational improvements. This category is roughly equivalent to the F_SCORE's "operating efficiency" section, except that the focus in our FS_SCORE is on improvements. We include in our recent operational improvements category the following:

- ΔROA is the current year's ROA less the prior year's ROA. If ΔROA is greater than zero, the variable F_ΔROA is marked one, and zero otherwise.
- ΔFCFTA is the current year's FCFTA less the prior year's FCFTA. If ΔFCFTA is greater than zero, the variable FS_ΔFCFTA is marked one, and zero otherwise.
- ΔMARGIN is the stock's current gross margin ratio (gross margin divided by total sales) less the prior year's gross margin ratio. The indicator variable FS_ΔMARGIN equals one if ΔMARGIN is positive, and zero if otherwise.
- ΔTURN is the stock's current year asset turnover ratio (total sales scaled by beginning of the year total assets) less the prior year's asset turnover ratio. The indicator variable FS_ΔTURN equals one if ΔTURN is positive, and zero if otherwise.

We examine recent operational improvements to ascertain whether the business has *operational momentum*. We don't want to buy a seemingly cheap stock that gets increasingly expensive relative to its fundamentals because the business deteriorates. For example, a stock with $100 million in EBIT trading for $300 million is trading on multiple of 3. If operations deteriorate to the extent that next year's EBIT is only $50 million, the "bargain" multiple of 3 becomes a more expensive multiple of 6. If this halving of EBIT continues, we will be left holding a very expensive stock after a few years.

FS_SCORE Formula and Interpretation

Our FS_SCORE has ten metrics across the three categories of profitability, stability, and recent operational improvements. The final score is from 0 to 10, where 10 is a perfect score, and 0 is the worst score possible. The FS_SCORE formula is as follows:

$$FS\_SCORE = Sum(FS\_ROA, FS\_FCFTA, FS\_ACCRUAL, FS\_LEVER, \\ FS\_LIQUID, FS\_NEQISS, FS\_\Delta ROA, FS\_\Delta FCFTA, FS\_\Delta MARGIN, \\ FS\_\Delta TURN)$$

COMPARING THE PERFORMANCE OF PIOTROSKI'S F_SCORE AND OUR FS_SCORE

Here, we compare the performance of the F_SCORE and the FS_SCORE. We look at the returns from all stocks with an F_SCORE of 6, 7, 8, or 9 and compare those to the performance of all FS_SCOREs with a score of 7, 8, 9, or 10. We examine the returns to a portfolio containing the high scorers in each strategy over the period January 1, 1974, to December 31, 2011 (see Figure 6.1 and Table 6.1).

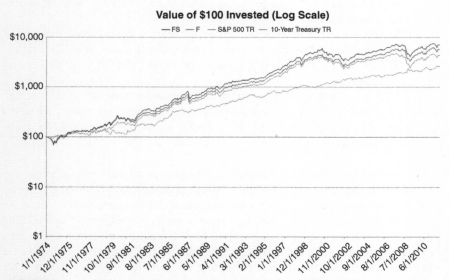

FIGURE 6.1 Cumulative Returns to the F_SCORE and the FS_SCORE

TABLE 6.1   Performance Statistics: F_SCORE and FS_SCORE (1974 to 2011)

	FS_SCORE	F_SCORE	S&P 500 TR	Ten-Year Treasury TR
CAGR	11.89%	11.29%	10.46%	8.99%
Standard Deviation	15.75%	15.80%	15.84%	10.90%
Downside Deviation	11.03%	11.11%	11.16%	6.55%
Sharpe Ratio	0.46	0.42	0.37	0.36
Sortino Ratio (MAR = 5%)	0.68	0.63	0.56	0.64
Worst Drawdown	−44.93%	−43.97%	−50.21%	−20.97%
Worst Month Return	−20.85%	−21.42%	−21.58%	−11.24%
Best Month Return	16.87%	15.71%	16.81%	15.23%
Profitable Months	60.75%	60.53%	60.53%	61.18%

The small tweaks we apply to the F_SCORE cause the FS_SCORE to outperform by a small, but economically meaningful amount. Additionally, the structure of the FS_SCORE is more intuitive and grounded in value-investing philosophy than the F_SCORE.

Next we use our FS_SCORE in a case study about Lubrizol Corporation, which Buffett acquired in March 2011.

CASE STUDY: LUBRIZOL CORPORATION

Lubrizol Corporation, a maker of lubricant additives, fits the Buffett mold in many ways. It was large and generated consistent earnings ($732 million in profit from $5.4 billion in revenue the year before Berkshire Hathaway acquired it). Its business is tractable, concentrated on producing automotive lubricants, and household products like lotions and dishwashing liquid. In 2010, the stock was also relatively cheap. On a total enterprise value to earnings before interest and taxes (TEV/EBIT) basis the stock traded at a multiple of 6.8.

Lubrizol's FS_SCORE speaks to its financial strength. In Table 6.2, we set out the FS_SCORE calculations for Lubrizol using December 31, 2010, data:

TABLE 6.2   Lubrizol Corporation's FS_SCORE Calculation

FS Variable	Lubrizol
FS_ROA	1
FS_FCFAT	1
FS_ACCRUAL	1
FS_LEVER	1
FS_LIQUID	1
FS_NEQISS	0
FS_ΔROA	1
FS_ΔFCFTA	1
FS_ΔMARGIN	1
FS_ΔTURN	0
FS_SCORE	**8**

The highest possible FS_SCORE is 10, which indicates a "financially strong" stock in our framework. An FS_SCORE of 8 indicates that Lubrizol has failed on two dimensions, but is still a very financially strong stock. For stocks with a less-than-perfect score, the FS_SCORE's utility is that it enables us to rapidly identify where the stock has fallen short. Lubrizol fails on the FS_SCORE variables NEQISS (from the "Stability" category) and ΔTURN (from the "Recent Operational Improvements" category). Lubrizol's FS_NEQISS score of zero indicates that repurchases did not exceed equity issuance. Lubrizol was a net issuer of stock, but the amount was minuscule ($32.9 million of stock on top of a market capitalization of nearly $5 billion). Given that Buffett controls Lubrizol's capital structure after the acquisition, it's unlikely that this would concern him. It's more important for a passive investor with no control over equity issuance. Also recall that ΔTURN is the stock's current year asset turnover ratio (total sales scaled by beginning of the year total assets) less the prior year's asset turnover ratio. The indicator variable FS_ΔTURN equals one if ΔTURN is positive, and zero if otherwise. Lubrizol's FS_ΔTURN score is zero, indicating that its current year asset turnover ratio did not exceed its prior year's asset turnover ratio, declining 25 percent. This may indicate a problem with slowing sales growth or ballooning assets that may require further investigation. Let's see how Lubrizol performed against the Standard & Poor's (S&P) 500 from July 1, 2010, through December 31, 2011 (see Figure 6.2).

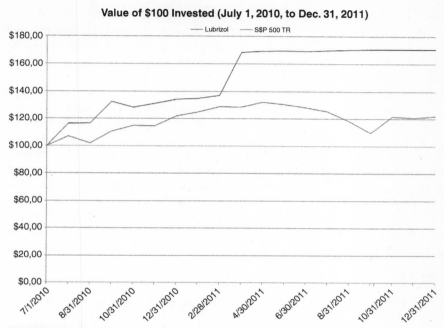

FIGURE 6.2   Invested Growth of $100 in Lubrizol and the S&P 500

This anecdote suggests that cheap stocks with strong FS_SCOREs can be attractive investments. While Lubrizol did outperform the market—and catch a bid from the world's greatest investor—we don't intend our FS_ SCORE to be used as a stand-alone metric. We use it as part of a suite of metrics to isolate the financial strength of a stock.

In this chapter, we have considered the second element of quality, financial strength. We've examined Piotroski's F_SCORE, a quantitative metric used to conduct fundamental analysis a stock's financial health, and shown that it is a powerful and intuitive metric for value investors. The Piotroski F_SCORE seeks to eliminate underperforming value stocks from the invest- able universe. The metric succeeds in doing so by classifying stocks accord- ing to their financial health. It uses a series of metrics that any value inves- tor would recognize, examining the stock's financial statements to assess its profitability, stability, and signs of operational improvements.

We modify the F_SCORE to create the financial strength or FS_SCORE. The FS_SCORE improves on the F_SCORE by substituting free cash flow for operating cash flow in two metrics, and by substituting net equity issu- ance for equity issuance. We also rearrange the metrics into a slightly more intuitive format to make them more useful to individual value investors. The changes allow us to take a more granular look at the financial strength of a stock, and to quickly identify potential problems in stocks with less-than-perfect FS_SCOREs. Our FS_SCORE outperforms Piotroski's F_SCORE, and so the changes objectively add value.

In this part, we have considered two elements of stock quality: franchise and financial strength. A franchise manifests in long-term return on investment measures and pricing power. Financial strength manifests in financial statement health and business improvement. By combining an analysis of a stock's franchise with an analysis of its financial strength, we get a comprehensive look at its quality. In the next part, we move on to price metrics. A high-quality stock is not necessarily a good investment. If we overpay, it can be a terrible investment. In Part Four, we examine a number of price metrics to find the best-performed metric and those that will help us to pay the lowest price, and thereby create the widest margin of safety.

NOTES

1. Warren Buffett, "Chairman's Letter," Berkshire Hathaway, Inc. Annual Report, 1990.
2. Warren Buffett, "Chairman's Letter," Berkshire Hathaway, Inc. Annual Report, 1985.
3. Warren Buffett, "Chairman's Letter," Berkshire Hathaway, Inc. Annual Report, 2011.
4. Benjamin Graham and David Dodd, *Security Analysis,* 5th ed. (New York: McGraw-Hill, 1988).
5. Joseph D. Piotroski, "Value Investing: The Use of Historical Financial Statement Information to Separate Winners from Losers." As published in *Journal of Accounting Research* 38(Supplement) (2000). Available at *http://ssrn.com/abstract=249455*.
6. J. Boudoukh, R. Michaely, M. Richardson, and M. R. Roberts, "On the Importance of Measuring Payout Yield: Implications for Asset Pricing." *Journal of Finance* 62 (2007): 877–915.

Four

The Secret to Finding Bargain Prices

In Part Four, we examine a variety of price ratios to determine which works the best. In Chapter 7, we use several statistical techniques to measure each metric's performance. First, we put the price ratios into a horse race, looking at raw, absolute compound growth over the full period. Next, we examine performance controlling for risk factors such as general market exposure. We also look at the risk profile of each price ratio, and its performance after adjusting for risk. Finally, we look at rolling performance statistics to ensure that the results are consistent over different subperiods of the sample time period. From these different analyses, we identify a winner.

Chapter 8 explores alternative and underresearched variations of price ratios. We examine longer-term price ratios. The price measures examined in Chapter 7 are all single-year metrics. There is some danger in using a single historical period of 12 months to calculate price. Such a thin slice of historical earnings data might cause our single-year price metrics to favor stocks that have had unusually good earnings in a 12-month period unrepresentative of the stock's typical earning power. Our price metrics might therefore select stocks at the peak of their business cycle, with the likelihood that earnings over subsequent periods revert down to at least their long-run average, and possibly lower.

We also research the use of composite price ratios. We investigate whether a combination measure of price ratios can outperform the best individual price ratios in each category of performance. The appeal of a compound measure using a variety of price ratios is the possibility that "ratio engineering" can offer a solution that dominates any particular measure. Such a compound measure could examine different price ratios, for example, looking at free cash flow yield, the unadulterated gross profits yield, and earnings before interest and taxes/total enterprise value (EBIT/ TEV). Seeking the cheapest stocks on a compound measure might provide a cross-check to help us avoid stocks with unusual accounting that look cheap on one metric but expensive on the other two. Further, if one metric under-performs for an extended period, the other two might counter its influence.

CHAPTER 7

Price Ratios: A Horse Race

*Value strategies yield higher returns because these strategies
exploit suboptimal behavior of the typical investor and not
because these strategies are fundamentally riskier.*
—Josef Lakonishok, Andrei Shleifer, and Robert Vishny,
"Contrarian Investment, Extrapolation, and Risk"[1]

The empirical evidence is unqualified: value stocks have beaten both glamour stocks and the market over the long term. This raises two obvious questions: (1) why would anyone buy glamour stocks, and (2) which measure of value has generated the best returns? The answer to the first question is behavioral. Expensive stocks are called "glamour" or "story" stocks for a reason. Glamour stocks seduce investors who ignore base rates and focus instead on the stock's "story." This can lead investors to extrapolate high historical earnings growth too far into the future, assume an upward trend in stock prices, overreact to good news, or simply conflate an exciting investment opportunity with an exciting technology or idea, irrespective of price. Investors can exploit these irrational behaviors by buying cheap or "value" stocks, but which price ratio should an investor use to assess cheapness? We explore in detail the answer to that question in this chapter.

Practitioners have relied on a variety of price ratios, including the price-to-earnings ratio, the price-to-cash flow ratio, and the enterprise multiple (total enterprise value to earnings before interest and taxes and depreciation and amortization). Academia has traditionally remained agnostic to the particular price ratio tested, leaning toward the book-to-market capitalization ratio to distinguish between value and glamour. Eugene Fama and Ken French consider book-to-market capitalization the slightly superior metric[2]:

> *We always emphasize that different price ratios are just different ways to scale a stock's price with a fundamental, to extract the*

information in the cross-section of stock prices about expected returns. One fundamental (book value, earnings, or cashflow) is pretty much as good as another for this job, and the average return spreads produced by different ratios are similar to and, in statistical terms, indistinguishable from one another. We like [book-to-market] because the book value in the numerator is more stable over time than earnings or cashflow, which is important for keeping turnover down in a value portfolio.

The empirical evidence does not support Fama and French's assertion. We have conducted a comprehensive examination of a wide variety of metrics and found economically and statistically significant differences between them, and found one price ratio stands head-and-shoulders above the rest.

THE HORSES IN THE RACE

Here, we describe the various price ratios under examination. We explain the rationale for each ratio, and, because there are often many ways of calculating each ratio, we set out the manner in which we perform our calculations. All the ratios in this chapter are expressed in "yield" format, which makes them comparable to the interest rate on a bank account or coupon on a bond.

Earnings Yield

The earnings yield is simply the inverse of the popular price-to-earnings (P/E) ratio. Following Fama and French (2001), we calculate it as follows:

$$Earnings\ Yield = E\ /\ M$$

where   E = earnings before extraordinary items – preferred dividends + income statement deferred taxes, if available
          M = market capitalization

The market capitalization (M) variable is used in several price ratios below.

Enterprise Yield (EBITDA and EBIT Variations)

The enterprise yield, or enterprise multiple, is sometimes called the "acquirer's multiple" because, in addition to market capitalization, it includes in the denominator all the liabilities taken on by an acquirer of the enterprise in its entirety. This calculation is called the total enterprise value, and is intended to reflect the true cost of total acquisition. We use earnings before interest, depreciation, and amortization (EBITDA) in the numerator because we wish to see the unadulterated operating earnings flowing to the acquirer postacquisition. The new owner can vary the mix of debt and equity in the capital structure, which will in turn impact the interest and tax paid. It also adjusts for depreciation and amortization because these charges are noncash, accounting charges that reflect historical investment decisions. The acquirer can take advantage of the earnings masked by these charges once in control, and so we add them back into the enterprise multiple calculation.

We calculate the enterprise yield as follows:

$$Enterprise\ Yield = EBITDA\ /\ TEV$$

where   EBITDA = earnings before interest, taxes, depreciation, and
                amortization
        TEV = market capitalization + total debt − excess cash +
                preferred stock + minority interests
    Excess cash = cash + current assets − current liabilities

We use total enterprise value (TEV) in a number of price ratios in this chapter.

We also examine another variation of the enterprise yield, EBIT/TEV, which substitutes EBIT for EBITDA:

$$EBIT\ /\ TEV$$

where   EBIT = earnings before interest and taxes.

Free Cash Flow Yield

Free cash flow yield is a similar calculation to the enterprise multiple, using total enterprise value as the denominator, but substituting free cash flow for the enterprise multiple's EBITDA. The rationale for free cash flow in the numerator is that, while depreciation and amortization are noncash, accounting charges reflecting historical investment decisions, some level of maintenance capital expenditure will be necessary after the acquisition. Free cash flow is the operating cash flow after capital expenditures have been removed, and so accounts for this maintenance capital expenditure.

We calculate the free cash flow yield as follows:

$$Free\ Cash\ Flow\ Yield = EBITDA\ /\ TEV$$

where   FCF = net income + depreciation and amortization − working
                 capital change − capital expenditures.

Gross Profits Yield

The gross profits yield is another variation of the enterprise multiple, but one that substitutes gross profitability for EBITDA. The rationale for gross profits is that it is the top-most profit figure in the financial statements, and so is the most difficult number to manipulate. It is the raw profit flowing back to the stock after the cost of goods sold is deducted from sales.

We calculate the gross profits yield as follows:

$$Gross\ Profits\ Yield = GP\ /\ TEV$$

where   GP = revenue − cost of goods sold.

Book-to-Market

The book value-to-market (BM) capitalization ratio is simply the inverse of the more familiar price-to-book value ratio. The argument for BM is that it is a stable metric. While income or cash flow can vary greatly from year to year, the assets remain relatively static. This should assist us in avoiding stocks that look cheap on some income-based metric, but are in actuality expensive because the income is at a cyclical peak. The rationale for BM is that, at a cyclical peak, such a stock should appear expensive on a BM basis.

We calculate BM capitalization as follows:

$$Book\ to\ Market = B\ /\ M$$

where   B = common equity + preferred stock par value or assets −
              liabilities − preferred stock (defined below) + balance
              sheet deferred taxes and investment tax credit, if available.
              Preferred stock means preferred stock redemption value
              or preferred stock liquidating value, or preferred stock
              par value.

Forward Earnings Estimate

The forward earnings estimate is similar to the earnings yield, but substitutes forward earnings estimates in place of historical earnings when calculating the earnings yield. The argument for forward earnings is that they look to the future, where historical measures record the past. As our investment will be made with an eye to the future, it therefore makes sense, so the argument goes, to use the forward estimate.

We calculated the forward earnings estimate as follows:

$$Forward\ Earnings\ Estimate = FE\ /\ M$$

where   FE = means consensus Institutional Brokers' Estimate System (I/B/E/S) earnings forecast of EPS for the fiscal year (available 1982 through 2010).

Next we describe the methods we use to study the performance of the price ratios.

RULES OF THE RACE

Here, we provide a brief overview of our methods of studying the performance of the various price ratios. Our full investment simulation criteria, our assumptions, and the rationale for each are set out in detail in Chapter 11. Our potential investment universe includes all stocks listed on the New York Stock Exchange (NYSE), American Stock Exchange (AMEX), and Nasdaq also with the requisite data in the University of Chicago's Booth School of Business Center for Research in Security Prices (CRSP) database and Compustat. We only examine stocks with ordinary common equity in CRSP and eliminate all real estate investment trusts, American depositary receipts, closed-end funds, utilities, and financial stocks.

We restrict our universe to include only those stocks with data for all the metrics described above (except for the forward earnings estimates yield, which we exclude because it highly restricts our universe due to limited I/B/E/S data). To ensure there is sufficient liquidity in the stocks in which we perform our tests, we restrict our analysis to stocks with a market capitalization greater than the 40th percentile NYSE breakpoint at June 30 of each year, which is the convention in finance research. This means that our analysis is limited to stocks with a market capitalization greater than the smallest 40 percent of NYSE stocks in each year, whether they are found on the NYSE, Nasdaq, or AMEX. To put this in context, on December 31,

2011, the smallest stock in our investable universe had a market capitalization of $1.4 billion.

We measure the stock returns from January 1964 through December 2011. We determine market capitalization by the value on June 30 of year t. We calculate stock fundamentals on December 31 of year $t - 1$. We sort the stocks into deciles on each measure on June 30 of year t, and then compute the buy-and-hold monthly returns from July of year t to June of year $t + 1$. We rebalance the portfolios annually.

THE RACE CALL

We analyze the compound annual growth rates of each price ratio over the 1964 to 2011 period for market capitalization–weighted decile portfolios. We find the best-performing price ratio measured on a raw compound annual growth rate is the EBIT variation of the enterprise multiple. The value decile of the EBIT enterprise multiple stocks generated a compound average growth rate of 14.55 percent per year over the full period. This compares favorably to the value decile of the next best performer, the EBITDA enterprise multiple, which generated 13.72 percent, the popular earnings yield, which generated on average 12.44 percent a year, and the academic favorite, BM, which earned 13.11 percent. The value decile of the gross profits yield performed admirably, earning 13.51 percent over the full period. The forward earnings estimate is the worst performed metric by a wide margin. The performance of the forward earnings estimate is uniformly poor, earning a compound annual growth rate of just 8.63 percent on average and underperforming the Standard & Poor's (S&P) 500 by almost 1 percent per year. Investors are wise to shy away from analyst forward earnings estimates when making investment decisions. We focus our analysis on historical valuation metrics throughout this chapter and leave the forward earnings estimates to the promoters on Wall Street.

Our finding is consistent with the research of Tim Loughran and Jay Wellman, who in 2009 found the enterprise multiple significantly outperformed the academic favorite BM over the period July 1964 to December 2009 (see Figure 7.1).[3] Loughran and Wellman identify good reasons for favoring the enterprise multiple. They cite a study by Damodaran (2006) of 550 equity research reports in which he notes that enterprise multiple, along with the earnings yield and the price-to-sales ratio, are the most common pricing metrics used. Damodaran states, "In the past two decades, [the enterprise multiple] has acquired a number of adherents among analysts for a number of reasons."[4]

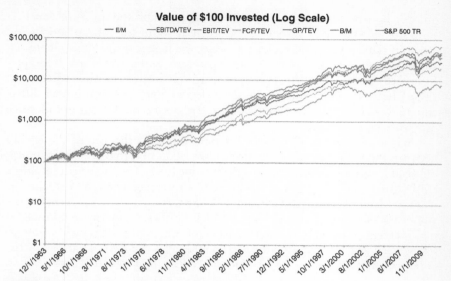

FIGURE 7.1 Enterprise Multiple (EBIT Variation) by a Length

One reason for the enterprise multiple's popularity cited by Damodaran is the ease with which stocks with differing leverage can be compared. Including debt is important. Damodaran gives the example of General Motors, which in 2005 had a market capitalization of $17 billion, but debt of $287 billion. Using market capitalization as a measure of size, General Motors was a midsized firm. Yet on the basis of enterprise value, General Motors was a very large firm. Market capitalization does not capture the effect General Motors' debt has on its returns, but enterprise value does.

Loughran identifies the enterprise multiple's use of EBITDA in the numerator as another reason for its popularity. EBITDA is not affected by nonoperating gains or losses. As a result, operating income before depreciation can be viewed as a more accurate and less easily manipulated measure of profitability than net income, allowing it to be used to compare firms within as well as across industries. On an absolute return basis, evidence suggests that the simplest form of the enterprise multiple (the EBIT variation) is superior to alternative price ratios.

Value Premium and Spread

The difference in returns between portfolios of value stocks and glamour stocks—the spread—is called the "value premium." Not only do we wish to find the best-performing price ratio, we wish to find the measure that best sorts stocks. The bigger the spread between the value (i.e., cheap) stocks and glamour (i.e., expensive) stocks, the better the metric differentiates between stocks primed for probabilistic outperformance and probabilistic underperformance. Table 7.1 sets out the returns to the decile portfolios sorted into value (decile 10) and glamour (decile 1) deciles. Each price ratio does differentiate to some degree between value and glamour stocks, but not all price ratios are created equal.

When we analyze the price ratios according to the size of the spread between the value and glamour stocks, we again find that enterprise multiple (EBIT variation) is the most effective measure. The enterprise multiple (EBIT variation) generates a spread of 7.45 percent per year because the glamour decile returns 7.09 percent per year versus the 14.55 percent for the value stocks. The next biggest spread is the EBITDA enterprise multiple at 6.17 percent. Interestingly, the top decile of the gross profits yield also performs very well on a stand-alone basis and gives the two variations of the enterprise multiples a run for their money, generating a spread of 6.09 percent.

TABLE 7.1 Compound Annual Growth Rates for All Price Measures (1964 to 2011)

	Earnings Yield	Enterprise Multiple (EBITDA Variation)	Enterprise Multiple (EBIT Variation)	Free Cash Flow Yield	Gross Profits Yield	Book-to-Market
S&P 500			9.52.%			
Glamour	7.77%	7.55%	7.09%	9.05%	7.42%	8.62%
2	8.04%	8.20%	8.58%	9.55%	7.08%	9.20%
3	10.70%	8.76%	8.77%	9.13%	7.96%	9.79%
4	8.76%	8.22%	8.29%	9.71%	9.18%	9.29%
5	9.20%	8.16%	9.70%	8.80%	9.86%	9.62%
6	9.00%	10.00%	11.04%	11.19%	10.89%	10.13%
7	11.75%	11.06%	11.00%	9.74%	12.02%	11.44%
8	12.45%	11.73%	11.63%	9.98%	13.71%	11.45%
9	12.92%	13.70%	12.08%	12.83%	13.43%	11.80%
Value	12.44%	13.72%	14.55%	11.68%	13.51%	13.11%
Value Premium (10-1)	4.67%	6.17%	7.45%	2.63%	6.09%	4.49%

This compares favorably to the spreads created by the earnings yield and BM, which create a 4.67 percent and 4.49 percent spread, respectively. The poorest performer on an absolute spread basis is the free cash flow yield, which stands at 2.63 percent.

"Alpha" and Adjusted Performance

Raw compound annual growth rates and spreads provide some information about the performance of the various price ratios, but its factor-adjusted performance provides a fuller picture of its utility. We want to know how each decile portfolio's exposure to the market contributes to each price ratio's performance over the market. To assess each portfolio's adjusted performance, we control for and calculate the capital asset pricing model (CAPM) estimate of "alpha," which we discuss in some detail below. We use the market capitalization-weight index of all NYSE/AMEX/Nasdaq as our market return. Our risk-free measure is the four-week Treasury bill.

Table 7.2 sets out our calculations of alpha. Bolded figures are statistically significant at the 5 percent level, which can be interpreted as the probability that these results appear by random chance.

TABLE 7.2 Factor-Adjusted Performance for All Price Measures (CAPM Alpha)

	Earnings Yield	Enterprise Multiple (EBITDA Variation)	Enterprise Multiple (EBIT Variation)	Free Cash Flow Yield	Gross Profits Yield	Book-to-Market
Glamour	−1.45%	−1.64%	−2.19%	−0.20%	−1.52%	−0.53%
2	−1.35%	−0.95%	−0.72%	0.40%	−1.87%	−0.05%
3	1.23%	−0.32%	−0.34%	−0.06%	−0.86%	0.44%
4	−0.34%	−0.84%	−0.64%	0.43%	0.15%	0.20%
5	**0.24%**	−0.75%	0.74%	−0.38%	0.70%	0.39%
6	0.16%	1.03%	2.01%	2.10%	1.71%	1.15%
7	**2.66%**	2.15%	1.99%	0.74%	**2.63%**	2.36%
8	**3.42%**	2.70%	2.69%	0.94%	**4.20%**	2.51%
9	4.02%	4.50%	2.98%	3.65%	4.02%	3.01%
Value	3.30%	4.46%	5.23%	2.45%	4.03%	4.09%
S&P 500			9.52%			

The value decile of the EBIT variation of the enterprise multiple generates the greatest alpha at 5.23 percent per year, beating out the EBITDA variation at 4.46 percent, and BM at 4.09 percent. The gross profits yield also performs well, generating alpha of 4.03 percent per year. The free cash flow yield strategy shows the lowest "alpha" at 2.45 percent. The highest alphas come from the enterprise multiples and the gross profit yield. The earnings yield also performs admirably.

We understand that for many value investors alpha is considered nonsense; however, it should have some informal, intuitive appeal. A portfolio that consists simply of the market purchased with some leverage will outperform the market over the long term, but we would not intuitively understand the portfolio to possess alpha, and the simple CAPM will capture this fact.

Risk-Adjusted Performance and Absolute Measures of Risk

Here we examine several common measures of risk for each of the price metrics: the *Sharpe* and *Sortino* ratios, and several slightly different measures of *drawdown* risk. These measures seek to gauge different aspects of the riskiness of each price metric. The Sharpe and Sortino ratios are risk/reward metrics. They seek to describe how much additional performance each metric generates for each additional unit of risk. The drawdown metrics look at absolute risk in the form of the largest historical drop in the portfolios. We examine drawdown risk either from peak to trough, or over several different time periods. By investigating the price metrics along these lines, we seek to find any problems not uncovered by the raw or adjusted performance measures.

William Sharpe created the Sharpe ratio in 1966, intending it to be used to measure the risk-adjusted performance of mutual funds.[5] Sharpe was interested in the extent to which managers took on extra risk to generate additional return. He wanted to find some measure that would adjust the return for the risk taken to generate it. He created the Sharpe ratio, which does this by examining the historical relationship between *excess return*—the return in excess of the risk-free rate—and *volatility*, which stands in for risk. The higher the Sharpe ratio, the more return is generated for each additional unit of volatility, and the better the price metric.

The Sortino ratio, like the Sharpe ratio, measures risk-adjusted return. The difference is that the Sortino ratio only measures downside volatility, while the Sharpe ratio measures both upside and downside volatility. The Sortino ratio doesn't adjust return for upside volatility, only for downside volatility, which we wish to avoid. The Sortino ratio also measures excess returns in excess of a minimum acceptable return. We use 5 percent per year as the minimum acceptable return in our analysis. The Sortino ratio therefore measures the *excess return over a minimum acceptable return* per unit of *downside* risk.

The drawdown risk examines the extent to which each portfolio has fallen in the past. "Worst Drawdown" measures the largest peak-to-trough drop in the history of the data under examination. The drawdown risk measures seek to describe the worst absolute performance of the price metric. Drawdowns are an excellent way to determine how well a strategy protects against a losses of capital that are so significant as to be effectively permanent.

Table 7.3 sets out the Sharpe and Sortino ratios and historical drawdown risk metrics for the market capitalization-weighted value decile portfolios of each price ratio.

Table 7.3 shows that the enterprise multiples have the top risk-adjusted performance, whether we examine the results using the Sharpe ratio or the Sortino ratio. The enterprise multiple (EBIT variation) monthly Sharpe ratio of 0.58 is the highest, and its monthly Sortino ratio of 0.89 is also the highest. This means the enterprise multiple (EBIT variation) metric offers the best risk/reward ratio, whether we define risk as volatility (Sharpe ratio) or just downside volatility (Sortino ratio). The EBITDA variation also stands out with favorable Sharpe and Sortino ratios of 0.53 and 0.82, respectively.

TABLE 7.3   Risk Measures for the Value Decile of All Price Ratios

	Earnings Yield	Enterprise Multiple (EBITDA Variation)	Enterprise Multiple (EBIT Variation)	Free Cash Flow Yield	Gross Profits Yield	Book-to-Market	S&P 500 TR
CAGR	12.44%	13.72%	14.55%	11.68%	13.51%	13.11%	9.52%
Standard Deviation	17.62%	17.25%	17.20%	16.42%	18.35%	17.39%	15.19%
Downside Deviation	12.17%	11.49%	11.34%	11.00%	12.93%	11.12%	10.66%
Sharpe Ratio	0.46	0.53	0.58	0.44	0.50	0.50	0.33
Sortino Ratio (MAR = 5%)	0.68	0.82	0.89	0.68	0.73	0.80	0.50
Worst Drawdown	−49.01%	−43.45%	−37.25%	−44.54%	−56.87%	−49.20%	−50.21%
Worst Month Return	−22.02%	−18.66%	−18.43%	−20.83%	−24.86%	−22.37%	−21.58%
Best Month Return	25.75%	16.95%	17.21%	16.56%	29.74%	28.59%	16.81%
Profitable Months	60.42%	62.85%	61.46%	61.11%	61.63%	61.63%	60.94%

The BM ratio has the worst risk-adjusted performance, with a Sharpe ratio of 0.33 and a Sortino ratio of 0.50.

The enterprise multiples also perform well relative to all other metrics in drawdown risk. Both the EBITDA and EBIT variations have the lowest worst drawdowns and monthly drawdowns. The EBIT variation performs the best with a worst drawdown of only 37.25 percent, compared with BM, which has the biggest worst drawdown of 50.21 percent.

Table 7.4 sets out the Sharpe and Sortino ratios and historical drawdown risk metrics for the market capitalization–weighted glamour decile portfolios of each price ratio.

The results in Table 7.4 make one thing painfully clear: buying expensive stocks is hazardous to your wealth. The Sharpe and Sortino ratios are uniformly worse for expensive stocks relative to cheap stocks, regardless of the price ratio examined. Glamour stocks woefully underperform the market. They also have terrible drawdown risk, suffering gut-wrenching peak-to-trough and monthly drawdowns. Whether we examine them on a risk-adjusted or absolute risk basis, Table 7.4 makes strong argument for avoiding glamour stocks.

TABLE 7.4   Risk Measures for the Glamour Decile of All Price Measures

	Earnings Yield	Enterprise Multiple (EBITDA Variation)	Enterprise Multiple (EBIT Variation)	Free Cash Flow Yield	Gross Profits Yield	Book-to-Market	S&P 500 TR
CAGR	7.77%	7.55%	7.09%	9.05%	7.42%	8.62%	9.52%
Standard Deviation	19.54%	20.92%	22.53%	19.40%	18.74%	18.47%	15.19%
Downside Deviation	13.44%	15.60%	16.43%	14.27%	14.15%	12.69%	10.66%
Sharpe Ratio	0.22	0.21	0.19	0.28	0.20	0.26	0.33
Sortino Ratio (MAR = 5%)	0.33	0.29	0.27	0.39	0.28	0.40	0.50
Worst Drawdown	−59.45%	−80.18%	−83.73%	−57.73%	−73.17%	−67.00%	−50.21%
Worst Month Return	−27.82%	−34.07%	−33.51%	−28.00%	−23.19%	−21.56%	−21.58%
Best Month Return	23.31%	22.23%	23.12%	22.05%	24.72%	23.31%	16.81%
Profitable Months	57.64%	58.16%	57.99%	58.85%	58.16%	59.03%	60.94%

A PRICE RATIO FOR ALL SEASONS

Over the full period, the EBIT variation of the enterprise multiple seems to be the best-performing price ratio on both raw and risk-adjusted bases. Here, we examine whether what is true for the full period is true for all business cycles. We want to know how the business cycle impacts the performance and the predictive power of each price ratio. Does the free cash flow yield perform better during economic downturns than accounting-based price ratios like earnings or EBITDA? Does an asset-based ratio like BM outperform when the economy is centered on manufacturing like it was in the 1970s and 1980s, and start to struggle as the economy becomes more oriented to "human capital" and services? To test these hypotheses, we analyze the returns of the valuation metrics during economic expansions and contractions. Our definitions for expanding or contracting economic periods are from the National Bureau of Economic Research.

Table 7.5 presents the compound annual growth rates for various price ratios during economic expansions.

Table 7.5 shows no consistent winner during economic expansions. The BM performance pattern offers no evidence for the hypothesis that balance-sheet-based value measures perform better than income or cash flow statement

TABLE 7.5 Price Ratio Performance During Economic Expansions

	Earnings Yield	Enterprise Multiple (EBITDA Variation)	Enterprise Multiple (EBIT Variation)	Free Cash Flow Yield	Gross Profits Yield	Book-to-Market	S&P 500 TR
July 1971–Oct. 1973	6.01%	11.83%	10.20%	1.19%	−3.89%	9.11%	6.70%
Apr. 1975–Dec. 1979	23.54%	20.83%	19.03%	16.19%	18.79%	18.39%	10.62%
Aug. 1980–June 1981	18.11%	6.54%	6.83%	20.61%	16.49%	17.69%	14.54%
Dec. 1982–Jun. 1990	22.57%	22.51%	24.76%	19.37%	24.66%	24.16%	17.73%
Apr. 1991–Feb. 2001	13.98%	18.19%	20.15%	17.29%	17.94%	13.92%	15.52%
Dec. 2001–Nov. 2007	18.16%	17.49%	20.14%	14.08%	10.85%	8.85%	6.52%
Jul. 2009–Dec. 2010	21.80%	24.12%	21.55%	14.87%	28.00%	42.60%	25.85%

TABLE 7.6   Price Ratio Performance during Economic Contractions

	Earnings Yield	Enterprise Multiple (EBITDA Variation)	Enterprise Multiple (EBIT Variation)	Free Cash Flow Yield	Gross Profits Yield	Book-to-Market	S&P 500 TR
Nov. 1973– Mar. 1975	−11.24%	−6.89%	−7.20%	−11.72%	−6.10%	−0.27%	−13.00%
Jan. 1980– July 1980	13.28%	42.72%	32.38%	25.29%	17.88%	23.99%	29.90%
Jul. 1981– Nov. 1982	−2.24%	−2.11%	−2.92%	4.92%	16.10%	17.89%	10.53%
Jul. 1990– Mar. 1991	1.45%	3.47%	2.27%	13.30%	9.56%	9.51%	10.44%
Mar. 2001– Nov. 2001	−8.83%	−5.21%	−9.68%	−3.44%	−0.06%	−3.27%	−9.19%
Dec. 2007– June 2009	−16.38%	−18.71%	−15.06%	−18.21%	−21.64%	−18.26%	−23.62%

value metrics when the economy generates more returns from tangible assets (e.g., property, plant and equipment) relative to intangible assets (e.g., human capital, research and development, and brand equity). Overall, there is little evidence that a particular price ratio delivers better performance than all other metrics during expanding economic periods.

Table 7.6 again shows no clear evidence that a particular price ratio consistently outperforms all other strategies in contracting economic periods. For example, during the July 1981 to November 1982 and March 2001 to November 2001 contractions the gross profits yield and BM showed strong outperformance over alternative price ratios, but these same metrics had terrible performance through the December 2007 to June 2009 recession.

Overall, there is little systematic evidence that a particular strategy outperforms all other metrics during economic contractions and expansions. However, there is evidence that value strategies as a whole do outperform passive benchmarks in good times and in bad.

THE OFFICIAL WINNER

The evidence is not conclusive, but the EBIT version of the enterprise yield seems to outperform the other price ratios on our full suite of analyses. It stands out in our analysis of raw performance. The portfolio created from the EBIT variation value decile generates a compound average growth rate of 14.55 percent per year over the full period. The closest competitors are the EBITDA variation of the enterprise multiple at 13.72 percent, and the gross profits yield, which generates 13.51 percent on average. The academic favorite, book-to-market, lags at 13.11 percent. All value deciles outperform the market. When we examine each metric's ability to sort stocks, we also find that the EBIT enterprise multiple generates the biggest spreads between value and glamour stocks at 7.45 percent.

When we examine the price ratios on a factor-adjusted basis using CAPM alpha, we again find that EBIT enterprise multiple is a top-performing metric, showing statistically and economically significant alpha of 5.23 percent for the top decile stocks. Here, the alternative EBITDA enterprise yield, earnings yield, and gross profits yield also perform well. BM and the free cash flow yield show smaller alphas than the other metrics.

The EBIT enterprise multiple shines on a risk-adjusted basis using the Sharpe and Sortino ratios. The EBIT enterprise multiple shows a Sharpe ratio, which calculates risk-to-reward by examining excess return against volatility, of 0.58. When we examine the metric's risk/reward ratio using the Sortino ratio, which ignores upside volatility, and measures only excess return against downside volatility, we again find the augmented enterprise multiple to be the best-performed metric, with a Sortino ratio of 0.89.

While the EBIT enterprise multiple is a comprehensive winner across a variety of analyses, the other metrics are also worth a second look. The coronation of a winner is not easy, but we can make one reliable claim: the portfolios formed from the value decile comprehensively outperform the portfolios formed from the glamour decile. Whether we examine raw performance, risk-adjusted performance, or absolute risk, the glamour portfolio is a poor bet. In combination, the metrics show value stocks to be better additions to the portfolio.

NOTES

1. J. Lakonishok, A. Shleifer, and R. W. Vishny, "Contrarian Investments, Extrapolation, and Risk." *Journal of Finance* 49(5): 1541–1578, 1994.
2. Eugene F. Fama and Kenneth R. French, "Fama and French Forum," June 27, 2011. Available at *www.dimensional.com/famafrench/2011/06/qa-why-use-book-value-to-sort-stocks.html*.
3. Tim Loughran and Jay W. Wellman, "New Evidence on the Relation between the Enterprise Multiple and Average Stock Returns." *Journal of Financial and Quantitative Analysis* 46, 1629–1650, 2010.
4. Ibid.
5. William F. Sharpe, "The Sharpe Ratio." *Journal of Portfolio Management* 21(1) (Fall 1994): 49–58.

CHAPTER 8

Alternative Price Measures— Normalized Earning Power and Composite Ratios

"The market level of common stocks is governed more by their current earnings than by their long-term average. This fact accounts in good part of the wide fluctuation in common-stock prices, which largely (though by no means invariably) parallel the changes in their earnings between good years and bad. Obviously the stock market is quite irrational in thus varying its valuation of a company proportionately with the temporary changes in its reported profits."

—Benjamin Graham, *Security Analysis* (1934)

In the preceding chapter, we examined several common single-year, individual price ratios to find the best-performing measure. While we found that the earnings before interest and taxes (EBIT) variation of the enterprise multiple was arguably the best metric, we found that it did not outperform in every category. For example, the gross profits yield performed admirably on raw and risk-adjusted return analyses.

In this chapter, we examine the performance of a combined price measure constructed from different individual price ratios. We investigate whether some combination of price ratios can outperform the best individual price ratios in each category of performance. The appeal of a compound measure using a variety of price ratios is in the possibility that it offers better risk and return characteristics than its constituent individual price ratios. Such a compound measure could examine different price ratios, for example, looking at free cash flow yield, the unadulterated gross profits yield, and the EBIT variation of the enterprise multiple. Seeking the cheapest stocks on a compound measure might provide a cross-check to help us avoid stocks with unusual accounting that look cheap on one metric, but expensive on the other two. Further, if one metric underperforms for an extended period, the other two might counter its influence.

We also consider the use of longer-term price ratios. The price measures in the previous chapter were all single-year metrics. There is some danger in using a single historical period of 12 months to calculate price. Such a thin slice of historical earnings data might cause our single-year price metrics to favor stocks that have had unusually good earnings in a 12-month period unrepresentative of the stock's typical earning power. Our price metrics might therefore select stocks at the peak of their business cycle, with the likelihood that earnings over subsequent periods revert down to at least their long-run average, and possibly lower. For example, an oil and gas producer might look attractive while oil and gas prices are high. Quality measures will likely be favorable, and the stock may also look cheap relative to peak earnings. Commodity prices are cyclical, however, so the oil and gas producer's elevated earnings are not sustainable over the cycle. It may be a bad bet to buy them at the peak of the cycle. If we were to examine these stocks at a trough in the cycle, they may look unattractive, when, all else being equal, we'd probably rather purchase them in the trough, than at the peak.

In *Security Analysis*, Benjamin Graham counseled that current earnings should not be the primary basis of appraising a stock[1]:

> *This is one of the most important lines of cleavage between Wall Street practice and the canons of ordinary business. Because the speculative public is clearly wrong in its attitude on this point, it would seem that its errors should afford profitable opportunities to the more logically minded to buy common stocks at the low prices occasioned by temporarily reduced earnings and to sell them at inflated prices created by abnormal prosperity.*

Graham suggested a methodology to avoid such errors and to exploit the variation in earnings: normalized earnings power. He recommended that investors calculate normalized earnings power by taking the average of earnings over a period of between 5 and 10 years. Robert Shiller extended Graham's recommendation by suggesting that investors adjust average earnings for inflation, and use a longer-term average with a minimum period of 10 years. Such a long-run, inflation-adjusted average smooths the peaks and valleys in earnings, making the earnings appear higher in the trough, and lower at the peak, than a single-year metric.

In this chapter, we analyze long-run and composite price metrics. We then test their predictive power and compare their performance against the single-year metrics. We analyze them along the same lines as the single-year metrics in the previous chapter.

NORMALIZED EARNING POWER

In *Security Analysis*, Graham advocated the use of "normalized" earnings over a single-year earnings ratio, suggesting that "[earnings] should cover a period of not less than five years, and preferably seven to ten years." By "normalizing" earnings, Graham sought to adjust for the impact of the business cycle, which pushes earnings up in the boom and down in the bust. The rationale is that the extremes found at the peak and trough of the business cycle do not represent the "normal" earning power of the business, which is likely lower than at the peak and higher than at the trough. Earnings tend to be mean reverting, so we need to normalize the extremes to make them less attractive at the peak and more attractive at the trough. We can achieve this taking an average of earnings over the business cycle. We can't know how long a business cycle will last, so Graham recommended using an average of between 5 and 10 years.

More recently, Robert Shiller, author of the book *Irrational Exuberance*, which took for its title the phrase then-chairman of the Federal Reserve Alan Greenspan used to warn of the dot-com bubble in 1996, collaborated with John Campbell to argue[2] that annual earnings are too "noisy" to use as the denominator in price-to-earnings (P/E) ratios. Campbell and Shiller point out that extremes in a price ratio can be remedied only by the denominator's or numerator's moving in a direction that restores the ratio to a more normal level. For example, high prices relative to earnings—a low earnings yield—must forecast some combination of unusual increases in earnings or declines in prices. In a 2001 update,[3] Campbell and Shiller asked which was more likely—an increase in earnings or a decline in prices? They found that the P/E ratio was a poor forecaster of earnings growth, which means that it has typically been the stock price that has moved to correct the ratio. They suggest that the underlying earning power of the business may be better captured by using "permanent" rather than "transient" earnings, meaning a longer-term average, rather than a shorter one. Shiller proposed 10 years.

Keith Anderson and Chris Brooks, respectively, from the ICMA Centre, University of Reading and Cass Business School, City University, in the United Kingdom, conducted a 2006 study[4] of long-term P/E ratios in the U.K. stock market from 1975 to 2003. Anderson and Brooks found evidence that substituting a long-term average of earnings (in their case, eight years) in place of single-year earnings increased the spread in returns between value and glamour stocks by 6 percent per year. We test the argument that using long-term price ratios to "normalize" earnings decreases the noise of the valuation signal and therefore increases the predictive power of the metric.

Our Long-Term Price Ratio Study

We calculate each long-term average price ratio by summing the numerator for each year under consideration, dividing it by the number of years examined, and then dividing the average by the most recent denominator. The single-year price ratio is constructed using the current numerator and current denominator for each price ratio. These are the same single-year price ratios we discussed in the last chapter. We calculate the longer average price ratios (two years to eight years) by taking the average of the numerator over the past n years, and divide this average by the current denominator. For example, we construct the eight-year enterprise multiple (EBITDA/TEV) by averaging the past eight years of EBITDA for each stock (including the current observation), and dividing the result by the stock's current total enterprise value. Formally, we calculate its average with the following equation:

$$\frac{EBITDA}{TEV_n} = \frac{\dfrac{\sum_{j=1}^{n} EBITDA}{n}}{TEV},$$

where EBITDAj is the average of j years of EBITDA, and where n equals the number of years.

We divide the universe into deciles for each price ratio and construct a portfolio from the value decile (i.e., the cheapest 10 percent of stocks) and the glamour decile (i.e., the most expensive 10 percent of stocks).

We set out the results in Table 8.1. Each column heading in Table 8.1 represents a long-term average calculated from a different number of years. As we read from left to right, in each column we increase the number of years of fundamental data in each average price ratio. So, for example, the first column of data contains the single-year price ratio we reported in the last chapter. The second column—"2yr"—contains the average of the numerator for years one and two divided by the denominator in year one. The "3yr" column contains the average of three years' of numerators divided by the year one denominator and so on. We highlight in bold the top-performing average for each price ratio.

TABLE 8.1 Results of Differing Long-Term Average Price Ratios (1972 to 2011)

9.95%

S&P 500 TR	1yr	2yr	3yr	4yr	5yr	6yr	7yr	8yr
Value Portfolios								
Earnings Yield	13.24%	12.55%	12.67%	13.24%	14.24%	14.19%	14.85%	14.35%
EBITDA/TEV	14.72%	14.96%	14.88%	15.16%	14.93%	14.68%	14.35%	14.02%
EBIT/TEV	15.53%	14.26%	14.38%	14.75%	14.82%	14.32%	13.79%	13.34%
FCF/TEV	12.24%	11.63%	12.00%	12.86%	12.26%	12.17%	12.29%	12.26%
GP/TEV	13.59%	14.04%	14.70%	14.42%	14.68%	14.41%	13.87%	13.93%
B/M	13.79%	13.65%	13.99%	14.28%	14.85%	15.57%	15.61%	15.79%
Glamour Portfolios								
Earnings Yield	7.09%	7.68%	8.47%	8.37%	8.13%	7.49%	6.42%	7.38%
EBITDA/TEV	6.92%	6.96%	7.11%	7.74%	8.24%	7.91%	7.79%	7.76%
EBIT/TEV	6.71%	6.42%	6.36%	6.58%	6.85%	6.46%	6.93%	6.98%
FCF/TEV	9.94%	10.61%	10.24%	9.80%	9.54%	9.14%	9.61%	9.70%
GP/TEV	7.02%	7.46%	6.85%	6.77%	6.89%	6.92%	6.76%	6.64%
B/M	8.26%	7.95%	8.27%	7.96%	7.49%	7.09%	6.92%	6.67%
Spread (Value − Glamour)								
Earnings Yield	6.15%	4.87%	4.20%	4.87%	6.11%	6.70%	8.43%	6.97%
EBITDA/TEV	7.80%	8.00%	7.77%	7.42%	6.69%	6.77%	6.56%	6.26%
EBIT/TEV	8.82%	7.84%	8.02%	8.17%	7.97%	7.86%	6.86%	6.36%
FCF/TEV	2.30%	1.02%	1.76%	3.06%	2.72%	3.03%	2.68%	2.56%
GP/TEV	6.57%	6.58%	7.85%	7.65%	7.79%	7.49%	7.11%	7.29%
B/M	5.53%	5.70%	5.72%	6.32%	7.36%	8.48%	8.69%	9.12%

Our evidence suggests that "normalizing"—taking the average of the numerator for a price ratio—might enhance the predictive power of some price ratios, but the results are not conclusive. The performance of any given normalized ratio is not consistently better than any other single-year price ratio or multiyear average. In addition, the spread or the value premium—the difference in performance between the value decile and the glamour decile—does not seem to be consistently greater at any other point. The spread results look almost random to the naked eye. We are unable to replicate the findings from the Anderson and Brooks study, who find evidence in the U.K. stock market that long-term price ratios increase the spread between the value and glamour portfolios by 6 percent per year. In contrast, we find that the spreads between value and glamour portfolios are very similar regardless of the length of the normalized average. Our results are roughly consistent with the results from a recent paper by Gray and Vogel, who examine long-term price ratios, but included smaller, less liquid stocks.[5] Gray and Vogel determined that long-term ratios add little to the predictive ability of single-year price ratios.

While we find some weak evidence that longer-term ratios have historically performed slightly better, we take those long-term results with a grain of salt because the data are mixed, and there is some disagreement between independent studies. The empirical evidence hints that using long-term ratios might add some marginal predictive ability to price ratios, but not much.

COMPOUND PRICE RATIOS: IS THE WHOLE GREATER THAN THE SUM OF ITS PARTS?

James O'Shaughnessy proposed the idea of composite price ratios in the fourth edition of his book *What Works on Wall Street*.[6] O'Shaughnessy stumbled onto the idea of combining price ratios after reading a 2001 paper by Siva Nathan, Kumar Sivakumar, and Jayaraman Vijayakumar called "Returns to Trading Strategies Based on Price-to-Earnings and Price-to-Sales Ratios."[7] In the paper, Nathan et al. examined the returns to a strategy that identified stocks using a combined price-to-earnings and price-to-sales ranking strategy to select stocks. They tested the combined ratio by creating five equal quintile portfolios of stocks rebalanced yearly using data from the period 1990 to 1996. They found that the value quintile portfolio of stocks with low price-to-earnings and price-to-sales ratios generated excess returns of 1.36 percent per year on average. The glamour quintile portfolio of stocks with high price-to-earnings and price-to-sales ratios fell below the market by a whopping –27.53 percent per year on average. The spread between the two portfolios—the value premium—was an enormous 28.89 percent per year (1.36 minus –27.53 = 28.89). As compelling as these results are, the period analyzed is simply too short to be reliable as a trading strategy. What is interesting, however, is that combining the price ratios outperformed both of the individual ratios.

Nathan et al. found that the value portfolio of stocks with low P/E ratios underperformed the market by –2.54 percent per year on average, while the glamour portfolio fell by –8.14 percent per year, creating a spread of 5.60 percent. Meanwhile, the price-to-sales ratio value portfolio outperformed by 5.34 percent per year on average, while the glamour portfolio fell below the market by –21.07 percent per year on average, creating a spread of 26.41 percent. Note that the spread between the value and glamour portfolios—the value premium—for each of P/E (5.60 percent) and price-to-sales (26.41) is lower than the spread for the combined ratio at 28.89 percent. We are more interested here in the sorting power of the ratio than the raw returns, and on this analysis the combined ratio outperforms both the individual ratios that constitute it.

O'Shaughnessy analyzed several different composite ratios formed from individual ratios and found that the composites outperformed the best-performing individual ratios. Composites are a promising idea. A composite price ratio provides diversification across its constituent ratios. All ratios, even the best-performing ones, underperform on occasion. As the example in the Nathan et al. paper demonstrates, the value portfolio of the price-to-sales ratio performed very well, significantly outperforming the market, while the P/E ratio underperformed, lagging both the price-to-sales ratio and the market. A composite ratio reduces the chance that an investor is stuck in a price ratio that lags. O'Shaughnessy finds that portfolios formed using composite price ratios outperform the individual constituent price ratios 82 percent of the time on a rolling 10-year basis from 1964 through 2009. While an individual price ratio might outperform over the long run, a composite measure increases the chances that the portfolio consistently outperforms. Next, we set out our analysis of composite ratios and their performances. We undertake a comprehensive empirical exercise to identify the composite measures that perform the best. The results are a little surprising.

Analyzing Our Composite Price Ratio

Here we analyze the performances of the composite price ratios over the 1972 to 2010 period.[8] Our study consists of two parts. First, we examine composite ratios formed on from all the price ratios. Second, we look at composite ratios formed from the most promising individual price ratios. We calculate our composite ratios by first ranking all stocks in our universe on each price metric. For example, if we are testing a composite that consists of single-year EBIT variation of the enterprise multiple, single-year earnings yield, and five-year gross profits yield, we calculate each stock's ranking in the universe on each individual price ratio. Next, we take the sum of all the rankings for the stocks, and rerank them on the combined rankings. Take, for example, a 2,000-stock universe. If stock XYZ is ranked 5/2,000 on the single-year EBIT enterprise multiple, 200/2,000 on the single-year earnings yield, and 1,500/2,000 on the five-year average gross profits yield, the composite ranking for XYZ is 1,750 (5 + 200 + 1,500). Stocks are then reranked on their composite ranking. Lower is better. In the case of XYZ, this stock performs well on the single-year EBIT enterprise multiple, on which it earns a very high ranking (5 out of 2,000), but on a composite basis, it ends up in the middle of the pack because it performs poorly on a five-year average gross profits yield. The beauty of the composite ranking is in its ability to examine "cheapness" from multiple perspectives. The downside is that, to successfully calculate the results, we need to undertake some additional data manipulation that introduces more complexity into the final calculation.

Composite Ratios Formed from All Metrics

In this section, we look at three comprehensive composite ratios:

- *Single-year combo,* which is the average of ranks based on all single-year price ratios (earnings yield, both forms of the enterprise multiple, the free cash flow yield, gross profits yield, and book-to-market).
- *Five-year average combo,* which is an average of ranks based on all five-year average price ratios.
- *Comprehensive combo,* which is an average of ranks based on all single-year and five-year prices ratios.

Figure 8.1 highlights the growth of the composite ratios.

Table 8. 2 shows the results for the portfolios constructed from the value decile of the composite price ratios.

Table 8.2 demonstrates that composite price ratios can generate excellent performance. For example, the comprehensive composite portfolio earns 14.96 percent a year, significantly outperforming the S&P 500 and slightly outperforming the alternative composite ratios. The single-year combo composite is arguably the best price ratio, with the highest compound annual growth rate, and strong outperformance on 5-year and 10-year rolling windows. The strategy beats the 5-year combo 66.27 percent of the time over all 5-year rolling windows. The comprehensive combo, which is formed from all single-year ratios and all 5-year ratios, also performs well, with the highest Sharpe ratio and the lowest maximum drawdown. Figures 8.2(a) and 8.2(b) show the rolling 5-year and 10-year returns for the composite price ratios for the period 1972 to 2011. The ratios are all very competitive, but

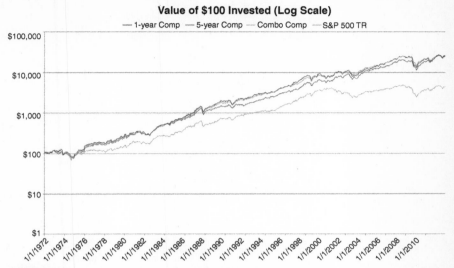

FIGURE 8.1 Comprehensive Composite Ratio Performance Chart (1972 to 2011)

the single-year composite has the highest winning percentage over 5-year and 10-year rolling windows. The clear loser is the S&P 500, which, aside from a brief period of outperformance through the Internet bubble in the late 1990s, has been a perennial loser relative to simple price ratios.

TABLE 8.2 Performance Statistics for the All-Inclusive Composite Ratios (1972 to 2011)

	Single-Year Combo	Five-Year Combo	Comprehensive Combo	S&P 500
CAGR	14.88%	14.81%	14.96%	9.95%
Standard Deviation	17.58%	16.44%	16.52%	15.66%
Downside Deviation	13.35%	11.65%	12.07%	11.12%
Sharpe Ratio	0.58	0.60	0.61	0.35
Sortino Ratio (MAR = 5%)	0.79	0.88	0.86	0.52
Worst Drawdown	−48.43%	−45.77%	−43.28%	−50.21%
Worst Month Return	−22.05%	−18.63%	−18.61%	−21.58%
Best Month Return	20.36%	18.49%	19.05%	16.81%
Profitable Months	65.21%	65.63%	65.00%	60.42%
Rolling 5-Year Win %	—	53.92%	58.67%	90.97%
Rolling 10-Year Win %	—	54.02%	49.58%	91.97%

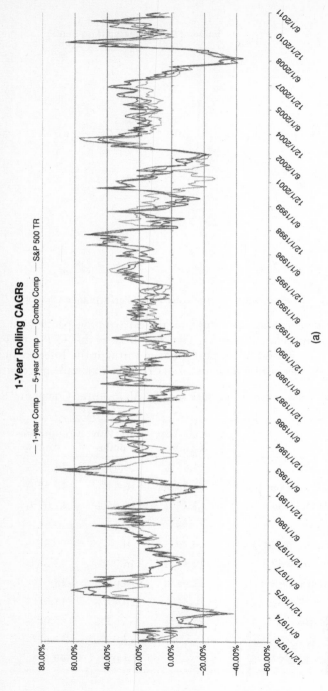

FIGURE 8.2(a) Five-year Rolling Period Performance Statistics: All-Inclusive Composite Ratios (1972 to 2011)

154

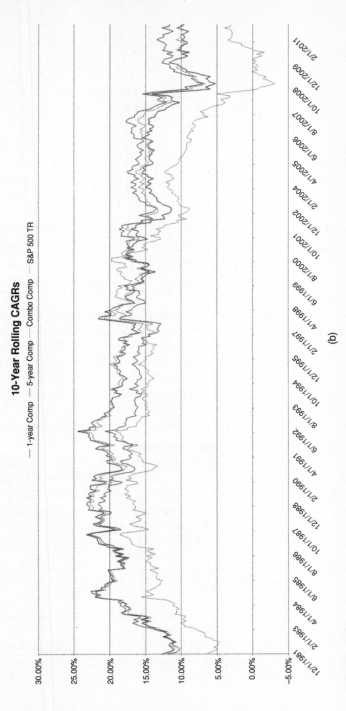

FIGURE 8.2(b) Ten-year Rolling Period Performance Statistics: All-Inclusive Composite Ratio (1972 to 2011)

155

TABLE 8.3 Top and Low Decile Performance Statistics: All-Inclusive Composite Ratios (1972 to 2011)

	Five-Year Combo (Value)	Five-Year Combo (Glamour)	Comprehensive Combo (Value)	Comprehensive Combo (Glamour)
CAGR	14.81%	7.08%	14.96%	7.11%
Standard Deviation	16.44%	22.50%	16.52%	22.16%
Downside Deviation	11.65%	16.83%	12.07%	16.24%
Sharpe Ratio	0.60	0.18	0.61	0.18
Sortino Ratio (MAR = 5%)	0.88	0.27	0.86	0.27
Worst Drawdown	−45.77%	−77.42%	−43.28%	−77.52%
Worst Month Return	−18.63%	−33.24%	−18.61%	−30.74%
Best Month Return	18.49%	23.68%	19.05%	23.91%
Profitable Months	65.63%	56.67%	65.00%	58.33%

Table 8.3 shows the summary performance statistics for the value and glamour deciles for the top comprehensive composite ratios: Single- year combo and comprehensive combo for the period 1972 to 2011. Both of the composite ratios do an exceptional job separating the universe into "good" and "bad." The spread in compound annual growth rates is 8.81 percent and 8.67 percent, respectively, for the single-year combo and the comprehensive combo. These results compare favorably to those in Table 8.1, which show the compound annual growth rate spreads for a variety of single-year price ratios.

Composite Ratios Formed from the "Best" Price Ratios

The analyses from Chapter 7 and in the first section of this chapter suggest that the EBIT enterprise multiple, the gross profits yield, and the earnings yield are the most promising stand-alone price ratios for stock selection. In this section, we ignore the lesser price ratios and look at simple composites of just these price ratios to see if they add value above the comprehensive composites. To focus our results, we present the following "best composites."

- *Best single-year combo,* which is an average of all ranks based on the best one-year price ratios (EBIT enterprise multiple, earnings yield, and gross profits yield).
- *Best five-year combo,* which is an average of all ranks based on the best five-year price ratios.
- *Best comprehensive combo,* which is an average of all ranks based on single-year and five-year EBIT enterprise multiple, earnings yield, and gross profits yield.

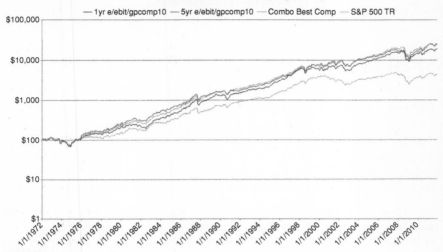

FIGURE 8.3   Best Composite Ratio Performance Chart (1972 to 2011)

Figure 8.3 highlights the growth of the best composite ratios.

Table 8.4 shows the summary statistics for our best composite ratios. The strongest-performed best composite is the comprehensive best combo, which is a combination ranking for single-year and 5-year EBIT enterprise multiple, earnings yield, and gross profits yield. The comprehensive best combo earns the highest compound annual growth rate, has the highest risk-adjusted statistics and has a good batting average relative to the other best composites over 5-year and 10-year rolling windows.

TABLE 8.4   Performance Statistics for the Best Composite Ratios (1972 to 2011)

	Best Single-Year Combo	Best Five-Year Combo	Best Comprehensive Combo	S&P 500
CAGR	13.97%	14.79%	14.89%	9.95%
Standard Deviation	18.00%	17.26%	17.36%	15.66%
Downside Deviation	13.51%	12.39%	12.87%	11.12%
Sharpe Ratio	0.53	0.58	0.58	0.35
Sortino Ratio (MAR = 5%)	0.72	0.84	0.81	0.52
Worst Drawdown	–45.20%	–43.34%	–43.13%	–50.21%

(continued)

TABLE 8.4   *(continued)*

	Best Single-Year Combo	Best Five-Year Combo	Best Comprehensive Combo	S&P 500
Worst Month Return	–21.59%	–19.52%	–20.76%	–21.58%
Best Month Return	21.23%	21.37%	21.12%	16.81%
Profitable Months	63.13%	63.96%	65.63%	60.42%
Rolling 5-Year Win %	—	51.54%	29.93%	82.42%
Rolling 10-Year Win %	—	46.26%	32.96%	93.07%

Table 8.5 shows the summary performance statistics for the value and glamour deciles for the strongest performing "best" composite ratios: best comprehensive combo and best single-year combo for the period 1972 to 2011. The spread in compound annual growth rate is 8.30 percent and 9.13 percent for the best comprehensive combo and best single-year combo, respectively. The best single-year combo results are particularly good at separating the wheat from the chaff.

TABLE 8.5   Value and Glamour Decile Performance Statistics: Best Composite Ratios (1972 to 2011)

	Best Comprehensive Combo (Value)	Best Comprehensive Combo (Glamour)	Best Five-Year Combo (Value)	Best Five-Year Combo (Glamour)
CAGR	14.89%	6.61%	14.79%	6.64%
Standard Deviation	17.36%	22.46%	17.26%	23.13%
Downside Deviation	12.87%	16.51%	12.39%	17.15%
Sharpe Ratio	0.58	0.16	0.58	0.17
Sortino Ratio (MAR = 5%)	0.81	0.24	0.84	0.25
Worst Drawdown	–43.13%	–76.64%	–43.34%	–80.49%
Worst Month Return	–20.76%	–33.01%	–19.52%	–34.34%
Best Month Return	21.12%	23.46%	21.37%	23.16%
Profitable Months	65.63%	57.71%	63.96%	57.08%

Which Ratio Wins the Composite Horserace?

Table 8.6 compares the top composite ratios against the best-performed metric, the EBIT enterprise multiple. The results are, frankly, humbling. After dissecting price ratios in every manner possible, we found the EBIT enterprise multiple comes out on top, particularly after we adjust for complexity and implementation difficulties. The EBIT enterprise multiple has a better compound annual growth rate, higher risk-adjusted values for Sharpe and Sortino, and the lowest drawdown of all measures analyzed. Joel Greenblatt nailed the correct price ratio with the Magic Formula, and sidestepped the back-testing of hundreds of other price ratio combinations that could presumably unseat it as the best price ratio.

Figures 8.4(a) and 8.4(b) show rolling five- and ten-year performance for the top-performing price ratios.

Figures 8.4(a) and (b) illustrate how close the race is between the top-performing price ratios. The EBIT enterprise multiple is the best performed over any rolling 5- or 10-year window. In the first half of the sample, however, the composite ratios beat the EBIT enterprise multiple. Over the entire sample the EBIT enterprise multiple stands out. The results are mixed, but there is a small edge to the EBIT enterprise multiple in terms of performance. If we also consider its ease of calculation, that small edge should be enough to push it over the top.

TABLE 8.6 Composite Ratio Horserace (1972 to 2011)

	Five-Year Combo	Comprehensive Combo	Best Comprehensive Combo	EBIT Enterprise Multiple
CAGR	14.79%	14.96%	14.89%	15.53%
Standard Deviation	17.26%	16.52%	17.36%	17.35%
Downside Deviation	12.39%	12.07%	12.87%	11.96%
Sharpe Ratio	0.58	0.61	0.58	0.62
Sortino Ratio (MAR = 5%)	0.84	0.86	0.81	0.92
Worst Drawdown	–43.34%	–43.28%	–43.13%	–37.25%
Worst Month Return	–19.52%	–18.61%	–20.76%	–18.43%
Best Month Return	21.37%	19.05%	21.12%	17.21%
Profitable Months	63.96%	65.00%	65.63%	62.71%

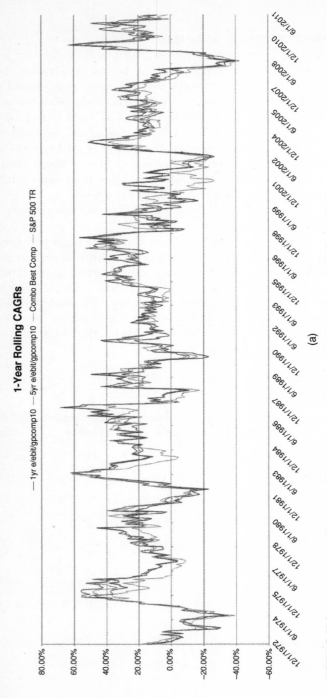

FIGURE 8.4(a) Five-Year Rolling Period Performance Statistics: Best Price Ratios (1972 to 2011)

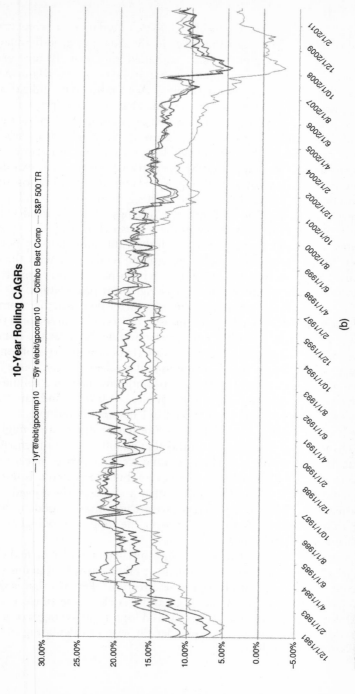

FIGURE 8.4(b) Ten-Year Rolling Period Performance Statistics: Best Price Ratios (1972 to 2011)

In this chapter we have considered some alternative interpretations of price ratios to see if we can improve on the single-year, individual price ratios from the last chapter. We first examined long-term average price ratios to test Graham's recommendation that an investor favor "normalized" earnings over trailing single-year earnings. We found some indication that Graham was right. The evidence suggests that five-year price ratios are slightly superior to single-year price ratios on a compound annual growth rate basis. Unfortunately, the evidence is pretty weak. The proposition that the five-year ratio is the best-performed long-term ratio, and better than the single-year ratio, is not supported by the spread analysis. If we examine the value premia generated by the all single-year and long-term ratios, the five-year ratio does not stand out, with the results looking almost random to the naked eye. We could not replicate the findings from the Anderson and Brooks study, who found evidence in the U.K. stock market that long-term price ratios increased the spread between the value and glamour portfolios by 6 percent per year. Our results are roughly consistent with the results from recent research by Gray and Vogel, who concluded that long-term ratios add little to the predictive ability of single-year price ratios.

Next, we explored composite ratios to determine whether combining multiple price ratios into a single composite ratio could outperform the best individual price ratio, the EBIT enterprise multiple. We beat the data like a mad dog with mange, examining many different combinations of long-term and single-year average ratios, and could find no clear winner. There is some weak evidence that composite price ratios outperformed on a rolling 5- and 10-year basis at the beginning of the sample, but little to indicate that any composite outperforms the single-year EBIT enterprise multiple.

We had hoped that our analysis of alternative price ratios might yield a long-term or combination price ratio that significantly outperformed the price ratios in common use. There is some weak evidence that a five-year average ratio adds some value at the margin, but the evidence is not strong enough, and neither is it supported by other analyses, to be considered reliable. While it was a humbling exercise, we are now more confident than ever buying value stocks beats the market over the long haul, whichever price ratio we choose to examine.

Albert Einstein once said that, "Any intelligent fool can make things bigger, more complex, and more violent. It takes a touch of genius—and a lot of courage—to move in the opposite direction." Perhaps that is the message. While our results are mixed, one thing is clear: the single-year EBIT enterprise multiple performs very well, and long-term averages or composites can do no better. If we also consider the ease of calculating it, it looks like the strongest candidate.

With our examination of quality and price completed, we now move to the final phase of our investment checklist: finding stocks with signals that corroborate our valuation. In the next part, we consider several different signals sent by market participants to find those that forecast market-beating performance. We examine buy-backs, insider buying, activism, institutional investors, and short selling.

NOTES

1. Benjamin Graham, and David Dodd, *Security Analysis: The Classic 1934 Edition* (McGraw-Hill, 1996).
2. J. Y. Campbell and R. J. Shiller, "Valuation Ratios and the Long-Run Stock Market Outlook." *Journal of Portfolio Management* (Winter 1998): 11–26.
3. John Y. Campbell and Robert J. Shiller, "Valuation Ratios and the Long-Run Stock Market Outlook: An Update (April 2001)." *NBER Working Paper Series,* Vol. w8221, 2001. Available at *http://ssrn.com/abstract=266191.*
4. K. P. Anderson and Chris Brooks, "The Long-Term Price-Earnings Ratio." *Journal of Business Finance & Accounting* 33(7–8) (September/October 2006): 1063–1086. Available at *http://ssrn.com/abstract=934618* or *http://dx.doi.org/10.1111/j.1468-5957.2006.00621.x.*
5. Wesley Gray and Jack Vogel, "Analyzing Valuation Measures: A Performance Horse-Race over the Past 40 Years." *Journal of Portfolio Management,* forthcoming.
6. James O'Shaughnessy, *What Works on Wall Street: The Classic Guide to the Best-Performing Investment Strategies of All Time,* 4th ed. (New York: McGraw-Hill, 2011).
7. S. Nathan, Kumar Sivakumar, and Jayaraman Vijayakumar, "Returns to Trading Strategies Based on Price-to-Earnings and Price-to-Sales Ratios." *Journal of Investing* 10(2) (Summer 2001): 17–28.
8. Our sample starts here in 1972 (1964 plus eight years) to accommodate the eight-year price ratios, and to make all other price ratios comparable.

Corroborative Signals

In this part, we explore the signals sent by other market participants. Here, we parse the signals sent by buybacks, insider purchases, and buying and selling from institutional investment managers like activists and other fund managers and short sellers. We examine the literature and the data to find the most predictive signals. We can use these signals to corroborate our quality and price analyses, perhaps to confirm our theory that a given stock is undervalued, or to identify potential problems.

CHAPTER 9

Blue Horseshoe Loves Anacott Steel: Follow the Signals from the Smart Money

"The companies in which we have our largest investments have all engaged in significant stock repurchases at times when wide discrepancies existed between price and value. As shareholders, we find this encouraging and rewarding for two important reasons— one that is obvious, and one that is subtle and not always understood. The obvious point involves basic arithmetic: major repurchases at prices well below per-share intrinsic business value immediately increase, in a highly significant way, that value.

...

The other benefit of repurchases is less subject to precise measurement but can be fully as important over time. By making repurchases when a company's market value is well below its business value, management clearly demonstrates that it is given to actions that enhance the wealth of shareholders, rather than to actions that expand management's domain but that do nothing for (or even harm) shareholders."
—Warren Buffett, Shareholder Letter, 1984

Henry Singleton is most notable for two achievements: building Teledyne from scratch into one of the most profitable and successful stocks in the United States at the time he stepped down 29 years later, and for his "almost arrogant scorn for most conventional business practices."[2] Warren Buffett has described Singleton as a "managerial superstar,"[3] saying that he had "the best operating and capital deployment record in American business."[4] That is high praise indeed, coming from one of the world's greatest capital allocators.

Singleton founded Teledyne in 1960 with just $225,000. He continually adapted his capital management strategy to the prevailing climate on Wall Street. In the conglomerate era, he used Teledyne's soaring stock to make cheap acquisitions and raise earnings per share. In the 1970s, when the stock slumped, Singleton bought back Teledyne's undervalued stock hand over fist. Said Singleton in a 1979 *Forbes* article[5]:

> *In October 1972 we tendered for 1 million shares and 8.9 million came in. We took them all at $20 and figured that was a fluke and that we couldn't do it again. But instead of going up, our stock went down. So we kept tendering, first at $14 and then doing two bonds-for-stock swaps. Every time one tender was over the stock would go down and we'd tender again and we'd get a new deluge. Then two more tenders at $18 and $40.*
>
> ...
>
> *I don't believe all the nonsense about market timing. Just buy very good value and when the market is ready that value will be recognized.*

Investors, heeding Singleton's signal that the stock was cheap, made out like bandits. Teledyne stock, which had sold for less than $14 in 1972, the year of Singleton's first buyback, was by 1987, when adjusted for splits and distributions, worth well over $930 a share (see Figure 9.1).[6] The gain in Teledyne stock following the buyback represents a total return of more than 6,500 percent, or a compound yearly return of more than 32 percent. This is not an isolated example. In fact, it's emblematic of stocks that repurchase shares. Those with the greatest number of shares bought back in any given year outperform the market in general. The market, it seems, is aware of this phenomenon. The mere announcement of a buyback is often enough to move a stock up. Stocks announcing a buyback—whether they follow through with the buyback or not—outperform immediately following the announcement and over the longer term. This means that announcement has informational value. It sends a signal to the market, perhaps about how insiders view the health of the stock, or its price relative to its underlying value.

If we think more broadly, buybacks are not the only signals sent by insiders. Insider purchases also send a signal. Insiders are presumably well informed about the health and prospects of their stock. It should come as no surprise, then, that insiders tend to make money when they buy stock in their own companies. But is insider buying predictive of future returns, or has the gain been made by the time the stock gives notice to the market?

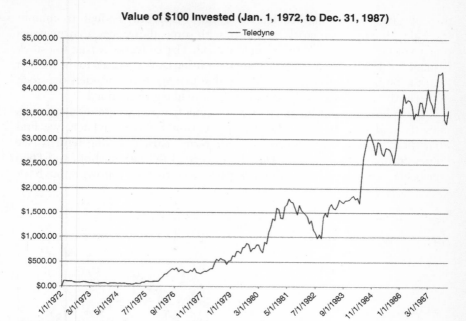

FIGURE 9.1   Teledyne Performance Chart (1972 to 1987)

What about the smart money? Does buying and selling from institutional investment managers like activists and other fund managers signal future returns? How about short sellers? Here we examine the literature and the data to find those signals most predictive of market-beating returns. We can use these signals in two ways. We can simply include the information with our quality and price analyses, using the signals from other market participants to confirm our theory that a given stock is undervalued. Alternatively, we can use the signals as stand-alone indicators to identify candidates primed to deliver near-term market-beating returns. Investors might then use those candidates as the starting point for a full fundamental analysis. Either way, signals are very useful to investors.

STOCK BUYBACKS, ISSUANCE, AND ANNOUNCEMENTS

Many studies have found stock repurchases to be predictive of market-beating returns. The corollary is also true. Stocks issuing shares tend to underperform the market. There are two events to consider: (1) the announcement itself, and (2) the actual buyback or issuance. The utility of the buyback announcement is in its signal to the market that the business is healthy enough to commit capital to buying back stock, and also, with some allowances, that management considers the stock to be undervalued. The converse is true for stock issuance. An announcement that a stock is raising capital signals to the market that the business needs capital, and also that management considers the stock to be, at the very least, fairly valued and, more likely, overvalued.

If we look only at buyback announcements made where managements identify undervaluation as the primary reason for the buyback, we find that these stocks go on to produce long-term, market-beating returns (see Figure 9.2). In a 1995 paper,[7] David Ikenberry, Josef Lakonishok, and Theo Vermaelen examined long-run stock price performance following buyback

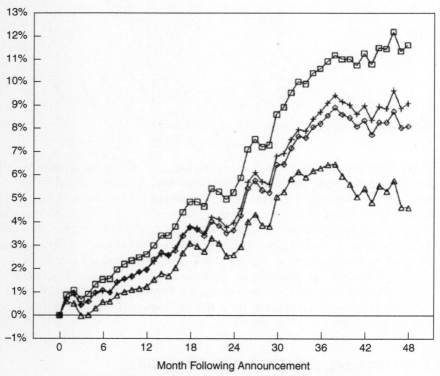

FIGURE 9.2 Stock Repurchase Abnormal Returns (1980–1990)
Source: David L. Ikenberry, Josef Lakonishok, and Theo Vermaelen, "Market Underreaction to Open Market Share Repurchases." *NBER Working Paper Series,* Vol. w4965, pp. 181–208, 1994.

announcements in value stocks. They found that stocks that announce share repurchases because of undervaluation generate substantial market-beating returns over the four years following the announcement. This analysis did not consider whether management actually completed the buyback, only whether the buyback was announced.

Managers know that announcing a buyback is good for the stock price, and so some announce a buyback and then fail to complete it. Like the boy who cried wolf, managers who do this often enough see diminishing returns to such a strategy. This is the finding of Alice Bonaime in her 2010 paper, "Repurchases, Reputation and Returns."[8] In 2010, Bonaime examined whether managements' reputations for completion rates (the ratio of actual to announced repurchases) predicted their actual completion rates, and whether the stock market discounts announcements made by less reputable managements. Bonaime found that managements' reputation for completing buybacks does seem to predict their actual completion rates. This suggests that managements who have previously announced buybacks and not completed them continue to use this tactic. Further, Bonaime found that the market considers this reputation when evaluating new buyback announcements, and discounts the announcements made by managements with bad reputations (see Figure 9.3).

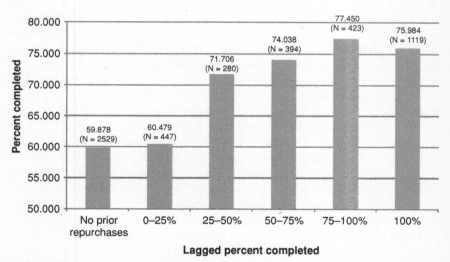

FIGURE 9.3 Predicting Repurchase Completion with Past Repurchase Completion
Source: Alice A. Bonaime, "Repurchases, Reputation, and Returns" *Journal of Financial and Quantitative Analysis (JFQA)* (December 21, 2010).

The second event to consider is the actual repurchasing or issuing of stock. There are two pitfalls here. First, where shares are issued to employees exercising options, some managers undertake buybacks to keep outstanding stock from ballooning up. Real capital is spent acquiring the shares, but, when the smoke clears, the share count is not reduced because the number of shares repurchased equals the number of shares issued from exercising options. Second, some managers will undertake buybacks at any price regardless of value. If we examine in aggregate only the dollar amount spent in undertaking buybacks, we find that managements have a poor record repurchasing shares, tending to spend most at peak valuations and least at trough valuations. Buyback spending among Standard & Poor's (S&P) 500 companies hit a record high in the third quarter of 2007, near the market peak. It shrank 86 percent over the next seven quarters as share prices tumbled.[9] This behavior turns the stomach of value investors, but it's par for the course for most managements. The Henry Singletons are few and far between.

Another method for measuring the performance of stocks is to measure the change in the stock's outstanding shares from one period to the next, rather than the amount of stock issued or repurchased or the dollar amount spent or raised, and then to examine the subsequent performance of the stock price. James O'Shaughnessy uses this method in his book *What Works on Wall Street*,[10] calling it "buyback yield." O'Shaughnessy examined the period from January 1927 through December 2009. He finds that the decile of stocks that repurchase the most shares in a year gain on average 13.69 percent in the following year against a market return of 10.46 percent for the same period, an outperformance of 3.8 percent. O'Shaughnessy also finds that stocks in the decile of stocks issuing the most shares in a year gain on average just 5.94 percent, underperforming the market return by 4.52 percent per year. Investors should be wary of stocks issuing lots of shares.

Capital management is a little understood, yet critical, issue for shareholder value creation. The research is clear: Investors should seek the rare stocks with a manager like Singleton or Buffett at the helm, who buy back shares only at trough valuations, are miserly with options, and issue shares only when the share price exceeds the stock's intrinsic value. Investors should keep a close eye on a management's capital allocation behavior. Typically, net purchasers of shares will turn out to be better investments than net issuers of shares. Managers who blindly buy back shares, however, are less than ideal. A manager who buys back stock at a peak valuation destroys value as surely as the manager who issues shares at a trough valuation. Investors should avoid managers who play games with buyback announcements, if only because such behavior suggests that they are more focused on the share price than the underlying value and might be squandering an opportunity to enhance shareholder value by not completing the buyback.

INSIDER TRADERS BEAT THE MARKET

In addition to undertaking buybacks, managements can express their view on the under- or overvaluation of their stock through their own trading. The trading activity of "insiders" (corporate officers, directors, and large stockholders) has attracted the interest of both academics and practitioners for over 40 years. For our purposes, insider trading is the *legal* buying or selling by corporate insiders.

It is well established through many studies that insiders are better informed and earn market-beating returns.[11] The conventional wisdom is that insiders have access to private information about the future prospects of stocks that outsiders do not have. Our interest in insider trading activity is in the signal it sends to the market. In this section, we examine how we, as outside investors, can benefit from this information about insider trading activity. In particular, we look for systematic rules that identify the insider transactions that best signal market-beating returns.

There are certain insider transactions that do not signal market-beating returns. For example, options, warrants, and convertibles transactions typically relate to insiders' remuneration packages and whether the options are in-the-money. They don't provide much information about the insiders' view of the valuation of the stock. It seems that stock sales also provide little information about insiders' views on valuation. While we might expect that sales signal overvaluation, we find that they don't necessarily send a negative signal. The reason is that there are a variety of other motives for sales besides valuation, including the liquidity needs of the insider or the insider's need to reduce risk by diversifying. Our main inquiry here is to find the characteristics of the insider trades with the biggest impact on the market.

Lauren Cohen, Chris Malloy, and Lukasz Pomorski sift through the insider trading literature and data in their insightful paper, "Decoding Inside Information."[12] The authors use a simple algorithm to differentiate between "routine" insider trading and "opportunistic" insider trading. Insiders who are trading on a regular schedule for diversification or liquidity needs, or within the confines of a 10b5-1 plan, are engaging in "routine" insider trading that may not be sending signals to the market that their stock is misvalued. Opportunistic trading is a different, and more profitable, signal. The trick is to separate the routine trades from the opportunistic trades. Cohen, Malloy, and Pomorski developed an algorithm that classified insider trades as routine if the insider placed a trade in the same calendar month for a certain numbers of years in the past. It treats all other trades as opportunistic. For example, if an insider has been buying stock every April for the past three years, this is treated as a routine trade. If the same insider buys stock every April, but then makes a large purchase in September, the September trade is treated as opportunistic. The authors find that these opportunistic trades generate *all* the market-beating returns. In fact, trading on opportunistic insider buys and sells generates around 8 percent market-beating return per year. Trading on routine insider buys and sells generates no additional return.

Daniel Giamouridis, Manolis Liodakis, and Andrew Moniz consider whether insider trading works in markets outside the United States. They examine the U.K. market and discuss it in a 2008 paper, "Some Insiders Are Indeed Smart Investors."[13] The authors find that stocks in the United Kingdom tend to outperform the market by 0.7 percent immediately after the insiders' purchase announcement, by 1.2 percent between days 1 to 60 and by 2.9 percent between days 1 and 120. They then examine which transactions yielded the biggest impact. They find that the larger the absolute value of the insider trade, the better the subsequent returns. It makes some intuitive sense that insiders with high conviction about the relative undervaluation of the stock would buy more of it, and that such trades would signal greater subsequent outperformance. This signal was reduced, however, when the trade was large in relation to the size of the stock, indicating that the market may be wary of trades that result in free-float reduction and possible deterioration in corporate governance. Giamouridis, Liodakis, and Moniz also find that the recent history of purchases is a key driver of outperformance. Insiders' trades in stocks where there have been many purchases over the preceding three months outperform. Notably, stocks that announce a buyback where insiders simultaneously purchase stock have a significant incremental outperformance, perhaps indicating that the insiders' purchases give credence to management's view that the company is undervalued. Several other factors indicate greater outperformance, including stocks that positively surprised at the last annual results, insiders purchasing within 20 days of the annual earnings announcement, and trades in value stocks are more profitable than those in growth stocks. Following insider trades can be very rewarding.

Investors seeking to use insider-trading signals need to be able to parse the signal from the noise. Insider trades like the exercise of options or warrants, or the sale of stock, carry little to no information. Purchases do send signals. The greater the value of a single purchase or series of purchases, the stronger the signal. Insider trades combined with buybacks offer the potential for significant outperformance, as do insider trades in undervalued stocks. While such insider behavior might be less worthy than the initiation of a buyback, investors who follow insiders who trade for their own accounts on information that the market seems to have ignored can outperform the market (see Figure 9.4).

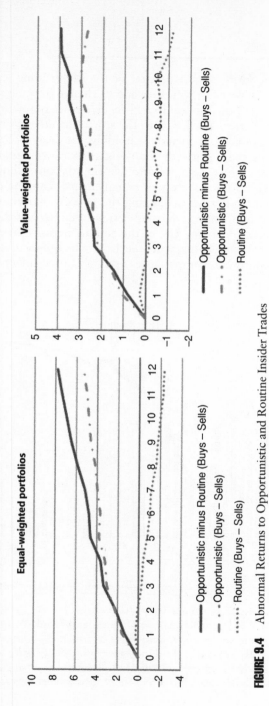

Equal-weighted portfolios

— Opportunistic minus Routine (Buys – Sells)
– · – Opportunistic (Buys – Sells)
· · · · · · Routine (Buys – Sells)

Value-weighted portfolios

— Opportunistic minus Routine (Buys – Sells)
– · – Opportunistic (Buys – Sells)
· · · · · · Routine (Buys – Sells)

FIGURE 9.4 Abnormal Returns to Opportunistic and Routine Insider Trades

Source: Lauren Cohen, Christopher Malloy, and Lukasz Pomorski, "Decoding Inside Information," NBER Working Paper No. w16454. Available at *http://ssrn.com/abstract=1692517.*

ACTIVISM AND CLONING

Investors purchasing more than 5 percent of the outstanding shares of a stock must file a notice with the Securities and Exchange Commission (SEC) disclosing the purpose of the transaction. If the investor has a plan to undertake some corporate action in relation to the stock, the investor must file a Schedule 13D notice indicating an activist holding. Those corporate actions may include acquiring more stock; undertaking an extraordinary corporate transaction, such as a merger, reorganization, or liquidation; selling material assets; changing the board of directors or management; changing the stock's capitalization or dividend policy; changing the stock's charter or bylaws; or other actions that may impede the acquisition of control. If the investor does not plan to undertake some any of the actions outlined in the Schedule 13D notice, the investor files a Schedule 13G, which indicates a passive holding. Institutional investment managers exercising investment discretion

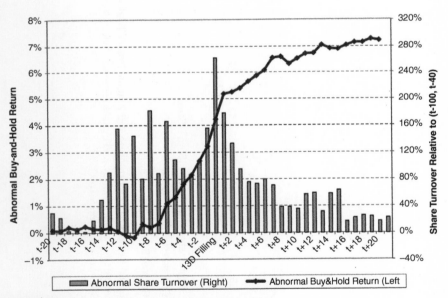

FIGURE 9.5   Abnormal Returns around 13D Filings
Source: Alon P. Brav, Wei Jiang, Randall S. Thomas, and Frank Partnoy, "Hedge Fund Activism, Corporate Governance, and Firm Performance." *Journal of Finance* 63 (May 2008): 1729; ECGI Finance Working Paper No. 139/2006; Vanderbilt Law and Economics Research Paper No. 07-28; FDIC Center for Financial Research Working Paper No. 2008-06. Available at SSRN: *http://ssrn.com/abstract=948907.*

over $100 million or more in securities must also file with the SEC a Form 13F, which sets out their holdings in various stocks.

Research suggests that stocks that are the subject of an activist Schedule 13D notice generate market-beating returns. In a 2008 paper, Brav, Jiang, Thomas, and Partnoy[14] found that the "market reacts favorably to hedge fund activism." The authors find market-beating returns upon the announcement of potential activism in the range of 5 to 7 percent, with no return reversal during the subsequent year (see Figure 9.5).

In a 2009 paper, April Klein and Emanuel Zur[15] examined "confrontational activism campaigns" by "entrepreneurial shareholder activists" and concluded that such strategies generate "significantly positive market reaction for the target firm around the initial Schedule 13D filing date" and "significantly positive returns over the subsequent year." The paper suggests that the filing of a Schedule 13D notice by an activist hedge fund is a catalytic event for a firm that heralds substantial positive returns in the stock. Klein and Zur find that targeted stocks outperform the market by an average of between 10.2 percent and 5.1 percent during the period surrounding the initial Schedule 13D. These findings suggest that, on average, the market believes activism creates shareholder value. Most interesting, the market-beating returns do not dissipate in the one-year period following the initial Schedule 13D. Instead, target stocks earn an additional 11.4 percent to 17.8 percent above-market return during the year following the activists' interventions. The market-beating returns may be due to changes in stock operations implemented at the behest of the activist investors (see Table 9.1).

In a 2008 paper, Jerry Martin and John Puthenpurackal[16] examine the performance of a hypothetical portfolio that mimics Berkshire Hathaway's investments after they are disclosed to the market. Martin and Puthenpurackal write that Buffett's investment record suggests he is one of the most successful investors of all time, with a stock portfolio in 2007 worth over $50 billion in publicly traded companies whose value would equate to the ninth-largest equity mutual fund. Observing that Berkshire Hathaway's equity portfolio had beaten the S&P 500 in 28 out of 31 years from 1976 to 2006, exceeding its average annual return by 14.65 percent over this period, the authors wondered whether it was possible to follow Buffett into the stocks the month after the filing of the Form 13F and outperform the market. They conduct a rigorous analysis of Berkshire Hathaway's investment performance, analyzing Buffett's investment style, which they characterize as "large-cap growth" contrary to the popular notion of Buffett's being a traditional "value" or "contrarian" investor. They conclude that Berkshire Hathaway's performance does not appear to be driven by buying traditional "value" stocks but by buying stocks whose growth potential is undervalued by the market.

TABLE 9.1 One-Year Abnormal Returns and Profitability Changes Following Activism

	Hedge Fund Activist Target Firms (1)	Hedge Fund Control Sample (2)	Other Entrepreneurial Activist Target Fims (3)	Other Entrepreneurial Activist Control Sample (4)	t-statistc [Z-statistc] for diff. between columns (1) and (3) (5)
Profitability					
Abnormal Stock Return	11.35%*** [4.90%]***	3.17% [2.38%]	17.82%*** [7.09%]***	2.87% [2.11%]	1.97** [1.85]**
ΔEBITDA/ Assets	−0.024* [−0.008]**	0.009 [0.002]	−0.008 [−0.002]*	−0.013 [−0.001]	−1.36 [−0.19]
ΔIndusry-Adjusted	−0.031** [−0.015]**	0.003 [−0.003]	−0.015 [−0.002]*	−0.020 [−0.001]	−1.51 [−0.23]
ΔCFO/ Assets	−0.001 [−0.001]	0.005 [−0.000]	−0.020 [−0.008]**	−0.004 [0.000]	0.87 [1.00]
ΔIndustry-Adjusted	−0.013 [−0.007]*	−0.003 [−0.001]	−0.022 [−0.011]**	−0.005 [−0.000]	0.69 [−0.43]

Source: April Klein and Emanuel Zur, "Entrepreneurial Shareholder Activism: Hedge Funds and Other Private Investors." *Journal of Finance* 64 (2009): 187–229. doi: 10.1111/j.1540-6261.2008.01432.x

This table summarizes changes (Δ) in firm characteristics between the fiscal year following and prior to the filing of the schedule 13D for firms targeted by hedge funds (column 1) and other entrepreneurial activists (column 3), as well as each group's control sample (based on industry, size and book-to-market, columns 2 and 4). For each variable the mean [median] is reported. All data are winsorized at the 1% and 99% levels. The abnormal stock return is from 30 trading days after the 13D filing date to one year after day 0, where day 0 is the SEC 13D filing date. The accounting data are during (for flows) or (for balances) on the end of the year previous to the filing of the initial Schedule 13D. Columns 1 and 3 also contain significance levels for tests for differences between the means [medians] between sample and control firms. Column 5 shows the t-statistic (Z-statistic) testing for differences between hedge fund and other entrepreneurial activists' means [maidans]. See Appendix A for variable definitions. ***significant at the 0.01 level; **significant at the 0.05 level; *significant at the 0.10 level.

Martin and Puthenpurackal evaluate the performance of an investment strategy that mimics Berkshire's investments after they are publicly disclosed to evaluate how quickly information produced by skilled investors gets incorporated into stock prices. They found that an investor who mimicked Berkshire's investments from 1976 to 2006 after they were publicly disclosed in regulatory filings could beat the market. The researchers find that such a portfolio created a month after Berkshire's investments are publicly disclosed earns returns that beat the market by 14.26 percent per year. This would suggest that the market underreacts to the information that Berkshire has bought a stock and indicates that the market is slow in incorporating the information produced by skilled investors.

There are many "cloning" services that offer brokerage accounts that allow investors to automatically follow other well-known investors. While this approach seems to be quite useful, there are two potential pitfalls: First, investors must select the "right" investment manager to follow. Many studies have investigated the performance of mutual funds and various financial professional recommendations to determine if they outperform the market or other suitable benchmarks.[17] Most papers have found that mutual funds, on average, do not outperform their benchmarks. Researchers have found, however, that investors who have in the past beaten the market will continue to do so. This suggests that some fund managers possess superior investment skills, and these skills will persist. These are the managers to follow. The second potential pitfall is in aggregating institutional investment manager stock purchases to the point that the target stocks are heavily concentrated with institutional investment managers. Some cloning services allow investors to create a portfolio that takes the most popular ideas from a number of institutional investment managers that have historically performed very well.

SHORT MONEY IS SMART MONEY

Short selling is the practice of selling a stock in anticipation of a decline in its price. The stock sold short is borrowed from another market participant and must eventually be bought back and returned to the lender, which is called *covering*. If the price declines as anticipated, the short seller covers to realize a profit. If the price advances, the short seller must still cover, but realizes a loss. Short interest (or the change in short interest) is measured by the short interest ratio (SIR), which is a monthly snapshot of the proportion of outstanding shares of any given stock sold short. A heavy or high SIR indicates that a large number of shares of a stock are sold short. A light or low SIR indicates that few or no shares of a stock are sold short.

There are several theories about the implications of the level of short interest in a stock. Some market pundits believe that high short interest is a *bearish* indicator for the obvious reason: lots of stock sold short means lots of investors think the stock will fall. Others suggests that short interest is a neutral indicator, simply signifying high demand from hedgers or arbitragers trading convertible bonds, options, mergers, or indices, and thus, the level of short interest says nothing about the future price of the stock. The third view is that high short interest is a *bullish* indicator because it implies there will be heavy buying demand in the future when the short sellers must cover. The empirical evidence on short selling is decisive. While many indicators produce counterintuitive results, short interest is not one of those indicators. High short interest is predictive of future poor returns, and therefore high short interest is a *bearish* indicator. In short: short money is smart money.

Research into stocks with high short interest finds that, while a high short interest indicates the stock price will decline, it is difficult to profit by shorting the stock in practice because of trading costs and other "short constraints." Short constraints include the difficulty or inability to borrow the stock essential to sell short. It is not possible to short a stock without borrowing stock first. If the stock is difficult to borrow, it is also likely to be expensive to borrow. Researchers have found that the borrowing costs can be so high as to remove most of the profit on the short side. The utility of high short interest is as a contrarian indicator. Investors seeking to take a long position in a stock should avoid those with high short interest.

In "The Good News in Short Interest,"[18] authors Ekkehart Boehmer, Zsuzsa Huszar, and Bradford Jordan, examined the performance of stocks with low short interest. On any given day, there are many relatively large and liquid stocks that could be easily and cheaply shorted, but nonetheless have few or no shorted shares (i.e., little or no short interest). Boehmer, Huszar, and Jordan speculated that if an easily shorted stock was completely avoided by short sellers it might suggest that short sellers did not have particularly negative information about it, and that the stock was, at a minimum, not overvalued. Could it be that the absence of short selling might indicate that the stocks are undervalued and likely to generate market-beating returns? Well, that's exactly what they found. Short sellers are able to identify overvalued stocks to sell and also seem adept at avoiding undervalued stocks, which is useful information for the investor seeking to take a long position.

Here, we present the results of Boehmer, Huszar, and Jordan's study into short interest for the period from June 1988 to December 2005. To conduct this study, each month Boehmer et al. ranked stocks on the proportion of stock sold short relative to the shares outstanding for each stock. Once ranked, the stocks were divided into percentiles, and examined at the 1st, 5th, and 10th percentile (indicating low short interest), and the 90th, 95th, and 99th percentile (indicating high short interest).

Figure 9.6 shows the monthly market-beating performance for short interest. The chart shows that annualized market-beating returns for a strategy focused on lightly shorted stocks is around 6 percent per year. A strategy concentrated in heavily shorted stocks generates market-beating returns of around 10 percent per year.

This analysis demonstrates that in the aggregate the lower a stock's short interest ratio, the better performance will be in the following year. Most interesting, the authors report that the returns to stocks with low short interest ratio and high liquidity are often larger (in absolute value) than the negative returns on portfolios of heavily shorted stocks, and they are robust to issues such as portfolio weighting, the timing of portfolio formation, the risk-adjustment procedure, listing venue, and the inclusion or exclusion of recent new listings or the 1998 to 2000 period. While short-sale constraints inhibit the short sellers from profiting from negative information about stocks, because there are no constraints to going long, it is easier to

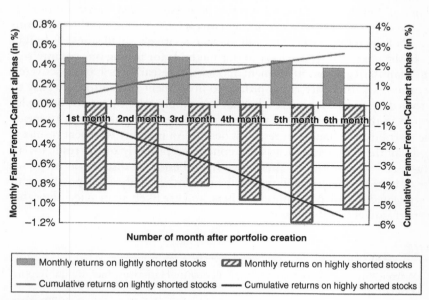

FIGURE 9.6 Monthly Alphas for Short Interest Strategy
Source: Ekkehart Boehmer, Zsuzsa R. Huszar, and Bradford D. Jordan, "The Good News in Short Interest," May 15, 2009. Available at *http://ssrn.com/abstract=1405511* or *http://dx.doi.org/10.2139/ssrn.1405511.*

profit from short interest signals on the long side. Although counterintuitive, value investors will find it worthwhile to examine short interest when analyzing potential long investments.

It makes sense to follow the smart money. For investors seeking to actively manage their own portfolio, there are several signals that indicate near-term market-beating returns. Buybacks, insider purchases, activist activity, and low SIRs indicate that the smart money may be excited about a stock. These signals combined with quantitative signals that a stock price is depressed below its valuation are very positive for future returns. There are also several corroborative market signals associated with future underperformance. Stock issuance and high SIRs indicate the smart money believes the stock is overvalued and ready for a tumble. These more negative signals may not indicate a good candidate for shorting because there are other factors to consider on the short side. Their utility lies mostly in finding stocks to avoid on the long side.

Investors seeking a less hands-on approach to their own portfolio can do well following high-performance institutional investment managers. Many cloning services exist that allow investors to automatically follow one or many institutional investment managers, or an investor can read the Form 13Fs on the SEC EDGAR website *(www.sec.gov/edgar.shtml)* for free. Investors should seek only institutional investment managers who have consistently beaten the market and still manage relatively small sums of capital.

In the next chapter, we look at our methods for testing our comprehensive quantitative value investment model. As researchers have discovered over the years, there are many pitfalls to investment simulation. It's easy to be fooled by great-looking results that are simply false or cannot be implemented in the market. Worse yet, many back-tested results are not repeatable or robust to changes in research design. An inability to repeat results is a red flag that the research was not conducted properly or the results were data-mined to confirm an alternative hypothesis. We discuss the steps we take to increase the probability that the returns we analyze are possible, can be replicated by independent researchers, and are likely to provide favorable live performance in the future.

NOTES

1. Warren Buffett, "Shareholder Letter," Berkshire Hathaway, Inc. Annual Report, 1984.
2 Robert J. Flaherty, "The Singular Henry Singleton," *Forbes*, July 9, 1979.
3. Warren Buffett, "Shareholder Letter," Berkshire Hathaway, Inc. Annual Report, 1982.
4. John Train, *The Money Masters* (New York: HarperBusiness, 1994).

5. Flaherty.
6. Alison Leigh Cowan, "Wall St. Eyes Are on Teledyne." *New York Times*, July 9, 1987.
7. David L. Ikenberry, Josef Lakonishok, and Theo Vermaelen, "Market Underreaction to Open Market Share Repurchases." NBER Working Paper Series, Vol. w4965 (December 1994), pp.181-208. Available at *http://ssrn.com/abstract=226564.*
8. Alice A. Bonaime, "Repurchases, Reputation, and Returns." *Journal of Financial and Quantitative Analysis* (JFQA), forthcoming. Available at *http://ssrn.com/abstract=1361800* or *http://dx.doi.org/10.2139/ssrn.1361800.*
9. Jack Hough, "Buy Signals: How to Decipher Stock Buybacks." *Wall Street Journal*, Upside, January 21, 2012. Available at *http://online.wsj.com/article/SB10001424052970203750404577171231151712236.html.*
10. James O'Shaughnessy, *What Works on Wall Street: The Classic Guide to the Best-Performing Investment Strategies of All Time*, 4th ed. (New York: McGraw-Hill, 2011).
11. Ako Doffou, "Insider Trading: A Review of Theory and Empirical Work." *Journal of Accounting and Finance Research* 11(1) (Spring 2003). Available at *http://ssrn.com/abstract=1028898.*
12. Lauren Cohen, Christopher Malloy, and Lukasz Pomorski, "Decoding Insider Information." *Journal of Finance*, forthcoming.
13. Daniel Giamouridis, Manolis Liodakis, and Andrew Moniz, "Some Insiders Are Indeed Smart Investors," July 29, 2008. Available at *http://ssrn.com/abstract=1160305* or *http://dx.doi.org/10.2139/ssrn.1160305.*
14. Alon P. Brav, Wei Jiang, Randall S. Thomas, and Frank Partnoy, "Hedge Fund Activism, Corporate Governance, and Firm Performance." *Journal of Finance* 63 (May 2008): 1729; ECGI Finance Working Paper No. 139/2006; Vanderbilt Law and Economics Research Paper No. 07-28; FDIC Center for Financial Research Working Paper No. 2008-06. Available at *http://ssrn.com/abstract=948907.*
15. April Klein and Emanuel Zur, "Entrepreneurial Shareholder Activism: Hedge Funds and Other Private Investors." *Journal of Finance*, forthcoming.
16. Gerald S. Martin, and John Puthenpurackal, "Imitation Is the Sincerest Form of Flattery: Warren Buffett and Berkshire Hathaway," April 15, 2008. Available at *http://ssrn.com/abstract=806246* or *http://dx.doi.org/10.2139/ssrn.806246.*
17. Ibid.
18. Ekkehart Boehmer, Zsuzsa R. Huszar, and Bradford D. Jordan, "The Good News in Short Interest," May 15, 2009. Available at *http://ssrn.com/abstract=1405511* or *http://dx.doi.org/10.2139/ssrn.1405511.*

Six

Building and Testing the Model

In this final part, we discuss how we construct and test our quantitative value investment model from the research we've examined in the book. In this chapter, we discuss our philosophy for conducting investment simulations, and survey the potential pitfalls in interpreting back-test results. We cast a suspicious eye on back-tested, and real, historical results, closely scrutinizing the steps we can take to ensure that results are genuine, and replicable.

In Chapter 11, we study the best way to combine the research we've already considered into a cohesive strategy. We examine the Magic Formula and the F_SCORE to see if we can find a better structure for our valuation model. Our process leads us to identify some potential structural issues with the Magic Formula.

In Chapter 12, the final chapter, we back-test the quantitative value model we created in Chapter 11. We take a comprehensive look at its raw results and its risk- and opportunity-cost-adjusted performance. We compare it to the Magic Formula's performance and the performance of other legendary investors. We also open up the black box, inspecting in granular detail the stocks bought by the strategy over the course of the back-test period.

CHAPTER 10

Bangladeshi Butter Production Predicts the S&P 500 Close

"I always find it extraordinary that so many studies are made of price and volume behavior, the stuff of chartists. Can you imagine buying an entire business simply because the price of the business had been marked up substantially last week and the week before? Of course, the reason a lot of studies are made of these price and volume variables is that now, in the age of computers, there are almost endless data available about them. It isn't necessarily because such studies have any utility; it's simply that the data are there and academicians have [worked] hard to learn the mathematical skills needed to manipulate them. Once these skills are acquired, it seems sinful not to use them, even if the usage has no utility or negative utility. As a friend said, to a man with a hammer, everything looks like a nail."

—Warren Buffett, "The Superinvestors of
Graham-and-Doddsville" [1]

In 1995, David J. Leinweber set out to find the metric that best predicted movements in the U.S. stock market.[2] He started with data about the annual closing price of the Standard & Poor's (S&P) 500 index for the 10 years from 1983 to 1993. He then consulted an archive of international data series published by the United Nations, which covered information like changes in interest rates, economic growth, and unemployment for all 140 United Nations (UN) member countries. Using a statistical technique called "regression analysis," Leinweber sought to find the data series that best predicted the annual closing price of the S&P 500.

Regression analysis is the main tool used by statisticians to uncover a linear relationship between two or more variables. There is some ambiguity as to its real inventor. It was first published in 1805 by Adrien-Marie Legendre, a French mathematician, as the "méthode des moindres carrés" or "least-squares method." Carl Friedrich Gauss, a German mathematician and physical scientist, is acknowledged as developing the basis for the least-squares method in 1795 at the astonishingly young age of 18. Gauss did not publish his method until 1809, and so, officially at least, Legendre got all the credit.

The measure of the explanatory power of a regression analysis is called "R-squared." A perfect relationship between two variables will show an R-squared of 1.00 or 100 percent. Strong relationships have an R-squared of greater than 50 percent. An R-squared of zero indicates the absence of any relationship. A regression analysis of, for example, height and weight in humans shows a strong, positive relationship of approximately 0.7 or 70 percent. The taller you are, the heavier you are likely to be.

After running a regression analysis of the UN's international data series for all 140 member countries, Leinweber made a stunning discovery. A simple dairy product from an unlikely country explained 75 percent of the variation in the S&P 500. What was it? Butter production in Bangladesh. Leinweber knew he was on to something. Maybe he could do better by including global data on a broader selection of dairy products. What about including cheese and U.S. production? Leinweber consulted the data. Amazingly, the R-squared vaulted to 95 percent accuracy. But what was driving these returns? By including a third variable— sheep population—Leinweber found that he could explain 99 percent of the movement in the S&P 500 for the period 1983 to 1993. Close to a perfect fit. Leinweber didn't immediately publish his findings. They seemed to good to be true. Reporters picked up on Leinweber's study, and the research finding found its way into the curriculum at the Stanford Graduate School of Business and elsewhere. Leinweber started getting calls from investors about the status of butter production in Bangladesh. With the charts fading from being copied time and time again, he decided to write up the study and publish it.

Leinweber's study was of course meant as a joke to illustrate the dangers of data mining. Data mining is the practice of analyzing huge amounts of data to find relationships between data series that are merely coincidental over the period analyzed. Bangladeshi butter production, for example, is useless as a predictor of the S&P 500 before 1983 or after 1993. Leinweber purposefully designed the study to illustrate that variables that couldn't possibly predict the S&P 500 could show a very strong relationship in a regression analysis. It was a chance association, and although he did not know what would show up as the best predictor of the S&P 500, he knew that some relationship would emerge if he looked at enough data series. The relationship between Bangladeshi butter production and the S&P 500 was the result of a lucky fishing expedition, and was entirely spurious.

The objective of this book is to develop a robust quantitative value investment strategy by combining the price and quality metrics we've already considered. Before we can create that strategy, we need to think about whether we can trust the research. Does the strategy make economic sense? We don't want to build our own Bangladeshi butter production-based strategy. It turns out that finding amazing simulated investment results is very easy. Finding measures that will lead to solid future performance in the real world is equivalently tough. In this chapter, we consider the pitfalls to avoid and present a framework for interpreting results.

SUSTAINABLE ALPHA: A FRAMEWORK FOR ASSESSING PAST RESULTS

It can be misleading to judge a fund manager's performance just on his or her historical returns. Historical returns can be deceptive, and they often have little correlation with future results. Yet investors tend to extrapolate a manager's near-term historical results into the future without considering the factors driving the manager's performance. Historical records can be so misleading that the Securities and Exchange Commission (SEC) requires fund managers to state on any document presented to investors that "past performance does not necessarily indicate future results." The empirical literature discussing this reality is vast. Here we highlight some of the more interesting research.

In their paper, "Morningstar Ratings and Mutual Fund Performance,"[3] Christopher Blake and Matthew Morey examined the ubiquitous Morningstar ratings to see if higher-ranking funds actually outperformed lower-ranked funds in the period after Morningstar assigned the rating. The authors found that the ratings were based on mere past performance, and had little ability to predict the next crop of top performers. Eugene Fama and Kenneth French in their work, "Luck versus Skill in the Cross Section of Mutual Fund Returns,"[4] conduct a comprehensive review of the returns of every mutual fund manager to assess whether performance is related to skill, which is repeatable, or luck, which is not. The evidence is sobering for investors and investment managers. Fama and French do detect some slight evidence that investment managers possess skill. However, once the fees charged by the investment managers are taken into account, they find that all value created through skill is paid to the investment manager.

As if the empirical evidence were not enough, Jonathan Berk and Richard Green pile on with a theoretical argument that chasing high-performance fund managers is a losing proposition, *even if managers are skilled*. Berk and Green argue in their paper, "Mutual Fund Flows and Performance in Rational Markets,"[5] that a truly skilled manager is unlikely to repeat past performance because good performance attracts assets, and the increased size of assets under management acts to lower subsequent returns. Buffett has regularly written in his Berkshire Hathaway Chairman's Letters about the difficulty of sustaining good returns with increased sums of capital. Here for example, in 1992:

> *Our ... conclusion—that an increased capital base will act as an anchor on our relative performance—seems incontestable. The only open question is whether we can drag the anchor along at some tolerable, though slowed, pace.*

If investors can't rely on past returns, what can they do? The answer is that we *can* rely on past results, *but* only after filtering them through our "Sustainable Alpha" model in Figure 10.1.

Figure 10.1 shows the Sustainable Alpha model as a pyramid with the most fundamental requirement at the base, and the least important requirement at the peak. Each level is less important than the level below.

- *Robust Idea Generation,* found at the base, is the most important requirement. A manager must have a sustainable "edge" or ability to beat the market. Why does the strategy work? Who is on the losing side of the trades? Can the manager generate an "edge" given their current

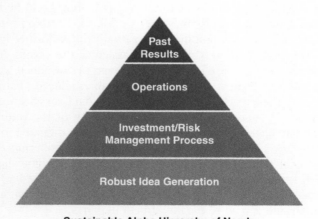

Sustainable Alpha Hierarchy of Needs

FIGURE 10.1 Sustainable Alpha

assets under management? A skilled manager controlling a small base of assets may actually have no skill with a larger asset base. Without a true edge, the only way that future returns will persist is by luck.

- *Risk Management* is the second level. To take advantage of the edge created by robust idea generation, a manager must have a sensible risk management process. Is it sensible to invest all of the capital (and use leverage) in a single best idea? If not, how much diversification is enough? A poorly designed risk management process can turn profitable ideas into loss makers because, for example, the margin on the position is called and the position can't be held to maturity.
- *Operations* looks at the infrastructure of an investment management business. Are communications clear between portfolio managers and the traders? Or is the portfolio manager asking to sell a stock, while the trading desk is buying the stock? Do the internal processes and workflows reflect the investment strategy? As the 27th Commandant of the Marine Corps Gen. Robert Borrow once said, "Amateurs talk about tactics, but professionals study logistics."
- Only after we have considered all of the previous stages can we examine *Past Results*. Historical results, interpreted from the top of the Sustainable Alpha pyramid, can be a useful indication of whether or not an investment strategy is repeatable in the future.

WHAT'S THE BIG IDEA?

As Leinweber's Bangladeshi butter example demonstrates, the use of statistical analysis to generate investment strategies can be dangerous. The risk for a quantitative investor's discovering an apparently strong relationship between a factor and subsequent returns is that the relationship is not real but a false positive found through data mining. It is possible, given a large enough body of data, to find relationships between variables that are merely the result of random chance. In fact, we can expect a known rate of false positives. As he points out in his 2009 book, *Nerds on Wall Street: Math, Machines and Wired Markets,* [6] if we look at 100 regressions that are significant at a level of 95 percent, five of them are there just by chance. John Freeman, in his 1992 paper, "Behind the Smoke and Mirrors: Gauging the Integrity of Investment Simulations," [7] writes that it is not unreasonable to assume that for every four completely spurious strategies tested, one will appear statistically significant. The challenge for the quantitative investor is to separate the bogus relationships from the genuine predictors. This is no small feat.

The reason it is so difficult to dismiss apparent patterns as mere randomness is the uncontrollable human impulse to explain everything we see.

Leinweber's Bangladeshi butter production was obviously not predictive of the direction of the S&P 500, but if he had created a model relating stock prices to interest rates, gross domestic product (GDP), trade, or housing starts, it might conceivably have had statistics that looked as good. Those statistics would be harder to dismiss because they might sound much more plausible, even though the relationship would be just as spurious as the Bangladeshi butter example. Taleb calls this the "narrative fallacy."[8] In the context of the Sustainable Alpha pyramid, generating a robust idea is not trivial. While most of us recognize that Bangladeshi butter example is an obvious canard, we are more likely to accept an explanation based on GDP or interest rates because the story makes more sense. It is impossible for us to avoid fitting an explanation to our spurious finding. How can we avoid the data-mining trap? First, don't dig up the investment idea in the data mine. The more scientific approach is to start with an idea and test it, which is exactly what we have done with our quantitative value strategy.

Start with Tried-and-True Value Investing Principles

The base of our Sustainable Alpha pyramid is a value-investment philosophy. We use as the basis for our quantitative value strategy seasoned value investing principles first discussed and successfully employed by Graham in the early 1930s. Warren Buffett's "wonderful company at a fair price" took Graham's value investing philosophy one step further. Buffett inspired Greenblatt to create the Magic Formula, a simple quantitative replication of Buffett's investment strategy. Value investing is not a new idea. Graham, Buffett, Greenblatt, and countless others have invested and written consistently and publicly over the last 80 years. Quantitative value has good investing DNA if we can trace its intellectual lineage back through Greenblatt to Buffett to Graham.

The individual quality and price measures we have considered are long-standing value investing methods. The price-to-book value and price-to-earnings ratios are so old we had to chisel them out of amber, and we found the enterprise multiple written on a cave wall. In other words, they are ancient in the value investment world. The quality metrics are newer because Buffett was the first to explain the importance of quality, but they have been used to great effect by Buffett, Greenblatt, and any reader of Buffett's Chairman's Letters or Greenblatt's *Little Book*. In other words, they have been used by many investors for many years.

In addition to the well-known value investing metrics we employ, we also restrict our strategy to measures previously suggested by academic or industry research. We did not conduct the free-for-all regression analysis cited by Leinweber as the primary cause of false statistical relationships.

We could have concocted some spurious combination of metrics that would have looked original and generated an outstanding performance. Instead, we started with publicly available research and then conducted our own out-of-sample tests on the findings with data through December 31, 2011. If we identify variables that disappear in our simulation, they were likely data-mined: we treat these variables with a great deal of suspicion. If a variable's performance persists, we proceeded cautiously on the basis that it hadn't been disproved yet.

Simplify, Simplify, Simplify

Researchers Claire Tsai, Joshua Klayman, and Reid Hastie[9] conducted a study in 2008. They wanted to examine how we make decisions about the outcome of uncertain future events as we are presented with additional information about the events. Specifically, they wanted to understand how the acquisition of additional information affects both the accuracy of our decisions, and our confidence about the accuracy of those decisions. We would expect to find that, as we are given more decision-relevant information, our accuracy improves, and our confidence increases accordingly. But is this the case?

Tsai, Klayman, and Hastie were aware of several preexisting studies that examined the relationship between increasing the information available to a decision maker and changes in their confidence and accuracy. In an unpublished study from 1973, researchers had provided horse-racing handicappers with 40 different statistical data points about the performance of horses in the races. From that set, the handicappers selected which specific data points they wanted to see in consecutive blocks of 5, 5, 15, and 15 data points each. As we would expect, the handicappers' confidence increased with each block of additional information, however, the handicappers' accuracy did not. Other studies had found a similar phenomenon with clinical psychologists and observers predicting the performances of baseball teams. In these studies, accuracy did slightly increase with the acquisition of more information, but confidence increased more than accuracy did. All these studies suggest an interesting general tendency for more information to lead to greater confidence, and overconfidence, but not to increased accuracy.

To conduct their study, Tsai, Klayman, and Hastie used students at the University of Chicago who had already demonstrated through a written test that they were "highly knowledgeable" about college football. Those "highly knowledgeable" students were then provided with statistical information about NCAA college football teams and asked to predict the winner and the point spread of 15 NCAA college football games without knowing the names of the teams. For each game, the researchers divided 30 data points into five blocks of six data points each such that each block contained new data points that the students were likely to regard as useful. After each block, the students made predictions about the game and assessed their confidence in their predictions. The researchers found that as the students were exposed to each new block of data, the accuracy of their predictions did not improve, but their confidence rose steadily. They concluded that the amount of available information affects our confidence more than it does our accuracy. More information simply leads to more overconfidence.

There are several factors at play here. The first is confirmation bias. This causes us to unconsciously collect information that agrees with our original decision and disregard information that disagrees with that decision. The researchers found that the students, when presented with new data, tended not to change their mind when the additional data warranted doing so. Another factor is Taleb's narrative fallacy. We weight the additional information on the degree to which we perceive it as coherent in the narrative we have constructed. If it fits into the story, it's included. If it doesn't, it's disregarded. The new evidence included in the existing story tends to corroborate the story, so we get increasingly confident that the story is accurate.

The implications for investors are obvious. The decision to purchase a stock or not is a decision about an uncertain future event. Collecting more and more information about a stock will not improve the accuracy of our decision to buy or not as much as it will increase our confidence about the decision. Hoarding additional data points in our intellectual attic makes us feel good, but it does nothing to improve our investment results. The better approach is to keep the strategy austere. Clean out the attic, and keep an eye on only the most important data. This is harder than it looks.

As investors, we should favor simplicity over complexity, but as humans we seem behaviorally destined to prefer complexity. In his 1977 book, *How Real Is Real?*,[10] Paul Watzlawick, an Austrian-American psychologist and philosopher, discussed a study in which two subjects, A and B, are asked to formulate, through trial and error, rules for distinguishing between "healthy" and "sick" cells shown to them. They are both seated facing a projection screen, but they cannot see each other and do not communicate. They are shown pictures of cells, some healthy and some sick, and asked to determine which is which. In front of each are two buttons marked "Healthy" and "Sick," respectively, and two lights marked "Right" and "Wrong." Every time a cell is shown, they must press one button, and one of the lights flashes on indicating whether the guess was correct or not.

The wrinkle to the experiment is that subject A gets real feedback, but subject B does not. A's lights tell him whether his guess was right or wrong. Subject B's feedback is based not on his own guesses, but on A's. It does not matter what he decides about a particular slide; he is told he is "right" if A guesses right, and "wrong" if A guessed wrong. B does not know this. He has been instructed that there is a way to make the distinction between the two, that he has to discover this method, and that he can do so by making guesses and finding out if he is right or wrong. He is searching for the rules where there are none that he can discover.

Subjects A and B are eventually asked to discuss their rules for distinguishing between healthy and sick cells. Subject A's explanations are simple and concrete, but B's are subtle and complex because B was forced to base his rules on weak and inconsistent guesses. The amazing thing is that A does not regard B's explanations as overly complex or illogical, but is impressed by their sophistication. Subject A tends to feel that his rules are inferior because they are so simple. And the more complex B's method, the more likely it is to convince A. Over the course of the first experiment, most A subjects learn to distinguish healthy from sick cells with good accuracy, getting the guess right approximately 80 percent of the time. Even more amazing is this: after hearing B's overly complicated explanations, A's accuracy drops significantly because he tries to incorporate B's more complex rules into his own rules. The moral of the story is that we should prefer simpler models over more complex models, but we can't help ourselves. We actually *prefer* complexity.

Recall from Chapter 2 Greenblatt's 2012 examination of the performance of small investors using the Magic Formula over the two years to April 2011.[11] The self-managed accounts, where clients could choose their own stocks from the preapproved list and then exercise discretion about the timing of the trades, slightly underperformed the market, returning 59.4 percent after all expenses, against the 62.7 percent performance of the S&P 500 over the same period. The aggregated professionally managed accounts returned 84.1 percent after all expenses over the same two years, beating the self-managed accounts by almost 25 percent (and the S&P by well over 20 percent)—a huge difference over a two-year period.

Greenblatt found the self-managed accounts took a model that outperformed in the real world and eliminated all the outperformance from their own portfolios. They achieved this by failing to buy the best performers. It's important to recognize that this was not a matter of random stock-selection errors. Rather, investors *systematically* avoided the best performers. All the outperformance provided by the simple model was eliminated for reasons beyond the model. This is another example of investors preferring complexity over simplicity. The talking heads on CNBC give brilliant reasons for avoiding the stocks, and investors trust those sophisticated answers over the pedestrian simplicity of the Magic Formula. A stock selected by the Magic Formula must be in error because the method is so simple, and the talking heads have such complex-sounding reasons for avoiding it. The self-managed investors eliminate stocks from the preapproved Magic Formula list because some self-appointed "expert" told them so, and those stocks turn out to be the biggest future winners.

This is true also for the experts. Recall from Chapter 1 the abundance of research that shows that simple models outperform expert judgments, even when those experts are given access to the models. This means that experts, in exercising their expertise, are actually detracting from the accuracy of the model. The reason is that models have a known historical error rate, and experts suffer from the same behavioral biases as the rest of us. Fiddling with the output of the model gives those biases a chance to be expressed in the results. Study after study finds that the model is the ceiling of performance from which the expert detracts, rather than the floor to which the expert adds. Even Greenblatt has said that he cannot outperform the Magic Formula.[12] He ran an experiment in which the Magic Formula selected stocks for him and his business partner to buy, and then they both went through the list and removed those stocks they "knew" to be value traps. They lost to the Magic Formula. Even a stock in which Greenblatt had personal experience fooled him. The model selected a pharmaceutical stock, but he knew that its main product was about to go off-patent, so he overruled the model. "And the thing doubled in six months. They say a little knowledge can be dangerous," says Greenblatt.[13] It is often the most counterintuitive stocks, those most hated by value investors, that generate the market-beating returns for the portfolio.

RIGOROUSLY TEST THE BIG IDEA

It makes sense that we would want to rigorously test our model. Many ideas that appear intuitive wilt under examination. The trap is that there are myriad ways that we can inadvertently fool ourselves with investment simulations. Bad data can introduce various biases into the results, and lead us to believe the returns would have been better than achievable in practice. Faulty assumptions made about portfolio construction, and turnover and transaction costs can also introduce errors into the results. In this section, we discuss the common errors made when conducting investment simulations and the means to avoid them.

Data Errors

In his 1992 article, "Behind the Smoke and Mirrors: Gauging the Integrity of Investment Simulations,"[14] John D. Freeman discusses several common errors made by researchers conducting investment simulations. Many are inadvertent and the result of faulty data. A good database can help us avoid most of these errors. One well-known error is caused by survivorship bias, so called because it stems from the inclusion of "survivors"—those stocks that are not delisted—to the exclusion of those that are delisted, which causes the study to be biased in favor of the survivors. Databases that don't include data on delisted stocks may cause returns to be overstated. Let's say, for example, that we test a strategy that buys stocks in financial distress. If the database does not include delisted stocks, our results will only include stocks that were in financial distress and survived. Those stocks likely produced incredible gains, which would overstate the results available in practice. Consider the stocks that were in financial distress and perished. If we bought those stocks, our results would be considerably lower but the database excludes them, so we cannot measure them, overstating the results we would have achieved in practice. In practice, we might not be able to distinguish between those that survive and those that perish at the time of acquisition, but the investment simulation performs as if we can.

To curb survivor bias, we must employ a database with data integrity. We use the Center for Research in Security Prices (CRSP) database, the gold standard for academic research and quantitative investors. CRSP includes "dead" companies and data on delisted stocks. This is, however, only the first stage. We need to incorporate the delisted security data into our returns. In their paper, "Delisting Returns and Their Effect on Accounting-Based Market Anomalies,"[15] Richard Price, William Beaver, and Maureen McNichols identified an algorithm that sensibly merges the CRSP delisting information into a final returns database. The authors highlight the importance of incorporating delisting data into a back-test analysis. They find that results change dramatically depending on whether or not delisted stocks are properly included in an analysis. For example, in the case of an analysis of portfolios formed according to book value-to-market price deciles, the performance of the value portfolio will be hugely overstated if delisting data is not properly incorporated because many of those stocks do not survive. Table 10.1 shows the impact of failing to incorporate delisted stocks in a book value-to-market (BM) price analysis.

Another pernicious error is caused by "look-ahead" or "point-in-time" bias. Look-ahead bias is simply the inclusion in a simulation of data not available during the period analyzed. For example, a database that does not account for the lag time in reporting may overstate results. Annual results are not typically announced until January or February of the following year. If we test a strategy that rebalances annually on January 1, we introduce look-ahead bias if we use the preceding year's annual results because they would not have been available on January 1 of this year.

Companies often restate financial statements after the fact, and this can introduce another form of look-ahead bias that can have a huge impact on back-tested results. Marcus Bogue and Morris Bailey in their white paper, "The Advantages of Using as First Reported Data with Current Compustat

TABLE 10.1   Delisting Effects on Book-to-Market Deciles

Returns of book-to-market deciles

	1987–2002			1962–2002		
BM_t decile	Mean R_{t+1}	Mean UR_{t+1}	t-Value	Mean R_{t+1}	Mean UR_{t+1}	t-Value
Panel A: excluding delisting firm-years						
1	0.102	−0.045	−3.78	0.083	−0.057	−7.62
2	0.088	−0.053	−5.57	0.092	−0.047	−7.85
3	0.197	−0.050	−5.74	0.106	−0.039	−7.09
4	0.136	−0.010	−1.05	0.133	−0.012	−2.04
5	0.137	−0.009	−1.03	0.141	−0.007	−1.18
6	0.154	0.003	0.29	0.161	0.008	1.28
7	0.174	0.019	2.04	0.177	0.019	3.45
8	0.186	0.024	2.25	0.189	0.023	3.63
9	0.246	0.074	6.01	0.230	0.056	7.77
10	0.301	0.114	9.41	0.272	0.086	11.73
10 − 1	0.199	0.158	8.20	0.189	0.143	13.34
n	74,087	74,087		139,164	139,164	
Panel B: including delisting firm-years						
1	0.024	−0.110	−10.23	0.030	−0.101	−14.48
2	0.077	−0.057	−6.16	0.085	−0.049	−8.25
3	0.083	−0.058	−6.99	0.097	−0.043	−8.15
4	0.127	−0.015	−1.68	0.131	−0.012	−2.04
5	0.129	−0.011	−1.42	0.138	−0.005	−0.92
6	0.153	0.007	0.84	0.161	0.013	2.28
7	0.166	0.016	1.89	0.174	0.021	3.93
8	0.183	0.026	2.53	0.189	0.028	4.46
9	0.227	0.062	5.43	0.223	0.055	8.04
10	0.246	0.075	6.74	0.242	0.067	9.71
10 − 1	0.222	0.185	10.58	0.212	0.168	16.96
n	81,755	81,755		150,046	150,046	

Source: William Beaver, Maureen McNichols, and Richard Price, "Delisting Returns and Their Effect on Accounting-Based Market Anomalies." *Journal of Accounting and Economics* 43 (2007): 341–368.

Data for Historical Research,"[16] highlight how restated financial statements impact back-test results for a simple price-to earnings ratio strategy. If the back-test fails to account for the difference in financial statement data as the data are first reported and then as they are subsequently restated, the back-test results vary dramatically. For example, from June 1987 through June 2001, failing to account for look-ahead bias caused by restatement of financial results led to an overstatement of returns achievable with the price-to-earnings ratio strategy by an incredible 28 percent. Figure 10.2 illustrates the impact of the failure to account for restated financial results.

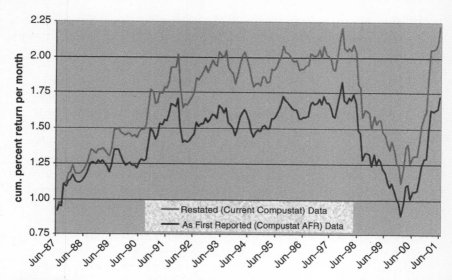

FIGURE 10.2 Impact on the Price-to-Earnings Ratio Strategy of Look-Ahead Bias Introduced by the Restatement of Financial Results (1987 to 2001)
Source: Marcus Bogue and Morris Bailey, "The Advantages of Using as First Reported Data with Current Compustat Data for Historical Research," Charter Oak Investment Systems, Inc., 2001.

In our investment simulations, we treat the data conservatively to protect against look-ahead bias. We do so by lagging the financial statement data by six months. This helps to ensure that all financial statement reports would have been available at the time the trading decision would have been made. For example, we often use annual data as of December 31, but assume the investor would not have this data available until June 30 of the following year. This is the standard practice in academic literature to ensure that researchers do not produce look-ahead bias that overstates the results.

Mo' Money, Mo' Problems

It is critical that any investment simulation considers the size of the portfolio, and the size and liquidity of the target stocks. The general rule is that the greater the sum of capital invested in a strategy, the smaller the potential investment universe, the more difficult the rebalancing, and, consequently, the worse the results. Smaller sums of capital can be invested in smaller, less liquid stocks, so the investment universe is larger. Smaller sums of capital can also be rebalanced more easily and without moving the price much or at all. A large universe and frequent rebalancing will produce better returns than a small universe and infrequent rebalancing, but the trade-off is that the strategy can only absorb smaller sums of capital. Take, for example, Benjamin Graham's original "net current asset value" strategy discussed in Chapter 1:

> *My first, more limited, technique confines itself to the purchase of common stocks at less than their working-capital value, or net-current-asset value, giving no weight to the plant and other fixed assets, and deducting all liabilities in full from the current assets. We used this approach extensively in managing investment funds, and over a 30-odd year period we must have earned an average of some 20 per cent per year from this source. For a while, however, after the mid-1950's, this brand of buying opportunity became very scarce because of the pervasive bull market. But it has returned in quantity since the 1973–74 decline. In January 1976 we counted over 300 such issues in the Standard & Poor's Stock Guide—about 10 per cent of the total. I consider it a foolproof method of systematic investment—once again, not on the basis of individual results but in terms of the expectable group outcome.*

Various researchers have found returns to the net-net strategy of approximately 30 percent per year.[17] Pretty amazing, right? The problem with the strategy is that it can only absorb very small sums of capital. Graham reported that the net current asset value strategy was "almost unfailingly dependable and satisfactory," but was "severely limited in its application" because the stocks were too small, infrequently available, and very illiquid. Research on a sample of stocks listed in the United Kingdom from June 1981 through June 2000 found liquidity and market capitalization had a huge impact on back-test results.[18] The returns to the smallest quintile of stocks were over 30 percent per year, but those returns were concentrated in stocks with little or no liquidity. The returns for the larger companies were still attractive at around 17 percent, but less reliable because there were fewer stocks in the study—only one or two in a given period. The research demonstrates that, while the net current asset value strategy might generate fantastic returns, it is, as Graham put it, severely limited in its application. Small, thinly traded stocks also often have wide bid and ask spreads, and it is often difficult to trade those stocks at the bid and ask prices recorded.

To combat the small capitalization issue, we use a New York Stock Exchange (NYSE) breakpoint rule that excludes the smallest 40 percent of stocks by market capitalization. We include in our study only common stocks that have a market capitalization larger than the 40th percentile of all stocks on the NYSE at any given point in time. For example, the 40th percentile of market capitalizations on the NYSE on December 31, 2011, is $1.4 billion.

We would exclude from our analysis on December 31, 2011, all stocks with a market capitalization smaller than $1.4 billion. We exclude smaller stocks because including them can create misleading performance data that could not be achieved in the real world. Small capitalization stocks tend to have wide bid/ask spreads and very little liquidity at the bid or ask. If we include them in the study, the program will assume that it was possible to trade at the price shown at the bid or ask, when in reality trading even a relatively small sum may have moved the price to a point that would dramatically impact the results. Simply stated, including very small or micro capitalization stocks hugely overstates the returns achievable in practice. We chose the 40th percentile because it can be objectively determined at any point in time, it represents a sufficiently large market capitalization to make it investable, and leaves a sufficiently large number of stocks in the study to make the results reliable. Our objective has been to study only those stocks sufficiently large and liquid to trade in the real world to make the results as reliable and repeatable as possible. This is the universe from which we study the various stock strategies. We could show greatly enhanced results by using a lower market capitalization cut off, including smaller, more illiquid stocks, but the results would not be as credible.

Benchmarking: Making the Numbers Sing

We analyze the universe and divide it into ten portfolios, each representing a decile ranked according to the investment criteria under consideration. Each decile portfolio contains 10 percent of the stocks studied, and each stock is weighted by market capitalization within the portfolio. So, for example, if the portfolio contains 350 stocks, each stock is represented by its market capitalization–weighted proportion of the total value of the 350-stock portfolio. If the total market cap of the 350-stock portfolio is $50 billion and a stock in the portfolio is $5 billion, it would represent 10 percent of the portfolio. "Decile 1" is the 10 percent of stocks most closely meeting the investment criteria, or possessing the best measure according to the investment criteria. "Decile 2" is the next 10 percent of stocks ranked according to the investment criteria. "Decile 10" is the worst 10 percent of stocks. For example, if we rank stocks according to the price-to-earnings (P/E) ratio, the stocks in decile 1 are the 10 percent with the lowest P/E ratios, the stocks in decile 2 are the 10 percent with the next lowest price-to-earnings ratios, and the stocks in decile 10 have the highest P/E ratios.

We compare the market capitalization–weighted returns generated by any given strategy to the Standard and Poor's 500 Total Return Index (S&P 500 TR), which is a market capitalization–weighted index that includes dividends. The S&P 500 TR contains relatively large stocks weighted by market capitalization, which means that the larger the market capitalization of a stock in the S&P 500 TR, the greater its movements influence the S&P 500 TR. If we were to present equally weighted results from our investment simulations and compare these results to the performance of the S&P 500 TR the results would be misleading because the strategy portfolios would weight more heavily smaller, more illiquid names. The strategy might have excellent back-test results relative to the S&P 500 TR, but the performance would not represent "alpha," or add value for the investor. For example, consider the performance of the purely passive portfolio in Table 10.2, which equally weights all NYSE/AMEX/Nasdaq stocks that meet the NYSE 40 percent market capitalization breakpoint.

Figure 10.3 shows that EW Portfolio, the passive, equal-weight portfolio, substantially outperforms the S&P 500 TR by almost 3 percent a year from January 1964 through December 2011. We could boost our returns by equal weighting, but our objective is to generate results that are robust, intellectually honest, and replicable by other researchers.

This discussion illustrates the need to control for investment managers' sleight of hand. Before investing with an investment manager, an investor should understand the investment manager's true "opportunity-adjusted" performance. Note that we are not adjusting performance here for risk, but rather for "opportunity." This is an important distinction. Let's say for the sake of this argument that small capitalization stocks provide favorable risk-adjusted returns (i.e., alpha). A manager who buys only small-capitalization

TABLE 10.2 Performance of a Passive, Equal-Weight Portfolio Compared to the S&P 500 TR and the Ten-Year Treasury TR (1964 to 2011)

	EW Portfolio	S&P 500 TR	10-Year Treasury TR
CAGR	12.19%	9.52%	7.52%
Standard Deviation	16.84%	15.19%	10.39%
Downside Deviation	12.09%	10.66%	6.23%
Sharpe Ratio	0.46	0.33	0.25
Sortino Ratio (MAR = 5%)	0.66	0.50	0.45
Worst Drawdown	−48.44%	−50.21%	−20.97%
Worst Month Return	−24.31%	−21.58%	−11.24%
Best Month Return	19.32%	16.81%	15.23%
Profitable Months	59.38%	60.94%	59.20%

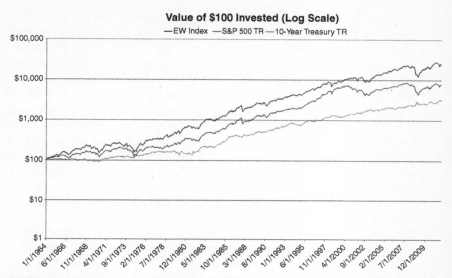

Value of $100 Invested (Log Scale)

—EW Index —S&P 500 TR —10-Year Treasury TR

FIGURE 10.3 Performance of Passive Equal-Weight Index Compared To S&P 500 TR (1964 to 2011)

stocks will perform in line with the performance provided by small-capitalization stocks. Should the manager be compensated simply because they invest in a particular market segment that happens to be performing well? We can replicate this manager's performance by investing in a small capitalization index with considerably lower fees. Why pay higher fees when the same investment performance can be achieved for less? To control for exposures to "indexable" opportunity costs, we use factor models to identify and measure true opportunity-cost beating performance. Factor models control for a variety of risks and opportunity costs, allowing us to observe the true, underlying performance of the strategy. We discuss these models briefly in Chapter 11 when we analyze the value added by our quantitative value strategy.

More Data Means More Confidence

There are many strategies that work for short periods of time, and then flame out. Think of dot-coms at the turn of the millennium. If we'd examined any strategy that sought telecommunications, media, or technology stocks over the 10 years to December 31, 1999, we'd have concluded that the strategy massively outperforms the market. If we included data from the 10 years before December 31, 1989, and the 10 years after December 31, 1999, we'd have found the strategy performed in line with the market. This is called *small sample bias*.

We examine the performance of all stocks traded on the NYSE, AMEX, and Nasdaq exchanges through the period 1964 to 2011.[19] Ideally, we'd use 1,000 years of return data from every stock market on earth because we want a comprehensive analysis of different time periods, exchanges, and countries. Unfortunately, the data prior to 1962 and outside the United States are unreliable or do not exist, so we make do with what we have. Compustat data for years prior to 1962 suffer from survivor bias and represent only large, historically successful stocks.[20] This raises an important point about the results in the book. Stock market returns in the United States through the period 1964 to 2011 may not be representative of those achievable in the future or in different countries. In the period examined, the United States experienced relative political stability and outstanding economic growth. The results would be wholly different if we included countries impacted by war, political instability, or hyperinflation. Philippe Jorion and William Goetzmann make this point in a very powerful research article called "Global Stock Markets in the Twentieth Century."[21] Jorion and Goetzmann show how lucky the amazing performance of the U.S. equity markets has truly been. Figure 10.4 shows the real returns to global stock markets.

Figure 10.4 illustrates that the performance of the U.S. stock market has been the exception, not the rule.

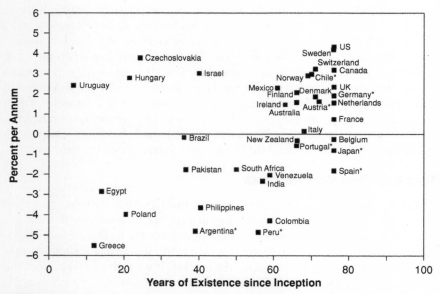

FIGURE 10.4 Real Returns on Global Stock Markets from 1921 to 1996
Source: Philippe Jorion and William Goetzmann, "Global Stock Markets in the Twentieth Century." *Journal of Finance* 54 (1999): 953–980.

Historical Data versus Forward Data

We use trailing 12-month figures, as opposed to forward estimates, and for good reason. Analysts tend to be too optimistic, and so systematically overestimate forward earnings figures. Figure 10.5 is a chart showing the results of research into analyst forecasts conducted by Roy Batchelor.[22]

As Figure 10.5 demonstrates, exceptions to the long pattern of excessively optimistic forecasts are rare. Only in 1995 and 2004 to 2006, when strong economic growth generated earnings that caught up with earlier predictions, do forecasts actually hit the mark. When economic growth accelerates, the size of the forecast error declines; when economic growth slows, it increases.

Transaction Costs

We must decide at the outset of the investment simulation how we will manage the weight of each stock in the portfolio, and how this will affect rebalancing and transaction costs. Even simple methods of weighting introduce complexity and will require substantial rebalancing and incur transaction costs. If, for example, we employ a constant equal-weighting scheme, and the portfolio holds 100 stocks in equal weights and at the next rebalancing, 20 stocks are sold off and replaced by 20 new stocks. The turnover is not 20 percent because the proportion of the sales will be greater than

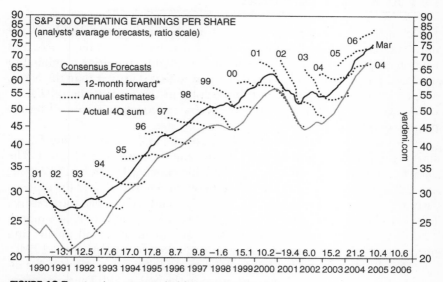

FIGURE 10.5 Analysts Are Reliably Overoptimistic
Source: Roy Batchelor, "Bias in Macroeconomic Forecasts." *International Journal of Forecasting* 23(2) (April–June 2007): 189–203.

20 percent if we sell winners, and less than 20 percent if we sell losers. To further complicate matters, the other stocks remaining in the portfolio will now have unequal weights, and will also need to be rebalanced to return them to equal weights. The situation is similar, although less trading intensive, if we use a market capitalization–weighting scheme.

In practice, all of this rebalancing incurs transaction costs. Investment simulations must take into account these transaction costs from the rebalancing. The more frequently the portfolio is rebalanced, the better the returns in the investment simulation, but the higher the transaction costs in the real world. It's possible that the transaction costs are so great as to erode all the expected return. Incorporating transaction costs into an investment simulation is difficult. Different investors will have different cost structures, tax statuses, and trading and execution skills. Cost assumptions for one group of investors will be a degree of magnitude larger (or smaller) for another set of investors. We try to minimize the distortions caused by transaction costs in our analysis by limiting ourselves to a yearly rebalance and trading in only relatively large, liquid stocks. Unless we explicitly state otherwise, we report all returns throughout this book without fees and transactions costs. Our philosophy is that investors are better able to gauge the expected costs of running their own portfolio than we are.

THE PARAMETERS OF THE UNIVERSE

For complete transparency, we outline in this section the details of the universe that we draw from to ensure that the back-test is repeatable and has integrity. Our universe is liquid and investable, requiring a minimum market capitalization at each rebalance period that is greater than the NYSE 40 percent market capitalization breakpoint at the time of the rebalance. Unless we state otherwise, these parameters are constant across all results presented in the book.

For our final investment simulation exercise in Chapters 11 and 12, we start the analysis on January 1, 1974, and end on December 31, 2011. The data for the NEQISS variable are available starting December 31, 1972, and we require a six-month lag period between report date and the time we assume an investor could see the data. We could technically start returns July 1, 1973; however, for ease of testing, we do not include the six-month "stub" in our final results. The numbers are identical for all intents and purposes whether we start testing on July 1, 1963, or on January 1, 1974.

The objective of this book is to develop a sensible quantitative value investment strategy that will deliver returns in the real world. There are many ways that we can fool ourselves with investment simulations: statistical

Universe Selection and Back-Test Assumptions

	Description
Market Capitalization	NYSE 40% breakpoint[23]
Exchanges	NYSE/AMEX/Nasdaq Real estate investment trusts (REITs) Business development companies (BDCs) Tracking stocks Limited partnerships (LPs) Master limited partnerships (MLPs)
Excluded Security Types	Mortgage REITs Royalty trusts Exchange-traded funds or notes (ETFs, ETNs) Closed-end funds American depositary receipts (ADRs) or American depository shares (ADSs) Special-purpose acquisition companies (SPACs)
Excluded Industries	Financials Utilities
Return Data	CRSP: Prices adjusted for dividends, splits, and corporate actions
Fundamentals Data	Compustat: Annual data starting December 31, 1962
Delisting Algorithm	"Delisting Returns and Their Effect on Accounting- Based Market Anomalies," by William Beaver, Maureen McNichols, and Richard Price [24]
Portfolio Weights	Market capitalization weighted One-year buy-and-hold returns
Formation Date	June 30 of year t
Fundamentals Date	December 31 of year $t - 1$. Firms with fiscal years ending before March 31 of year t use year t fundamentals, after March 31 use year $t - 1$ fundamentals
Data Requirements	Firms must have data for all core data items

analyses can identify spurious relationships; we can inadvertently introduce look-ahead or survivorship biases by using the wrong database; we
can overestimate the amount of capital the strategy can accommodate or the
liquidity of the target stocks; or we can underestimate the transaction costs

from frequent rebalancing. As Buffett and Graham have acknowledged, while the market is not *always* efficient, it is *frequently* efficient. Beating the market is difficult. Anyone who tells you otherwise is selling you something that will make them rich and you poor.

We don't generate our ideas through statistical analysis and curve fitting. We rely on tried-and-true security analysis techniques, and we supplement these metrics with academic research and common sense. We also tend toward simplicity in our measures where possible. In addition to the reasons we gave earlier, there are many other good reasons for preferring simplicity. Simpler models have fewer and more concrete rules, and so tend to be more robust. Complex models have more rules, which are more intuitive and open to interpretation. One of the reasons that quantitative investing works so well is that it prompts the investor to crystallize at the outset the means by which he or she will analyze a stock. This crystallization prevents the rules from being modified to accommodate stocks that don't meet the model's investment criteria, which might be tempting at market extremes.

Finally, we have sought to avoid the common pitfalls of back-test results. We model our testing on the best academic and industry finance research. In all cases, our null hypothesis is that the market is efficient, and only in the face of overwhelming evidence do we reject the null hypothesis. We use comprehensive databases free of survivorship bias, containing historical corporate action and delisting data, and we have lagged the data to control for look-ahead bias. We use a relatively large market capitalization cutoff ($1.4 billion as of December 31, 2011). We also assume an annually rebalanced, market capitalization–weighted portfolio at inception. We seek only genuine, repeatable results, and do so by replicating in our investment simulations as conservatively and authentically as possible the investment conditions confronted by investors in the real world.

NOTES

1. Warren Buffett, "The Superinvestors of Graham-and-Doddsville," *Hermes,* Columbia Business School alumni magazine, 1984. Available at *www7.gsb .columbia.edu/alumni/news/hermes/print-archive/superinvestors.*
2. David J. Leinweber, *Nerds on Wall Street: Math, Machines and Wired Markets* (Hoboken, NJ: John Wiley & Sons, 2009).
3. Christopher Blake and Matthew Morey, "Morningstar Ratings and Mutual Fund Performance." *Journal of Financial and Quantitative Analysis* 35 (2000): 451–483.

4. Eugene Fama and Kenneth French, "Luck versus Skill in the Cross Section of Mutual Fund Returns." *Journal of Finance,* forthcoming.

5. J. B. Berk and R. C. Green, "Mutual Fund Flows and Performance in Rational Markets." *Journal of Political Economy* 112 (2004): 1269–1295.

6. Leinweber.

7. J. D. Freeman, "Behind the Smoke and Mirrors: Gauging the Integrity of Investment Simulations," *Financial Analysts Journal* 48 (6) (November–December 1992): 26–31.

8. Nassim Nicholas Taleb, *The Black Swan: The Impact of the Highly Improbable* (New York: Random House, 2007).

9. Claire I. Tsai, Joshua Klayman, and Reid Hastie, "Effects of Amount of Information on Judgment Accuracy and Confidence." *Organizational Behavior and Human Decision Processes* 107 (2008): 97–105. Available at *http://ssrn.com/abstract=1297347.*

10. Paul Watzlawick, *How Real Is Real?* (Vintage, 1977).

11. Joel Greenblatt, "Adding Your Two Cents May Cost a Lot Over the Long Term." MorningStar, Perspectives, January 16, 2012. Available at *http://news.morningstar.com/articlenet/SubmissionsArticle.aspx?submissionid=134195.xml&part=2.*

12. Steven Friedman, "Joel Greenblatt and Robert Goldstein of Gotham Asset Management, LLC," *Santangel's Review,* Profiles of Undiscovered Investors, March 2011.

13. Ibid.

14. Freeman.

15. William Beaver, Maureen McNichols, and Richard Price, "Delisting Returns and Their Effect on Accounting-Based Market Anomalies." *Journal of Accounting and Economics* 43 (2007): 341–368.

16. Marcus Bogue and Morris Bailey, "The Advantages of Using as First Reported Data with Current Compustat Data for Historical Research." Charter Oak Investment Systems, Inc., 2001.

17. Oppenheimer, H. R. "Ben Graham's Net Current Asset Values: A Performance Update." *Financial Analysts Journal* 42 (1986): 40–47; and J. Greenblatt, R. Pzena, and B. Newberg, "How the Small Investor Can Beat the Market." *Journal of Portfolio Management* (Summer 1981): 48–52.

18. Xiao Ying and Glen Arnold, "Testing Benjamin Graham's Net Current Asset Value Strategy in London." *Journal of Investing* 17 (2008): 11–19.

19. Survivor bias–free fundamental data begins on December 31, 1962, which means we can initiate our portfolios on July 1, 1963; however, for ease of exposition and to eliminate a "stub" year, we present all results from January 1, 1964, through December 31, 2011. Conclusions and results are not affected by eliminating returns from July 1, 1963, through December 31, 1963.

20. Eugene Fama and Kenneth French, "The Cross-Section of Expected Stock Returns." *Journal of Finance* 47 (1992): 427–465.

21. Philippe Jorion and William Goetzmann, "Global Stock Markets in the Twentieth Century." *Journal of Finance* 54 (1999): 953–980.

22. Roy Batchelor, "Bias in Macroeconomic Forecasts." *International Journal of Forecasting* 23(2) (April–June 2007): 189–203.
23. NYSE breakpoints can be obtained from Ken French's website: *http://mba.tuck. dartmouth.edu/pages/faculty/ken.french/data_library.html*.
24. Beaver, McNichols, and Price.

CHAPTER 11

Problems with the Magic Formula

"The additional rise of this stock above the true capital will be only imaginary; one added to one, by any rules of vulgar arithmetic, will never make three and a half; consequently, all the fictitious value must be a loss to some persons or other, first or last. The only way to prevent it to oneself must be to sell out betimes, and so let the Devil take the hindmost."

—Anonymous[1]

We know that the Magic Formula comprises two equally weighted components: return on capital (ROC), a measure of quality; and the earnings before interest and taxes (EBIT) version of the enterprise multiple, a price ratio. After conducting an exhaustive back-test of different price ratios in Chapters 7 and 8, we saw that the EBIT enterprise multiple performed the best. Against formidable opposition in the form of other widely used individual price ratios, long-term average "normalized" price ratios promoted by Graham, and composite price ratios suggested by O'Shaughnessy, the humble EBIT enterprise multiple stood out. Greenblatt's selection of it as the price metric for the Magic Formula seems serendipitous. But what of the quality metric, ROC?

The stand-alone performance of the EBIT enterprise multiple is so strong that we wondered how much it actually contributed to the overall performance of the Magic Formula. We decided to test it by separating the Magic Formula into its constituent parts, and comparing the performance of the constituents to the performance of the complete Magic Formula. In Table 11.1, we set out the results of our examination.

TABLE 11.1 Comparing the Performance of the Magic Formula and Its Constituent Parts, the EBIT Enterprise Multiple and ROC (1974 to 2011)

	Magic Formula	EBIT Enterprise Multiple	MF ROC	S&P 500 TR
CAGR	13.94%	15.95%	10.37%	10.46%
Standard Deviation	16.93%	17.28%	17.04%	15.84%
Downside Deviation	12.02%	11.88%	11.35%	11.16%
Sharpe Ratio	0.55	0.64	0.35	0.37
Sortino Ratio (MAR = 5%)	0.80	0.96	0.56	0.56
Worst Drawdown	−36.85%	−37.25%	−47.15%	−50.21%
Worst Month Return	−23.90%	−18.43%	−22.76%	−21.58%
Best Month Return	14.91%	17.21%	19.27%	16.81%
Profitable Months	63.60%	63.38%	59.87%	60.53%
Rolling 5-Year Win %	—	15.11%	84.38%	80.10%
Rolling 10-Year Win %	—	11.28%	89.91%	96.44%
Cumulative Draw Downs	−9596.95%	−9299.02%	−10591.86%	−9562.93%
Correlation	—	0.927	0.806	0.872

Table 11.1 shows that the Magic Formula underperformed its price metric, the EBIT enterprise multiple, over the full period. The Magic Formula earns a lower compound annual growth rate (CAGR), higher downside volatility, and lower risk-adjusted performance based on the Sharpe and Sortino ratios. How much does the quality measure contribute to the Magic Formula? Shockingly, ROC actually detracts from the Magic Formula's performance. In other words, the strong showing from the price metric is dragged down by the weakness of the quality metric. The quality metric underperforms even the S&P 500 TR with lower returns and higher volatility. What if we were to substitute a better quality metric?

We know from our brief analysis in Chapter 2 that the Magic Formula's quality metric underperforms other quality metrics. Let's return to the individual quality measures from Chapter 2, set out in Table 11.2.

TABLE 11.2 Performance Statistics for Common Quality Measures (1974 to 2011)

	E/TA	FCF/TA	GPA	MF ROC	S&P 500 TR
CAGR	9.84%	10.80%	12.56%	10.37%	10.46%
Standard Deviation	17.82%	17.78%	16.93%	17.04%	15.84%
Downside Deviation	11.36%	12.00%	11.45%	11.35%	11.16%
Sharpe Ratio	0.32	0.37	0.47	0.35	0.37
Sortino Ratio (MAR = 5%)	0.53	0.57	0.73	0.56	0.56
Worst Drawdown	−51.11%	−56.02%	−43.96%	−47.15%	−50.21%
Worst Month Return	−20.64%	−21.07%	−20.68%	−22.76%	−21.58%
Best Month Return	18.99%	19.82%	21.58%	19.27%	16.81%
Profitable Months	59.43%	60.53%	58.99%	59.87%	60.53%
Rolling 5-Year Win %	—	45.84%	34.01%	50.63%	46.35%
Rolling 10-Year Win %	—	50.45%	4.15%	51.34%	50.15%
Cumulative Drawdowns	−11328.87%	−10990.16%	−9373.19%	−10591.86%	−9562.93%
Correlation	—	0.956	0.884	0.953	0.896

Other than gross profits on total assets (GPA), Table 11.2 shows that no quality measure performs well relative to the Standard and Poor's 500 Total Return Index (S&P 500 TR). Recall from Chapter 2 that the Quality and Price strategy outperformed the Magic Formula. Quality and Price worked, despite using an inferior price metric: the book value-to-market capitalization ratio. Is it the influence of the quality metric, GPA, which outperforms the Magic Formula's quality metric, MF ROC, that leads Quality and Price to outperform the Magic Formula? What if we take the best from each strategy, the Magic Formula's price ratio, the EBIT enterprise multiple, and Quality and Price's quality metric, GPA, and combine it into a new strategy that we'll call *Magic Quality*? Table 11.3 sets out our examination of Magic Quality and its constituent parts, the EBIT enterprise multiple, and GPA.

Oddly, while Magic Quality significantly outperformed the Magic Formula, with a better CAGR and improved Sharpe and Sortino ratios, it continued to underperform the simple EBIT enterprise multiple. Even worse, it does so at higher standard and downside deviations, giving it lower Sharpe and Sortino ratios than the EBIT enterprise multiple. Maybe it's time to pull out the howitzer, our full quantitative value quality measure.

Let's substitute for GPA our full suite of quality measures, and combine it with the EBIT enterprise multiple, into a strategy we'll call *Magic Quality on Steroids*. Table 11.4 sets out our examination of Magic Quality on Steroids and its constituent parts, the EBIT enterprise multiple, and our full quality suite.

TABLE 11.3 Comparing the Performance of Magic Quality and Its Constituent Parts, the EBIT Enterprise Multiple and GPA (1974 to 2011)

	Magic Quality	EBIT Enterprise Multiple	GPA	S&P 500 TR
CAGR	15.80%	15.95%	12.56%	10.46%
Standard Deviation	17.19%	17.28%	16.93%	15.84%
Downside Deviation	12.31%	11.88%	11.45%	11.16%
Sharpe Ratio	0.64	0.64	0.47	0.37
Sortino Ratio (MAR = 5%)	0.91	0.96	0.73	0.56
Worst Drawdown	−39.59%	−37.25%	−43.96%	−50.21%
Worst Month Return	−21.98%	−18.43%	−20.68%	−21.58%
Best Month Return	16.19%	17.21%	21.58%	16.81%
Profitable Months	62.06%	63.38%	58.99%	60.53%
Rolling 5-Year Win %	—	38.54%	68.01%	92.44%
Rolling 10-Year Win %	—	56.08%	62.31%	100.00%
Cumulative Drawdowns	−8204.94%	−9299.02%	−9373.19%	−9562.93%
Correlation	—	0.823	0.777	0.871

TABLE 11.4 Comparing the Performance of the Magic Quality on Steroids and Its Constituent Parts, the EBIT Enterprise Multiple and Our Full Quality Suite (1974 to 2011)

	Magic Quality On Steroids	EBIT Enterprise Multiple	Full Quality	S&P 500 TR
CAGR	15.47%	15.95%	11.46%	10.46%
Standard Deviation	16.39%	17.28%	16.66%	15.84%
Downside Deviation	11.55%	11.88%	11.04%	11.16%
Sharpe Ratio	0.64	0.64	0.42	0.37
Sortino Ratio (MAR = 5%)	0.94	0.96	0.66	0.56
Worst Drawdown	−42.46%	−37.25%	−45.45%	−50.21%
Worst Month Return	−18.98%	−18.43%	−22.64%	−21.58%
Best Month Return	15.84%	17.21%	19.43%	16.81%
Profitable Months	64.69%	63.38%	58.77%	60.53%
Rolling 5-Year Win %	—	38.04%	68.77%	88.66%
Rolling 10-Year Win %	—	43.62%	83.09%	91.69%
Cumulative Drawdowns	−8754.55%	−9299.02%	−8962.87%	−9562.93%
Correlation	—	0.914	0.748	0.850

Amazingly, the performance of Magic Quality on Steroids is essentially equivalent to the simpler Magic Quality on a risk-reward basis, and continues to underperform the simple EBIT enterprise multiple. No matter what we pit against the EBIT enterprise multiple, it wins by a knockout. What's going on here? Why does the simple EBIT enterprise multiple seem to consistently best all the competition?

There are two factors at play here. First, the EBIT multiple performed exceptionally well. The metric contains a lot of information about what we're paying—total enterprise value—and what we're getting—earnings before interest and taxes. It's difficult to improve upon it. We also know from Chapter 5 that single-year quality measures like MF ROC and profit margins are highly mean reverting. We can make a good argument that the quality measures don't warrant as much weight as the price ratio because they are more ephemeral. Why pay up for something that's just about to evaporate back to the mean? Yet this is exactly what the Magic Formula does, and it systematically leads to lower returns, as we'll demonstrate next.

GLAMOUR IS ALWAYS A BAD BET

The Magic Formula is a systematic value strategy designed to pay more for higher quality. The empirical question is, "Does the Magic Formula pay too much for quality?" As we have seen, stand-alone price ratios as a group, and EBIT/TEV in particular, are more profitable than MF ROC or any of the other quality measures. By using a measure to influence stock selection that is not as predictive of future returns as the EBIT enterprise multiple, the quality component of the Magic Formula injects lower returns and higher volatility into a favorable investment strategy. Our hypothesis is that the Magic Formula systematically overpays for high-quality firms.

To test that supposition, we examined the prices paid by the Magic Formula in our back-test. Figure 11.1 sets out a histogram showing those EBIT multiples paid by the Magic Formula.

Figure 11.1 demonstrates that the Magic Formula has tended to pay a higher EBIT enterprise multiple than the value decile of the EBIT enterprise multiple. The premium paid by the Magic Formula can be seen easily at the

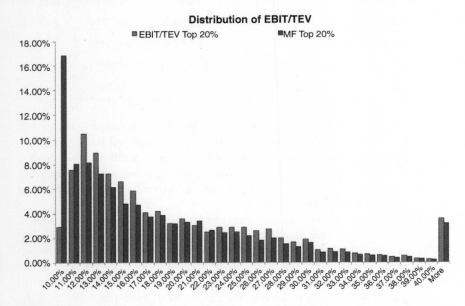

FIGURE 11.1 Histogram Showing EBIT Enterprise Multiples Paid by Magic Formula and Value Decile of EBIT Enterprise Multiple (1974 to 2011)

left-hand side of the histogram, where there is a spike for the Magic Formula (prices get more attractive as we move from left to right). The spike occurs at an EBIT/TEV yield of 10 percent or lower, which we consider the event horizon for "glamour."

We know that glamour stocks don't provide good returns in the aggregate. The logic behind the Magic Formula is that it pays up for quality. Do the highest-quality glamour stocks break the rule that buying expensive stocks is a bad bet? Table 11.5 shows the glamour decile of the EBIT enterprise multiple divided into high-quality and low-quality stocks using our full suite of quality measures.

Quality works. Table 11.5 shows that in the EBIT glamour decile, high-quality stocks have performed better than low-quality stocks, however the returns to the glamour decile—high quality, low quality, or the whole decile—are substantially lower than the returns to the S&P 500 TR. It seems that glamour is such a bad bet that, while high-quality glamour outperforms low-quality glamour, glamour inexorably leads to poor performance. The Magic Formula is designed to pay up for quality, but paying glamour prices doesn't work on average. The Magic Formula systematically overpays for quality. It is structurally flawed, leading us to fish in the wrong pond. So how do we fish in the right pond?

TABLE 11.5 Comparing the Performance of the EBIT Enterprise Multiple Glamour Decile High Quality and Low Quality Using Our Full Quality Suite (1974 to 2011)

	EBIT Glamour Decile	Low Quality	High Quality	S&P 500 TR
CAGR	7.16%	7.06%	7.63%	10.46%
Standard Deviation	24.18%	23.68%	24.99%	15.84%
Downside Deviation	17.52%	16.45%	17.84%	11.16%
Sharpe Ratio	0.19	0.18	0.21	0.37
Sortino Ratio (MAR = 5%)	0.28	0.28	0.31	0.56
Worst Drawdown	−83.73%	−72.64%	−85.59%	−50.21%
Worst Month Return	−33.51%	−29.23%	−35.71%	−21.58%
Best Month Return	23.12%	32.34%	22.68%	16.81%
Profitable Months	57.89%	56.36%	58.11%	60.53%

IMPROVING THE STRUCTURE OF A QUANTITATIVE VALUE STRATEGY

In Chapter 6, we examined Joseph Piotroski's 2002 study, "Value Investing: The Use of Historical Financial Statement Information to Separate Winners from Losers,[2] and his F_SCORE." Working on the theory established by Fama and French in 1992 that cheap stocks tend to beat the market—but only because they are more financially distressed, and therefore fundamentally riskier, than the average stock—Piotroski set out to find some way that investors could sort financially healthy stocks that are cheap from cheap stocks that are in financial distress.

One of his most interesting findings was that, despite the strong performance of low price-to-book value portfolios, a majority of the stocks (approximately 57 percent) underperformed the market over one- and two-year stretches. Piotroski concluded, therefore, that any strategy that could eliminate the left tail of the return distribution (i.e., the stocks that underperform the market), could greatly improve the portfolio's performance. Piotroski found that by identifying financially strong value stocks according to his F_SCORE, he could improve the return of a low price-to-book value portfolio by at least 7.5 percent per year, which is an astonishing outperformance.

We have adopted Piotroski's broad approach to value strategy implementation. We substitute for the price-to-book value price ratio favored by Piotroski the EBIT enterprise multiple, which, as we have seen, is the best-performing metric. Next we shift the return distribution of the EBIT enterprise value decile by separating winners and losers using our full suite of quality measures, rather than Piotroski's F_SCORE.

We start by eliminating from our investable universe stocks at risk of sustaining a permanent loss of capital, which we discussed in Part One. These firms are the frauds, the earnings manipulators, and those at a high risk of financial distress. We want to avoid these companies because they have no intrinsic value to equity holders, and provide no margin of safety at any price. Table 11.6 shows the effect of eliminating these stocks from our universe.

Table 11.6 shows that our universe of clean stocks significantly outperform the full universe. By eliminating the small number of frauds, the earnings manipulators, and stocks with a high risk of financial distress (roughly 5 percent of the universe), the remaining stocks generate superior performance.

We narrow our complete universe and pit it against the value decile of the EBIT enterprise multiple. Figure 11.2(a) shows the performance of the EBIT enterprise multiple value decile against the universe.

TABLE 11.6 Performance Statistics Comparing "Cleaned" Stocks and Universe (1974 to 2011)

	MW_INDEX "Cleaned"	MW_INDEX	S&P 500 TR
CAGR	11.04%	10.80%	10.46%
Standard Deviation	15.31%	15.49%	15.84%
Downside Deviation	10.85%	11.01%	11.16%
Sharpe Ratio	0.42	0.40	0.37
Sortino Ratio (MAR = 5%)	0.62	0.59	0.56
Worst Drawdown	−43.48%	−44.38%	−50.21%
Worst Month Return	−21.37%	−21.55%	−21.58%
Best Month Return	17.73%	17.66%	16.81%
Profitable Months	61.62%	61.84%	60.53%
Rolling 5-Year Wins	—	88.92%	63.48%
Rolling 10-Year Wins	—	99.70%	60.83%
Cumulative Drawdown	−9059.38%	−9224.27%	−9562.93%
Correlation	—	0.999	0.990

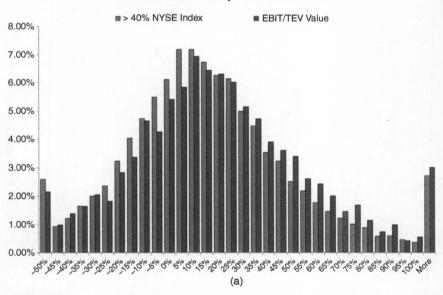

Distribution of 1-Year Buy-and-Hold Returns

FIGURE 11.2(a) Histogram Showing EBIT Enterprise Multiple Value Decile Compared to the Universe (1974 to 2011)

Figure 11.2(a) shows that value has consistently outperformed the universe. How does value do against glamour in our universe? Figure 11.2(b) shows a histogram of the EBIT enterprise multiple value decile compared to the glamour decile of the universe.

Figure 11.2(b) shows that value dominates glamour. Glamour is overrepresented on the left of the distribution, where returns are nil or lower, and underrepresented on the right of the distribution, where returns positive. The wings of the distribution are also notable. Glamour stocks were cut in half more than three times as often as value stocks; glamour stocks dropped 50 percent or more 7 percent of the time, while value stocks dropped 50 percent or more in approximately 2 percent of instances. Interestingly, glamour stocks have also tended to double more often than value, gaining 100 percent in 5.5 percent of the time against 3 percent for value. This is one of the reasons for investors' persistent attraction to glamour stocks despite glamour's generally poorer performance: glamour stocks have behaved like lottery tickets, providing big payoffs in about 1 in 20 occasions. Unfortunately, the glamour lottery tickets don't pay out often enough to overcome glamour's generally poor showing.

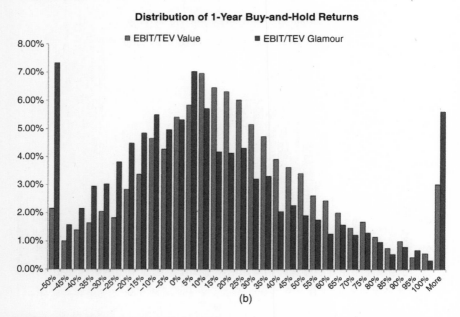

FIGURE 11.2(b)   Histogram Showing EBIT Enterprise Multiple Value Decile Compared to Glamour Decile (1974 to 2011)

We know that the EBIT enterprise multiple performs well and we know that a "cleansing" method can shift returns in our favor, but can we further separate the winners from the losers? We can. Within that cheapest tranche of "cleaned" stocks, we look for the highest-quality and lowest-quality stocks. Here, we seek the franchises with robust financial strength. Franchises have economic moats evidenced by excellent long-term returns on capital through the business cycle, and pricing power demonstrated by rapidly growing or high, stable margins. Financial strength is a question of operations and balance sheet liquidity. We examine financial strength along three broad axes using our FS_SCORE: profitability, stability, and operational improvement. Figure 11.3 shows the cumulative performance of the value decile of stocks ranked on the EBIT enterprise multiple separated into two groups: high quality and low quality, both of which are cleansed of frauds, manipulators, and financially distressed stocks.

Figure 11.3 demonstrates that separating the value decile of EBIT enterprise multiple stocks into high quality and low quality concentrates the better-performing stocks in the high-quality portfolio, which outperforms the whole EBIT enterprise multiple decile and the low-quality portfolio.

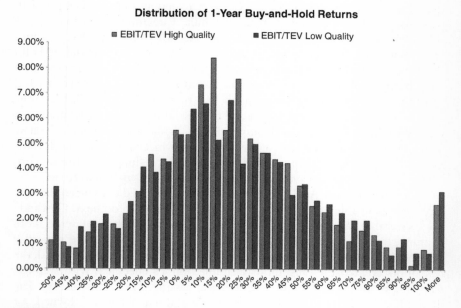

FIGURE 11.3 Invested Growth of EBIT Enterprise Value Separated into High-Quality and Low-Quality Portfolios (1974 to 2011)

OUR FINAL QUANTITATIVE VALUE CHECKLIST

In Chapter 2, we sought to make the case for employing an investment checklist using Atul Gawande's intensive care analogy. Recall that Peter Pronovost, the intensivist at Johns Hopkins Hospital who pushed so hard for the widespread adoption of checklists, drew his inspiration from the U.S. Army Air Corps's experience with the WWII-era test flight of the Boeing Corporation's B-17 model.

Prior to the test flight, Boeing's model had been the favored plane, beating out competing airplane designers vying to build the next-generation long-range bomber. According to Gawande's article, the model B-17 was far superior to the competition, carrying five times as many bombs as the Army Air Corps had requested, faster, and almost twice as far as previous bombers. It was apparently an impressive-looking machine, with a 103-foot wingspan and four engines, rather than the usual two. So impressive, in fact, that a Seattle newspaperman had coined it the "Flying Fortress" and the name stuck.

After the Flying Fortress crashed during its test flight on October 30, 1935, at Wright Air Field in Dayton, Ohio, investigators found that it was not a mechanical fault that brought the plane down, but "pilot error." This was an unexpected finding because the pilot, Major Ployer Hill, was the Army Air Corps's chief of flight testing and a very experienced pilot. The problem was clearly not in Ployer but in the machine. Gawande writes that it was substantially more complex than previous aircraft Major Hill had encountered. With four engines, it had twice as many instruments demanding Hill's attention. It also had a retractable landing gear, new wing flaps, electric trim tabs that needed adjustment to maintain control at different airspeeds, and constant-speed propellers whose pitch had to be regulated with hydraulic controls, among other contraptions, all of which Hill had to manipulate correctly from memory in order to stay airborne. While monitoring all the new instruments, he forgot to release the new locking mechanism on the elevator and rudder controls, which resulted in the plane's crashing just after takeoff. The Flying Fortress was simply "too much airplane for one man to fly."

A group of Army Air Corp test pilots who remained convinced that the aircraft was flyable got together and considered what to do next. Gawande points out that they could have required B-17 model pilots to undergo more training, but it was hard to imagine having more experience and expertise than Major Hill, the U.S. Army Air Corps' chief of flight testing. Instead, the test pilots created the "ingeniously simple" pilot's checklist, with step-by-step checks for takeoff, flight, landing, and taxiing. The rest is history. The Flying Fortress helped the Allies rule the air and win the war. It turned out the Flying Fortress was not "too much airplane for one man to fly," it was simply too much airplane for one man to fly *from memory*.

The problem in investing is similar in kind to the problem faced by modern pilots. A comprehensive fundamental analysis involves many critical steps, and it's easy to miss a step if we do it from memory. We don't want to build a Flying Fortress if we can't fly it. Next, we combine all of our analyses into a "human readable" checklist.

THE FINAL QUANTITATIVE VALUE CHECKLIST

Step 1: Avoid Stocks at Risk of Sustaining a Permanent Loss of Capital

1. Identify Potential Frauds and Manipulators

1.1 Accrual Screens

STA = Scaled Total Accruals = (CA (t) – CL (t) – DEP (t)) / Total Assets (t)

- CA = change in current assets – change in cash and equivalents
- CL = change in current liabilities – change in LT debt included in current liabilities – change in income taxes payable
- DEP = depreciation and amortization expense
- P_STA = percentile (STA) among all firms in the universe
- SNOA = (operating assets (t) – operating liabilities (t)) / total assets (t)
- P_SNOA = percentile (SNOA) among all firms in the universe
- **COMBOACCRUAL = average (P_STA, P_SNOA)**

1.2 Fraud and Manipulation Screen

Calculate variables:

- DSRI = days' sales in receivables index
- GMI = gross margin index
- AQI = asset quality index
- SGI = sales growth index
- DEPI = depreciation index
- SGAI = sales, general and administrative expenses index
- LVGI = leverage index
- TATA = total accruals to total assets

(continued)

Calculate probit probability of manipulation (PROBM) values:

- PROBM = $-4.84 + 0.92 \times$ DSRI $+ 0.528 \times$ GMI $+ 0.404 \times$ AQI $+ 0.892 \times$ SGI $+ 0.115 \times$ DEPI $- 0.172 \times$ SGAI $+ 4.679 \times$ TATA $- 0.327 \times$ LVGI

Calculate probability of manipulation from PROBM:

- **PMAN = CDF(PROBM)**, where CDF is the cumulative density function for a normal (0,1) variable.[3]

2. Identify Stocks at High Risk of Financial Distress

2.1 Probability of Financial Distress (PFD)

Calculate PFA variables:

- NIMTAAVG = weighted average (quarter's net income/MTA)
- MTA = market value of total assets = book value of liabilities + market cap
- TLMTA = total liabilities / MTA
- CASHMTA = cash & equivalents / MTA
- EXRETAVG = weighted average(log(1 + stock's return) − log(1 + S&P 500 TR return)
- SIGMA = annualized stock's standard deviation over the previous 3 months (daily)
- RSIZE = log (stock market cap / S&P 500 TR total market value)
- MB = MTA / adjusted book value
- Adjusted book value = book value +.1 × (market cap-book value)
- PRICE = log (recent stock price), capped at $15, so a stock with a stock price of $20, would be given a value of log(15) instead of log(20).

Calculate logit for the probability of financial distress (LPFD) values:

- LPFD = $-20.26 \times$ NIMTAAVG $+ 1.42 \times$ TLMTA $- 7.13 \times$ EXRETAVG $+ 1.41 \times$ SIGMA $- .045 \times$ RSIZE $- 2.13 \times$ CASHMTA $+ .075 \times$ MB $- .058 \times$ PRICE $- 9.16$

Calculate the probability of financial distress (PFD) value:

- PFD = $1/(1 + e^{(-LPFD)})$

3. Eliminate Stocks at Risk of Sustaining a Permanent Loss of Capital

Simultaneously conduct the following screens:

- Eliminate all firms in the top 5 percent of the sample based on COMBOACCRUAL.
- Eliminate all firms in the top 5 percent of the sample based on PMAN.
- Eliminate all firms in the top 5 percent of the sample based on PFD.

Step 2: Find Cheapest Stocks

To calculate PRICE we simply calculate EBIT enterprise value for each stock and then rank all stocks on PRICE.

- PRICE = EBIT/TEV

Step 3: Find Highest-Quality Stocks

1. Franchise Power

8yr_ROA = Eight-Year Return on Assets (Geometric Average).

- Return on assets = net income before extraordinary items (t) / total assets (t).
- P_8yr_ROA = percentile (8yr_ROA) among all stocks in the universe.

8yr_ROC = Eight-Year Return on Capital (Geometric Average).

- Return on capital = EBIT (t) / capital (t)
- P_8yr_ROC = percentile (8yr_ROA) among all stocks in the universe.

FCFA = Long-Term Free Cash Flow on Assets

- Sum (eight-year FCF) / total assets (*t*)
- P_CFOA = percentile (FCFA) among all stocks in the universe

(continued)

MG = Margin Growth

- Eight-year gross margin growth (geometric average)
- P_MG = percentile (MG) among all stocks in the universe

MS = Margin Stability

- Eight-year average gross margin % / eight-year gross margin % standard deviation
- P_MS = percentile (MS) among all firms in the universe

MM = Margin Max

- Max (P_MG, P_MS)

P_FP = Franchise Power

- Percentile (average (P_8yr_ROA, P_8yr_ROC, P_CFOA, MM) among all firms in the universe

2. Financial Strength (FS)

2.1 Current Profitability

- ROA = return on assets
  - Net income before extraordinary items (t) / total assets (t)
  - FS_ROA = 1 if ROA > 0, 0 otherwise
- FCFTA = free cash flow (t) / total assets (t)
  - FS_FCFTA = 1 if FCFTA > 0, 0 otherwise
- ACCRUAL = FCFTA – ROA
  - FS_ACCRUAL = 1 if ACCRUAL > 0, 0 otherwise

2.2 Stability

- LEVER = long-term debt $(t-1)$ / total assets $(t-1)$ – long-term debt (t) / total assets (t)
  - FS_LEVER = 1 if LEVER > 0, 0 otherwise
- LIQUID = current ratio (t) – current ratio $(t-1)$

- FS_LIQUID = 1 if LIQUID > 0, 0 otherwise
- NEQISS = net equity issuance from $t - 1$ to t
  - FS_NEQISS = 1 if NEQISS > 0, 0 otherwise

2.3 Recent Operational Improvements

- ΔROA = year-over-year change in ROA
  - FS_ΔROA = 1 if ΔROA > 0, 0 otherwise
- ΔFCFTA = year-over-year change in FCFTA
  - FS_ΔFCFTA = 1 if ΔFCFTA > 0, 0 otherwise
- ΔMARGIN = year-over-year change in gross margin
  - FS_ΔMARGIN= 1 if ΔMARGIN > 0, 0 otherwise
- ΔTURN = year-over-year change in asset turnover
  - FS_ΔTURN = 1 if ΔTURN > 0, 0 otherwise

2.4 P_FS = Financial Strength

- P_FS = Sum(FS_ROA, FS_FCFTA, FS_ACCRUAL, FS_LEVER, FS_LIQUID, FS_NEQISS, FS_ΔROA, FS_ΔFCFTA, FS_ΔMARGIN, FS_ΔTURN))/10

3. Identify Quality

To calculate quality we simply take an average of the franchise power score and the financial strength score.[4] We then rank all firms on QUALITY.

- QUALITY = .5 × P_FP + .5 × P_FS

There is a structural issue with the Magic Formula: it tends to overpay for quality, and the "quality" seems to be of dubious value, adding little to the performance of its price ratio. Glamour stocks, even high-quality glamour stocks, tend to provide suboptimal performance. Commingling glamour stocks with value stocks will reduce the performance of the value stocks but tend to disguise the underperformance of the glamour stocks. The problem, as Charlie Munger has said, is that, "When you mix raisins and turds, you still have turds." The attractiveness of a stock as an investment is always a function of its price to its value. This chapter simply confirms our view that *value* must always be the watchword.

The EBIT enterprise multiple has performed strongly throughout out our tests. It is difficult to improve upon the performance of its value decile. There are some things that we can do, however, to goose the performance of the universe. First, we found that removing from the universe even only a very small proportion of stocks that might be frauds, financial statement manipulators, or at high risk of financial distress improves the performance of the universe. We have also found separating the stocks remaining in the value decile into high and low quality, and then buying the high-quality stocks, leads to better performance. It makes intuitive sense that high-quality value stocks would outperform the average value stock and low-quality value stocks. Our examination of the cumulative returns bore this out in stunning fashion.

Our probing of the Magic Formula set the stage for the final step in the creation of our own quantitative value strategy. In "human readable" format, the strategy becomes our checklist, which is a useful tool for navigating complex problems. Next, we run our quantitative value model through our full battery of tests.

NOTES

1. Edward Chancellor, *Devil Take the Hindmost: A History of Financial Speculation* (New York: Penguin Group, 2000).
2. Joseph D. Piotroski, "Value Investing: The Use of Historical Financial Statement Information to Separate Winners from Losers." As published in *Journal of Accounting Research* 38(Supplement) (2000). Available at *http://ssrn.com/abstract=249455*.
3. The excel function NORMDIST can accomplish this transformation. For example, if PROBM = −1.26, then set the PMAN cell = NORMDIST(−1.26,0,1,TRUE), for a value of 10.38 percent, or a probability of manipulation of 10.38 percent.
4. Our initial tests involved a simple average of franchise power and financial strength. We studied various weighting schemes, and the final results presented are all quantitatively similar.

CHAPTER 12

Quantitative Value Beats the Market

"It is the long-term investor, he who most promotes the public interest, who will in practice come in for the most criticism, wherever investment funds are managed by committees or boards or banks. For it is in the essence of his behaviour that he should be eccentric, unconventional and rash in the eyes of average opinion. If he is successful, that will only confirm the general belief in his rashness; and if in the short run he is unsuccessful, which is very likely, he will not receive much mercy. Worldly wisdom teaches that it is better for reputation to fail conventionally than to succeed unconventionally."

John Maynard Keynes, *The General Theory of Employment, Interest and Money*[1]

In this chapter, we present the results of the examination into the Quantitative Value investment model described in the book. We've studied how to avoid stocks at risk of sustaining a permanent loss of capital, how to find the best value, and how to identify high-quality stocks. We've also analyzed the best approach to combine the components into a cohesive quantitative strategy. Here, we've conducted a range of analyses on the strategy to calculate its performance, and its risk/reward profile. We also conduct an exhaustive investigation into the robustness of the strategy by looking at its rolling 5- and 10-year returns, drawdowns, and alpha measurements, which we calculate across a variety of asset pricing models for robustness.

A criticism often leveled at quantitative strategies is that they are a "black box," which means that the manner in which the stocks are selected is not comprehensible. We want to make sure the Quantitative Value strategy is transparent and tractable by discussing its rules and the rationale for all of them throughout this book. We also offer a peek inside the black box, showing the names and basic details for the model's stock selections starting in 1974.

TABLE 12.1.   Analysis Legend

Word/Symbol	Description
Quantitative Value or QV	The quantitative value strategy described in the book.
MF	The Magic Formula strategy.
S&P 500 TR	Standard & Poor's 500 Total Return Index, the free-float, market capitalization–weighted index including the effects of dividend reinvestment.
MW Index	A total-return, market capitalization–weighted index that we construct from the universe of stocks included in the analysis. The MW Index's returns represent a passive investment in the universe of all stocks we analyze.
CAGR	Compound annual growth rate.
Standard Deviation	Sample standard deviation (annualized by square root of 12).
Downside Deviation	Sample standard deviation of all negative observations (annualized by square root of 12).
Sharpe Ratio	Monthly return minus risk-free rate divided by standard deviation (annualized by square root of 12).
Sortino Ratio (MAR = 5%)	Monthly return minus minimum acceptable return (MAR/12) divided by downside deviation (annualized by square root of 12).
Worst Drawdown	Worst peak-to-trough performance.
Worst Month Return	Worst monthly performance.
Best Month Return	Best monthly performance.
Profitable Months	Proportion of monthly performances that have a positive return.
Rolling 5-Year Wins	Proportion of rolling 5-year periods that a designated strategy beats the identified benchmarks.
Rolling 5-Year Wins	Proportion of rolling 10-year periods that a designated strategy beats identified benchmarks.
Cumulative Drawdown	Sum of the rolling 5-year period worst drawdowns for the designated strategy.
Correlation	Correlation coefficient for a designated strategy and the identified benchmarks, which demonstrates the extent to which a designated strategy and the identified benchmarks move together.

Finally, we investigate the performance of the Quantitative Value model portfolio, adding transaction fees and management fees, and comparing the performance to the long-term performance of three giants of the value investment world: the Sequoia Fund, the Legg Mason Value Trust, and the Third Avenue Value Fund.

We set out in Table 12.1 a legend of the key terms and acronyms we use throughout this chapter.

RISK AND RETURN

Table 12.2 sets out the standard statistical analyses of the Quantitative Value strategy's performance and risk profile, comparing it to the Magic Formula, the Standard & Poor's (S&P) 500 and the MW Index, the market capitalization–weighted index of the universe from which we draw the stocks in the model portfolios.

TABLE 12.2 Performance Statistics for Quantitative Value (1974 to 2011)

	Quantitative Value	MF	S&P 500 TR	MW Index
CAGR	17.68%	13.94%	10.46%	10.80%
Standard Deviation	16.81%	16.93%	15.84%	15.49%
Downside Deviation	10.83%	12.02%	11.16%	11.01%
Sharpe Ratio	0.74	0.55	0.37	0.40
Sortino Ratio (MAR = 5%)	1.18	0.80	0.56	0.59
Worst Drawdown	−32.06%	−36.85%	−50.21%	−44.38%
Worst Month Return	−19.00%	−23.90%	−21.58%	−21.55%
Best Month Return	16.55%	14.91%	16.81%	17.66%
Profitable Months	63.82%	63.60%	60.53%	61.84%
Rolling 5-Year Wins	—	91.44%	94.46%	96.22%
Rolling 10-Year Wins	—	98.81%	99.11%	99.70%
Cumulative Drawdown	−8683.58%	−9596.95%	−9562.93%	−9224.27%
Correlation	—	0.891	0.769	0.778

Table 12.2 shows that the Quantitative Value strategy generated a compound annual growth rate (CAGR) of 17.68 percent over the period 1974 to 2011, significantly outperforming the Magic Formula's 13.94 percent. The strategy also outperformed the S&P 500 TR at 10.46 percent, and the MW Index at 10.80 percent.

Importantly, the Quantitative Value portfolio achieved this return with a slightly lower volatility than the Magic Formula's portfolio. The model had a standard deviation of 16.81 percent against the Magic Formula's 16.93 percent. The combination of elevated return and slightly lower volatility gave the strategy an outstanding Sharpe ratio of 0.74, considerably better than the Magic Formula's 0.55, the S&P 500 TR at 0.37 and the

MW Index at 0.40. The strategy also had a lower downside volatility, with downside deviation at 10.83 percent to the Magic Formula's 12.02 percent. The combination of better return and lower downside volatility led to an extraordinary Sortino ratio of 1.18 for the Quantitative Value strategy, against 0.80 for the Magic Formula, 0.56 for the S&P 500 TR and 0.59 for the MW Index.

If we look at the drawdowns that have accompanied the returns, the Quantitative Value strategy also performed best. The worst drawdown suffered the Quantitative Value portfolio was −32.06 percent, considerably lower than the Magic Formula at −36.85 percent, the S&P 500 TR at −50.21 percent, and the MW Index at −44.38 percent.

Table 12.3 shows that the model Quantitative Value portfolio preserves capital better than the Magic Formula, the S&P 500, or the MW Index. Capital preservation is important for investors because a recovery following a drop in portfolio value requires a proportionately greater gain than the loss suffered in the drop. For example, a 33.3 percent drawdown requires a 50 percent recovery to break even; a 50 percent drawdown requires a heroic 100 percent recovery to break even.

TABLE 12.3 Recovery Required to Break Even Following Worst Drawdown (1974 to 2011)

	Quantitative Value	MF	S&P 500 TR	MW Index
Worst Monthly Drawdown	−19.00%	−20.57%	−18.43%	−21.58%
Worst 12-Month Drawdown	−25.83%	−42.19%	−31.20%	−42.54%
Worst 36-Month Drawdown	−14.22%	−23.81%	−19.63%	−40.35%
Worst Drawdown	−32.06%	−50.01%	−37.25%	−50.21%
Required Recovery (Worst Monthly)	23.45%	34.83%	16.58%	47.19%
Required Recovery (Worst Monthly)	25.90%	72.99%	31.26%	100.02%
Required Recovery (Worst Monthly)	22.59%	45.35%	24.42%	59.36%
Required Recovery (Worst Monthly)	27.52%	74.04%	67.63%	100.84%

Note in Table 12.2 that the cumulative drawdown of –9,596.95 percent over the entire period tested for the Magic Formula is considerably greater than the cumulative drawdown for the strategy at –8,683.58 percent. The model also has a lower cumulative drawdown than either the S&P 500 TR at –9,562.93 percent and the MW Index at –9,224.27 percent. The worst drawdown is a single event, while the cumulative drawdown looks at all drawdowns over the entire period tested. We need to be mindful of both. The Quantitative Value model outperforms whether we examine the single worst drawdown or the cumulative drawdowns.

The Quantitative Value strategy also outperforms on a rolling-average performance basis, beating out the Magic Formula on a rolling 5-year basis 91.44 percent of the time, and 98.81 percent of the time on a rolling 10-year basis. This means that Quantitative Value delivered a better return than the Magic Formula in 9 out of every 10 five-year periods, and approximately 49 out every 50 ten-year periods. It consistently outperformed the S&P 500 TR, generating a better return 94.46 percent of the time on a rolling 5-year basis and 99.11 percent of the time on a rolling 10-year basis. It also beat out the MW Index 96.22 percent of rolling 5-year periods and 99.70 percent of all rolling 10-year periods.

Figure 12.1 shows the cumulative performance of the Quantitative Value model portfolio compared to the performance of the Magic Formula, the S&P 500 TR, and the MW Index over the entire period.

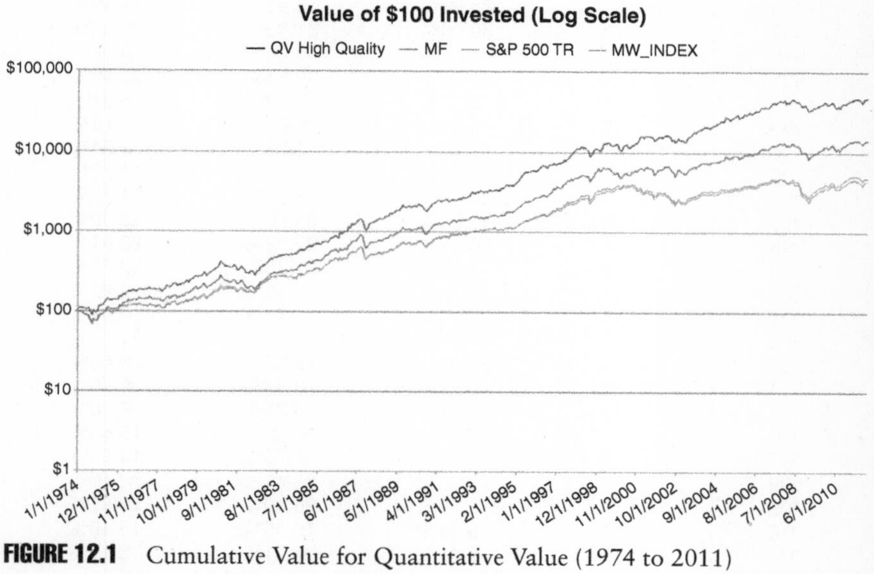

Value of $100 Invested (Log Scale)

— QV High Quality — MF — S&P 500 TR — MW_INDEX

FIGURE 12.1 Cumulative Value for Quantitative Value (1974 to 2011)

Figure 12.1 illustrates the effects of compounding a small edge over a long period of time. Quantitative Value portfolio's small advantage led to a yawning gap between it, the Magic Formula, the S&P 500 TR, and the MW Index at the end of the period.

Figure 12.2 shows the annual performance of the Quantitative Value portfolio, the Magic Formula, the S&P 500 TR, and the MW Index over the entire period. The model show consistent strong performance compared to the other benchmarks. The two periods of strongest underperformance come during the run-up to the Nasdaq crash in 1998 and 1999, and the knee-jerk recovery following the 2008 financial crisis.

	QV	MF	S&P 500 TR	MW_INDEX
1974	−1.96%	−24.35%	−26.42%	−26.80%
1975	42.21%	40.45%	36.95%	37.12%
1976	35.35%	37.03%	23.92%	23.90%
1977	0.37%	−2.30%	−7.43%	−5.54%
1978	12.14%	5.37%	6.40%	6.94%
1979	27.23%	31.68%	18.60%	20.94%
1980	48.43%	32.56%	32.60%	32.75%
1981	−14.50%	−12.97%	−4.88%	−5.35%
1982	9.05%	5.55%	22.15%	19.02%
1983	34.40%	33.24%	22.30%	22.69%
1984	18.54%	18.76%	6.69%	5.83%
1985	27.74%	33.79%	32.01%	30.63%
1986	30.80%	16.32%	18.07%	18.60%
1987	13.42%	11.42%	5.15%	6.69%
1988	41.53%	28.68%	16.95%	17.46%
1989	34.07%	30.08%	31.39%	29.35%
1990	−2.34%	−1.45%	−3.20%	−0.68%
1991	20.93%	24.76%	30.68%	30.45%
1992	24.78%	15.77%	7.73%	5.31%
1993	5.30%	3.56%	9.89%	9.19%
1994	15.98%	12.25%	1.35%	2.34%
1995	54.26%	45.86%	37.64%	33.60%
1996	19.34%	31.38%	23.23%	21.12%
1997	58.12%	40.73%	33.60%	28.90%
1998	−1.62%	20.41%	29.32%	28.81%
1999	13.78%	−3.49%	21.35%	22.79%
2000	14.90%	9.34%	−8.34%	−8.26%
2001	10.54%	−0.05%	−11.88%	−10.48%
2002	−10.44%	−4.42%	−21.78%	−21.70%
2003	39.92%	25.38%	28.72%	26.65%
2004	22.91%	10.98%	10.98%	9.46%
2005	15.94%	7.11%	5.23%	7.26%
2006	29.95%	27.52%	15.69%	15.63%
2007	24.66%	16.90%	5.76%	14.59%
2008	−14.75%	−22.32%	−36.46%	−33.15%
2009	8.51%	16.12%	26.49%	29.97%
2010	0.44%	9.65%	15.35%	16.48%
2011	13.35%	8.41%	2.11%	3.17%

FIGURE 12.2   Annual Performance for Quantitative Value (1974 to 2011)

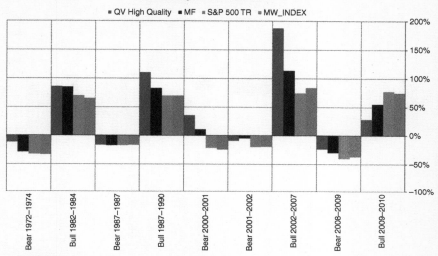

FIGURE 12.3 Market Cycle Performance for Quantitative Value (1974 to 2011)

Figure 12.3 shows the market cycle performance of the Quantitative Value strategy compared to the performance of the Magic Formula, the S&P 500 TR, and the MW Index over the entire period.

Table 12.4 shows the dates used to calculate market cycle returns.

TABLE 12.4 Market Cycle Definitions (1974 to 2011)

	Month Begin	Month End
Bull	June 1982	December 1984
Bear	July 1987	December 1987
Bull	December 1987	June 1990
Bear	March 2000	September 2001
Bear	September 2001	December 2002
Bull	September 2002	July 2007
Bear	August 2008	February 2009
Bull	March 2009	December 2010
Bull	June 1982	December 1984
Bear	July 1987	December 1987

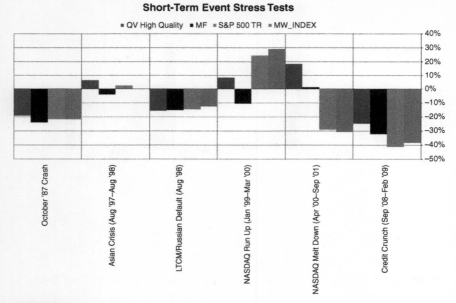

FIGURE 12.4   Short-Term Event Stress Tests for Quantitative Value (1974 to 2011)

Figure 12.3 demonstrates that the strategy protected capital in bear markets and grew capital in bull markets. While the strategy may occasionally struggle for short periods of time, it outperforms through a full market cycle.

Figure 12.4 shows the relative performances during short-term stress events of the Quantitative Value strategy, the Magic Formula, the S&P 500 TR, and the MW Index over the entire period. This analysis examines how a strategy tends to perform through extraordinary short-term market events.

There is no evidence that the model underperforms the benchmarks during stress events. The Quantitative Value strategy substantially outperformed over the Asian crisis, the Nasdaq meltdown, and the credit crunch during the 2008 financial crisis, suggesting the strategy is relatively resilient to market chaos.

Figure 12.5 shows the performance during down months of the Quantitative Value strategy, the Magic Formula, the S&P 500 TR, and the MW Index over the entire period. Like the stress event analysis, this test looks at performance when the broader market is falling. A perfect strategy would not follow the market down, but this is unrealistic in practice for a long-only strategy. We would settle here for an absence of underperformance. Figure 12.6 suggests that the strategy in fact outperforms, even generating positive returns during some negative performance months.

Performance during Down Month

■ QV High Quality ■ S&P 500 TR

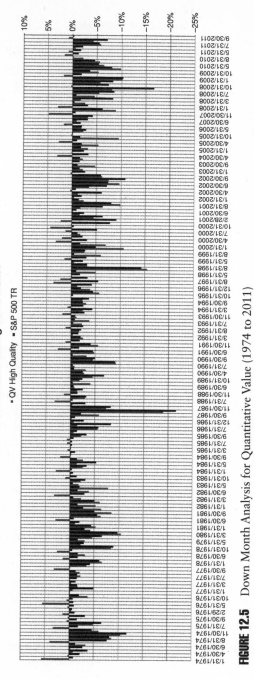

FIGURE 12.5 Down Month Analysis for Quantitative Value (1974 to 2011)

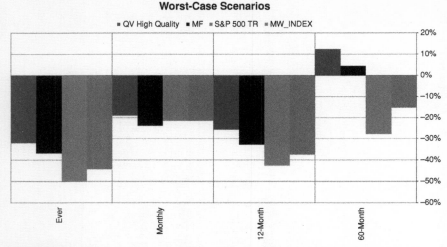

Worst-Case Scenarios

■ QV High Quality   ■ MF   ■ S&P 500 TR   ■ MW_INDEX

FIGURE 12.6   Worst-Case Scenario Analysis for Quantitative Value (1974 to 2011)

Figure 12.6 shows the worst-case scenarios of the Quantitative Value strategy, the Magic Formula, the S&P 500 TR, and the MW Index over a single month, a year, five years, and over the entire period. This figure is a graphical representation of many of the drawdown analyses in Tables 12.2 and 12.3.

The Quantitative Value strategy protects capital better than the competition. Its single worst drawdown was lower than the Magic Formula, the S&P 500 TR, and the MW Index. It also did better than all the others over rolling 1- and 12-month periods. The worst-case scenario for the strategy over a 5-year period was again slightly better than the Magic Formula, which was also positive, and considerably better than the S&P 500 TR and the MW Index, which were both down significantly. The 5-year drawdowns suggest that value strategies like ours and the Magic Formula are a better long-term bet than passive market indices.

Figure 12.7 shows the standard risk/reward trade-off chart for the Quantitative Value strategy, the Magic Formula, the S&P 500 TR, and the MW Index.

Figure 12.7 plots the CAGR against the standard deviation of each strategy, and the two measures of the market. The higher the CAGR, and the lower the standard deviation, the better. Figure 12.7 shows that the Quantitative Value strategy generates a higher return at a lower risk than the Magic Formula. It also generates a higher return than the two market indices, but does so at a higher risk. There is a trade-off between risk and

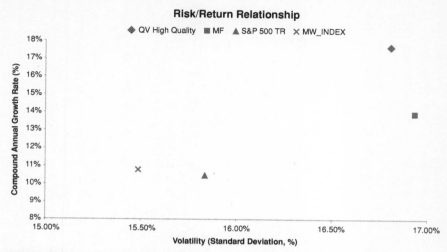

FIGURE 12.7 Risk/Reward for Quantitative Value (1974 to 2011)

return. The question we must ask after reviewing Figure 12.7 is whether the benefit of additional return is worth the cost of additional risk. We think it is justified.

Examined on a risk/reward basis, the model portfolio outperforms. It generates a CAGR over the full period of 17.68 percent with a standard deviation of 16.81 percent. The combination of elevated return and low volatility gave the strategy an outstanding Sharpe ratio of 0.74. The strategy also had low downside volatility, which, combined with its great return, led to its extraordinary Sortino ratio of 1.18. The Quantitative Value strategy also outperformed through bull and bear markets and short-term stress events. It also performed well on the drawdown analyses. In sum, the analyses demonstrate that the quantitative strategy outperformed, delivering great returns at lower risk.

ROBUSTNESS

Here we look at a variety of measures to assess the soundness of the conclusions from the study earlier in this chapter. Figures 12.8(a) and (b) show the rolling 1-, 5-, and 10-year CAGRs for the strategy. These figures show the relevant holding period return at different points in time. A robust strategy will show consistent outperformance regardless of timing; a "lucky"

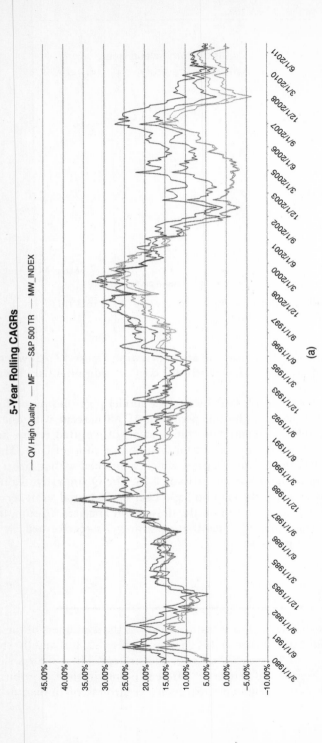

FIGURE 12.8(a) Five-Year Rolling CAGR for Quantitative Value (1974 to 2011)

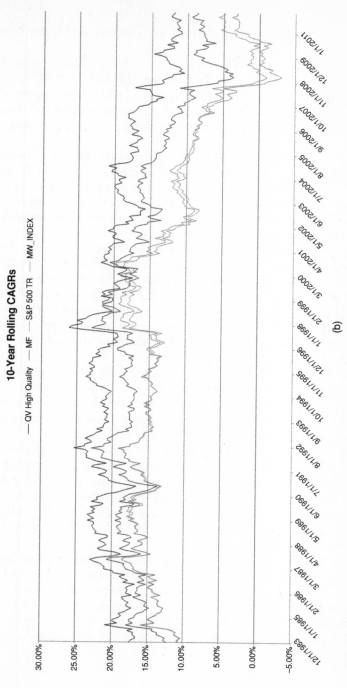

FIGURE 12.8(b) Ten-Year Rolling CAGR for Quantitative Value (1974 to 2011)

strategy may have extreme outperformance in one time period but flounder in others.

Figures 12.8(a) and (b) illustrate how consistently the strategy beats the Magic Formula, the S&P 500 TR, and the MW Index on rolling 5- and 10-year bases. Only rarely, and for brief periods, was it better to have been invested in the others. Over a short period, any strategy can outperform. In a single year, the winner is almost random chance, but over the long haul, skill wins out.

Figures 12.9(a) and (b) show the rolling 5- and 10-year maximum drawdowns for the strategy. These figures help researchers identify the frequency and intensity of a strategy's maximum drawdowns. Consider two strategies with similar worst drawdowns. If one strategy experiences big drawdowns several times through history, while the other experiences big drawdowns only once, this helps us identify the latter, better one.

The rolling drawdown analysis shows that the strategy suffers less intense drawdowns, less frequently than the competition. For example, in the early 1980s Quantitative Value took it on the chin alongside the Magic Formula, but to a lesser degree. In the early 2000s, the strategy also takes some pain, but it is less than the cardiac arrest experienced by the broader market. Finally, in the 2008 financial crisis, every strategy gets beaten up, but the strategy takes a lesser pummeling than the one suffered by the competition.

Figures 12.10(a) and (b) show the rolling 5- and 10-year alpha for the strategy. Alpha analysis is typically found in quantitative research articles published in academic journals. The procedures researchers use to estimate alpha can be complicated, but the idea is simple: How much value does a strategy create after controlling for a variety of risk factors?

To help with robustness, we estimate alpha using several different asset-pricing models. We control for general market risk using the capital asset pricing model[2]; we adjust for market, size, and value exposures with the Fama and French three-factor model[3]; we account for momentum using the four-factor model[4]; and, finally, we account for liquidity by adding the Lubos Pastor and Robert Stambaugh market-wide liquidity factor to create the comprehensive five-factor model.[5]

Figures 12.10(a) and (b) confirm that the Quantitative Value strategy consistently generates alpha on rolling 5- and 10-year bases, regardless of the model we choose to inspect. On a rolling 5-year basis there are only a few short instances where the strategy's performance does not add value after controlling for risk. The 10-year rolling chart tells the story vividly: over the long-term, Quantitative Value has consistently created value for investors.

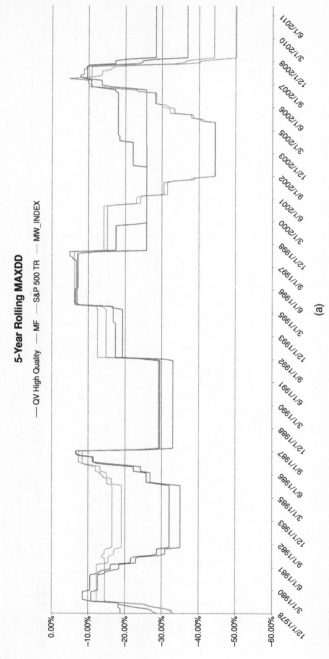

FIGURE 12.9(a) Five-Year Rolling Max Drawdown for Quantitative Value (1974 to 2011)

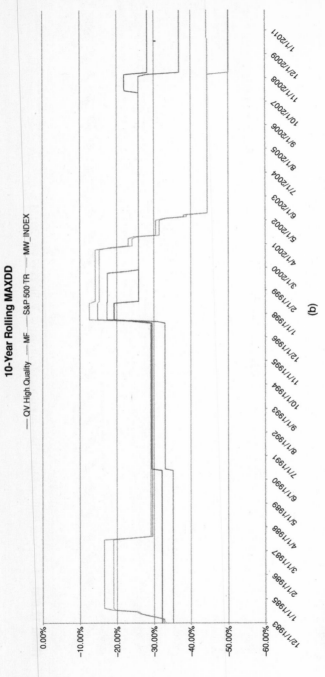

FIGURE 12.9(b) Ten-Year Rolling Max Drawdown for Quantitative Value (1974 to 2011)

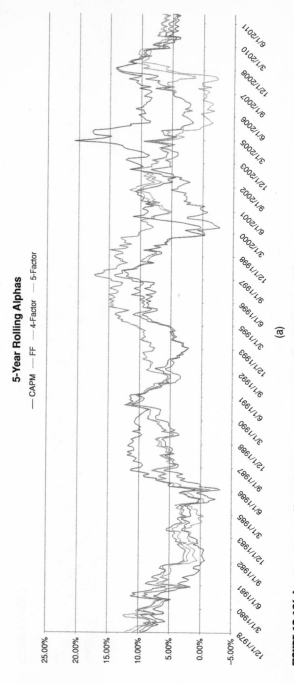

FIGURE 12.10(a) Five-Year Rolling Alpha for Quantitative Value (1974 to 2011)

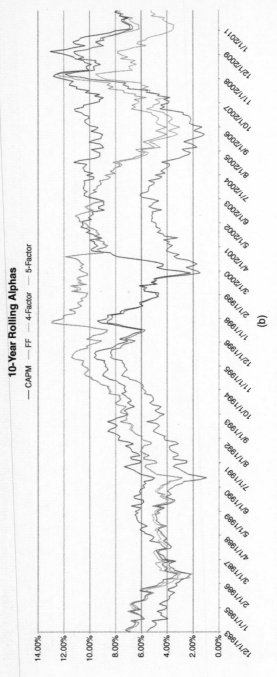

FIGURE 12.10(b) Ten-Year Rolling Alpha for Quantitative Value (1974 to 2011)

TABLE 12.5   Asset Pricing Coefficient Estimates for Quantitative Value (1974 to 2011)

	Alpha	MKT-RF	SMB	HML	MOM	LQD
CAPM	7.72%	0.78	—	—	—	—
	0.0000	0.0000	—	—	—	—
Three-Factor	6.80%	0.86	⊠0.14	0.23	—	—
	0.0001	0.0000	0.0025	0.0000	—	—
Four-Factor	7.26%	0.85	⊠0.14	0.21	⊠0.05	—
	0.0001	0.0000	0.0031	0.0000	0.1670	—
Five-Factor	6.66%	0.85	⊠0.14	0.21	⊠0.04	0.08
	0.0002	0.0000	0.0037	0.0000	0.1822	0.0417

Table 12.5 shows the full sample coefficient estimates for the four asset-pricing models. We set out *P*-values below each estimate and represent the probability of seeing the estimate given the null hypothesis is zero. MKT-RF represents the excess return on the market-weight returns of all New York Stock Exchange (NYSE)/American Stock Exchange (AMEX)/Nasdaq stocks. SMB is a long/short factor portfolio that captures exposures to small capitalization stocks. HML is a long/short factor portfolio that controls for exposure to high book value-to-market capitalization stocks. MOM is a long/short factor portfolio that controls for exposure to stocks that have had great performance over the recent year. LQD controls for exposure stocks have to market-wide liquidity.

Table 12.5 suggests that Quantitative Value generates between approximately 6 and 8 percent per year in "alpha," or performance not explained by exposures to known factors (the market, size, value, momentum, or liquidity). The strategy has a lower beta than the broader market (MKT-RF beta of around 0.85), tends to buy larger stocks (–0.14, mostly due to the universe parameters), clings to value (HML is 0.23, but we have built this into the model because we are looking at stocks in the top decile of earnings before interest and taxes/total enterprise value [EBIT/TEV]), and has no statistically significant exposure to momentum stocks or stocks affected by low liquidity (MOM and LQD betas are statistically insignificant).

In Figure 12.11, we compare the ability of each strategy's quality metrics to separate winners from losers. The better quality-identification method should generate a larger spread in returns between winners and losers. Figure 12.12 shows the cumulative invested growth for the high- and low-quality portfolios for both the Magic Formula and Quantitative Value strategies. The Magic Formula's high- and low-quality portfolios are separated using the Magic Formula's quality measure, MF ROC. Quantitative Value high- and low-quality portfolios are separated using the quality measures described in this book.

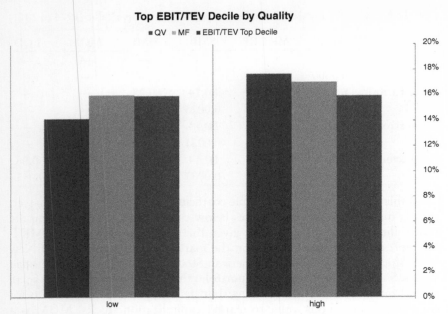

FIGURE 12.11   Decile Performance for Quantitative Value (1974 to 2011)

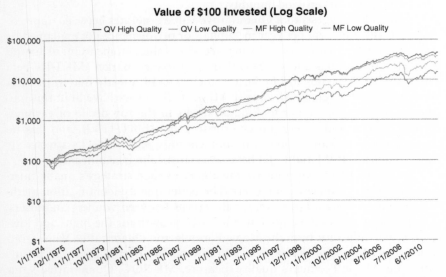

FIGURE 12.12   Quality Splits via Quantitative Value and Magic Formula Quality (1974 to 2011)

Figures 12.11 and 12.12 demonstrate that the quality measures described in the book do a better job separating the winners from the losers. The Quantitative Value high-quality value stocks outperform the Magic Formula high-quality stocks. Further, the Quantitative Value low-quality value stocks *underperform* the Magic Formula's low-quality value stocks by a substantial margin. This analysis shows that when we compare the strategy and the Magic Formula on a like-for-like basis, controlling for the investment structure, which separates the best value stocks into high- and low-quality portfolios, the book's quality measure does a much better job identifying the cheap stocks that will outperform and the cheap stocks that will not perform as well.

A PEEK INSIDE THE BLACK BOX

Many investors legitimately fear that quantitative analysis is an inscrutable "black box," from which emanate incomprehensible investment ideas, many of which don't look like winners. While we know the past results for Quantitative Value have been outstanding, it often feels like one or more of the current crop of stocks selected by the model are particularly weak and should be avoided. Surely we can pick and choose from the model's output? Jim Simons disagrees. The billionaire mathematician turned quantitative hedge fund titan, believes that much of his success is attributable to his strict adherence to the output of his models[6]:

> *Did you like what the model said or did you not like what the model said? That is a hard thing to backtest. If you are going to trade using models, you just slavishly use the models; you do whatever the hell it says no matter how smart or dumb you think it might be at that moment.*

We know from Chapters 1 and 2 that fiddling with the model's output is an error that leads inexorably to underperformance. We know rationally, but when we invest, we engage the irrational fear and greed portions of our brains. It's hard to follow the model when it feels like a magic show.

Aficionados of Warren Buffett's investment style have also been taught that they should stay in their "circle of competence"—the areas in which they are knowledgeable—and not invest in that which they don't understand. For example, Buffett wrote in his 1996 Shareholder Letter[7]:

> *You only have to be able to evaluate companies within your circle of competence. The size of that circle is not very important; knowing its boundaries, however, is vital.*

Quantitative Value seems to go against that grain. It's doubly hard to follow the model's output when every fiber of your being screams that you're outside your circle of competence.

To combat this, we have sought throughout this book to turn the black box into a perfectly transparent aquarium. We hope you now have a granular understanding of how and why the Quantitative Value investment model works. Now we want to open it up.

Table 12.6 lists the top five stocks selected by the model at the start of each year, starting in 1974.

TABLE 12.6   Selected Quantitative Value Portfolio Holdings

Date	EBIT/ TEV	Market Capitalization ($ million)	Stock Name	QV Rank
6/30/74	29.44%	$55	New Process Co.	1
6/30/74	43.42%	$59	CTS Corp.	2
6/30/74	29.35%	$79	Remington Arms Inc.	3
6/30/74	30.44%	$62	Harcourt Brace Jovanovich Inc.	4
6/30/74	30.24%	$77	Pittway Corp. Old	5
6/30/75	142.68%	$73	Amalgamated Sugar Co.	1
6/30/75	32.64%	$319	Cyprus Mines Corp.	2
6/30/75	28.89%	$105	Kennametal Inc.	3
6/30/75	27.87%	$1,000	Texasgulf Inc.	4
6/30/75	34.84%	$509	Cominco Ltd.	5
6/30/76	24.68%	$161	Norris Industries Inc.	1
6/30/76	26.39%	$2,511	Reynolds R J Industries Inc.	2
6/30/76	22.58%	$1,672	Pittston Co.	3
6/30/76	22.75%	$452	Champion Spark Plug Co.	4
6/30/76	22.59%	$206	Gerber Products Co.	5
6/30/77	27.31%	$896	Teledyne Inc.	1
6/30/77	25.17%	$126	Remington Arms Inc.	2
6/30/77	29.56%	$139	Stewart Warner Corp.	3
6/30/77	32.02%	$160	Weis Markets Inc.	4
6/30/77	24.69%	$355	Crown Cork & Seal Co. Inc.	5
6/30/78	27.70%	$731	Hudsons Bay Oil & Gas Ltd.	1
6/30/78	27.08%	$126	Copeland Corp.	2

Date	EBIT/ TEV	Market Capitalization ($ million)	Stock Name	QV Rank
6/30/78	27.48%	$250	Avnet Inc.	3
6/30/78	32.81%	$142	Hollinger Mines Ltd.	4
6/30/78	30.28%	$110	E Systems Inc.	5
6/30/79	35.79%	$296	Washington Post Co.	1
6/30/79	29.77%	$155	Transway International Corp.	2
6/30/79	34.10%	$313	Congoleum Corp.	3
6/30/79	36.86%	$131	Miller Wohl Inc.	4
6/30/79	29.83%	$123	Coleman Inc.	5
6/30/80	33.59%	$598	Northrop Corp.	1
6/30/80	37.64%	$142	Federal Co.	2
6/30/80	34.89%	$1,649	Teledyne Inc.	3
6/30/80	30.32%	$669	Winn Dixie Stores Inc.	4
6/30/80	48.17%	$209	Robins A H Inc.	5
6/30/81	28.88%	$281	VF Corp.	1
6/30/81	25.75%	$1,184	Carnation Co.	2
6/30/81	32.46%	$250	Stone & Webster Inc.	3
6/30/81	26.96%	$1,469	Levi Strauss & Co.	4
6/30/81	25.70%	$313	National Service Industries Inc.	5
6/30/82	43.13%	$185	S F N Companies Inc.	1
6/30/82	40.27%	$182	The Scott & Fetzer Co.	2
6/30/82	32.63%	$1,208	Cooper Industries Inc.	3
6/30/82	34.83%	$327	Wyman Gordon Co.	4
6/30/82	33.36%	$1,383	Colgate Palmolive Co.	5
6/30/83	29.26%	$567	Brown Forman Distillers Corp.	1
6/30/83	22.47%	$1,959	Kellogg Co.	2
6/30/83	20.57%	$2,629	American Brands Inc.	3
6/30/83	23.70%	$1,791	Carnation Co.	4
6/30/83	28.17%	$652	Cameron Iron Works Inc.	5
6/30/84	23.00%	$377	Wrigley William Jr. Co.	1
6/30/84	24.16%	$530	Maytag Co.	2

(continued)

Date	EBIT/ TEV	Market Capitalization ($ million)	Stock Name	QV Rank
6/30/84	31.73%	$798	V F Corp.	3
6/30/84	26.26%	$599	Parsons Corp.	4
6/30/84	32.28%	$271	Bassett Furniture Industries Inc.	5
6/30/85	22.63%	$3,213	General Dynamics Corp.	1
6/30/85	24.56%	$3,174	Halliburton Company	2
6/30/85	41.41%	$292	Western Pacific Industries Inc. De	3
6/30/85	20.11%	$301	Carlisle Corp.	4
6/30/85	24.37%	$514	Diebold Inc.	5
6/30/86	17.93%	$331	Lee Enterprises Inc.	1
6/30/86	31.60%	$13,128	Chevron Corp.	2
6/30/86	36.26%	$4,923	Standard Oil Co. Oh	3
6/30/86	31.85%	$7,516	Texaco Inc.	4
6/30/86	18.03%	$324	Carlisle Companies	5
6/30/87	18.71%	$343	Lee Enterprises Inc.	1
6/30/87	16.21%	$753	Wrigley William Jr. Co.	2
6/30/87	15.38%	$7,530	Rockwell International Corp.	3
6/30/87	16.04%	$345	Hon Industries Inc.	4
6/30/87	46.45%	$582	Subaru America Inc.	5
6/30/88	16.39%	$513	Shared Medical Systems Corp	1
6/30/88	21.91%	$707	Tektronix Inc.	2
6/30/88	19.71%	$513	Stone & Webster Inc.	3
6/30/88	21.94%	$3,397	Texaco Canada Inc.	4
6/30/88	21.22%	$2,717	Lockheed Corp.	5
6/30/89	17.01%	$378	N C H Corp.	1
6/30/89	19.49%	$2,846	Lockheed Corp.	2
6/30/89	23.23%	$15,417	Dow Chemical Co.	3
6/30/89	20.15%	$5,291	Phillips Petroleum Co.	4
6/30/89	18.80%	$923	Intergraph Corp.	5
6/30/90	16.42%	$954	Glatfelter P H Co.	1
6/30/90	16.75%	$4,070	Raytheon Co.	2
6/30/90	17.20%	$1,318	Sundstrand Corp.	3
6/30/90	18.48%	$2,179	Martin Marietta Corp.	4

Date	EBIT/ TEV	Market Capitalization ($ million)	Stock Name	QV Rank
6/30/90	19.86%	$316	Kimball International Inc.	5
6/30/91	34.74%	$295	Kimball International Inc.	1
6/30/91	19.08%	$866	Cray Research Inc.	2
6/30/91	20.30%	$4,876	Apple Computer Inc.	3.5
6/30/91	16.36%	$1,846	Computer Associates Intl Inc.	3.5
6/30/91	29.46%	$2,708	Compaq Computer Corp.	5
6/30/92	17.12%	$1,329	Brown Forman Corp.	1
6/30/92	14.86%	$800	Lotus Development Corp.	2
6/30/92	14.03%	$5,871	Raytheon Co.	3
6/30/92	24.82%	$409	National Presto Industries Inc.	4
6/30/92	25.22%	$5,152	Rockwell International Corp.	5
6/30/93	14.48%	$3,725	Martin Marietta Corp. New	1
6/30/93	21.29%	$2,679	Nike Inc.	2
6/30/93	17.53%	$1,251	King World Productions Inc.	3
6/30/93	16.07%	$2,491	Reebok International Ltd.	4
6/30/93	14.50%	$7,083	General Motors Corp.	5
6/30/94	13.04%	$2,282	Washington Post Co.	1
6/30/94	24.29%	$474	United Television Inc.	2
6/30/94	15.78%	$2,470	Reebok International Ltd.	3
6/30/94	13.83%	$967	Briggs & Stratton Corp.	4
6/30/95	14.37%	$612	Lee Enterprises Inc.	1
6/30/95	19.94%	$822	Bandag Inc.	2
6/30/95	12.24%	$2,481	Washington Post Co.	3
6/30/95	15.58%	$1,166	Georgia Gulf Corp.	4
6/30/95	16.76%	$729	Stratus Computer Inc.	5
6/30/96	28.38%	$581	Bandag Inc.	1
6/30/96	26.10%	$4,132	Phelps Dodge Corp.	2
6/30/96	17.46%	$19,001	Dow Chemical Co.	3
6/30/96	19.99%	$1,364	King World Productions Inc.	4
6/30/96	33.04%	$647	Sterling Chemicals Inc.	5

(continued)

Date	EBIT/ TEV	Market Capitalization ($ million)	Stock Name	QV Rank
6/30/97	13.34%	$651	Medusa Corp.	1
6/30/97	14.12%	$5,130	UST Inc.	2
6/30/97	13.29%	$713	Tootsie Roll Industries Inc.	3
6/30/97	12.38%	$853	Asa Holdings Ltd.	4
6/30/97	12.55%	$4,227	Morton International Inc. New	5
6/30/98	12.16%	$785	Superior Industries Intl Inc.	1
6/30/98	11.95%	$2,890	Deluxe Corp.	2
6/30/98	12.93%	$1,031	Wallace Computer Services Inc.	3
6/30/98	13.44%	$722	Georgia Gulf Corp.	4
6/30/98	21.90%	$1,626	Adaptec Inc.	5
6/30/99	13.24%	$1,293	Crompton & Knowles Corp.	1
6/30/99	14.33%	$696	Blount International Inc.	2
6/30/99	25.40%	$917	Tecumseh Products Co.	3
6/30/99	14.00%	$2,773	Times Mirror Co. New	4
6/30/99	14.55%	$5,162	UST Inc.	5
6/30/00	15.35%	$661	Manitowoc Co. Inc.	1
6/30/00	16.74%	$1,127	Lubrizol Corp.	2
6/30/00	16.34%	$965	Mueller Industries Inc.	3
6/30/00	19.22%	$673	Superior Industries Intl Inc.	4
6/30/00	16.94%	$623	Fossil Inc.	5
6/30/01	26.60%	$3,641	AVX Corp. New	1
6/30/01	14.13%	$2,042	Deluxe Corp.	2
6/30/01	13.71%	$2,524	Brown Forman Corp.	3
6/30/01	39.37%	$1,723	Kemet Corp.	4
6/30/01	17.00%	$1,246	Timberland Co.	5
6/30/02	13.27%	$2,720	Brown Forman Corp.	1
6/30/02	16.22%	$962	Universal Corp.	2
6/30/02	13.72%	$1,634	Readers Digest Association Inc.	3
6/30/02	11.83%	$4,318	VF Corp.	4
6/30/02	12.66%	$1,520	Autodesk Inc.	5
6/30/03	14.68%	$3,743	Jones Apparel Group Inc.	1
6/30/03	14.54%	$1,338	Valassis Communications Inc.	2

Date	EBIT/ TEV	Market Capitalization ($ million)	Stock Name	QV Rank
6/30/03	12.28%	$1,338	Polaris Industries Inc.	3
6/30/03	14.25%	$2,527	Brown Forman Corp.	4
6/30/03	15.14%	$1,127	Mcclatchy Co.	5
6/30/04	11.53%	$7,709	Mattel Inc.	1
6/30/04	12.62%	$2,466	Qlogic Corp.	2
6/30/04	11.39%	$290,443	Exxon Mobil Corp.	3
6/30/04	11.99%	$2,170	Deluxe Corp.	4
6/30/04	14.14%	$2,158	Reebok International Ltd.	5
6/30/05	12.93%	$2,145	Timberland Co.	1
6/30/05	11.27%	$7,548	UST Inc.	2
6/30/05	13.61%	$1,786	Briggs & Stratton Corp.	3
6/30/05	11.07%	$4,017	Lincare Holdings Inc.	4
6/30/05	12.16%	$365,839	Exxon Mobil Corp.	5
6/30/06	13.52%	$4,198	Check Point Software Techs Ltd.	1
6/30/06	18.25%	$1,884	Groupe CGI Inc.	2
6/30/06	12.91%	$15,772	Nike Inc.	3
6/30/06	13.17%	$3,873	Liz Claiborne Inc.	4
6/30/06	15.76%	$2,830	Career Education Corp.	5
6/30/07	14.00%	$4,663	Lexmark International Inc. New	1
6/30/07	17.73%	$17,695	Nucor Corp.	2
6/30/07	11.48%	$2,517	Thor Industries Inc.	3
6/30/07	25.98%	$2,545	Methanex Corp.	4
6/30/07	15.41%	$472,519	Exxon Mobil Corp.	5
6/30/08	24.49%	$1,610	Radioshack Corp.	1
6/30/08	15.34%	$2,786	Family Dollar Stores Inc.	2
6/30/08	33.14%	$2,485	Frontier Oil Corp.	3
6/30/08	14.90%	$5,470	Sherwin Williams Co.	4
6/30/09	19.60%	$101,220	Pfizer Inc.	1
6/30/09	24.57%	$2,100	Endo Pharmaceuticals Holdings Inc.	2
6/30/09	19.48%	$1,596	Lincare Holdings Inc.	3

(continued)

Date	EBIT/ TEV	Market Capitalization ($ million)	Stock Name	QV Rank
6/30/09	23.91%	$3,003	Polo Ralph Lauren Corp.	4
6/30/09	21.82%	$53,344	Occidental Petroleum Corp.	5
6/30/10	15.77%	$38,630	Lilly Eli & Co.	1
6/30/10	14.53%	$2,685	Total System Services Inc.	2
6/30/10	17.19%	$14,223	Best Buy Company Inc.	3
6/30/10	14.94%	$42,889	Bristol Myers Squibb Co.	4
6/30/10	15.04%	$1,515	Buckle Inc.	5
6/30/11	30.30%	$2,196	ITT Educational Services Inc.	1
6/30/11	13.49%	$217,776	Microsoft Corp.	2
6/30/11	16.86%	$2,485	American Eagle Outfitters Inc. NA	3
6/30/11	16.67%	$31,459	Dell Inc.	4
6/30/11	16.42%	$117,492	Intel Corp.	5

There are some storied names in this list. For example, the strategy bought Teledyne, Inc. in 1977 just as it was about to embark on the stellar run under Henry Singleton that we described in Chapter 9. It bought a long-term Berkshire Hathaway holding, the Washington Post Company, in 1979. In 1982, Quantitative Value also picked up another Buffett favorite, the Scott & Fetzer Company, owner of a diverse range of businesses from World Book encyclopedias to Kirby vacuum cleaners. Buffett later bought out Scott & Fetzer in 1986 for $320 million, describing it as owning "the sort of businesses that we wish to buy for Berkshire. Scott Fetzer is a prototype—understandable, large, well-managed, a good earner. ... Return on invested capital is good to excellent for most of these businesses."

Buffett, Warren. "Shareholder Letter," *Berkshire Hathaway, Inc. Annual Report*, 1985.

The strategy also bought Colgate Palmolive Company in 1982, another household name with an exceptionally strong long-term track record. It also bought Halliburton in 1985, Nike and Reebok in 1993, Family Dollar Stores in 2008, and Polo Ralph Lauren in 2009. All have outperformed, demonstrating that the strategy favors large, well-known stocks primed for market-beating performance.

The stocks in the simulated portfolios were often well-known, household names, selected at bargain basement prices. Looking back with the benefit of hindsight, it's deceptively easy now, given that we know that these household names eventually survived and prospered, to forget that these stocks were all depressed at the time for an apparently good reason. If not, they would not have been available at a sufficiently low valuation for the strategy to identify them. It's another strong argument for slavishly following the model.

MAN VERSUS MACHINE

How does the performance of the Quantitative Value model portfolio compare to the performance of three of the top value investors over the past 20 years? Does a quantitative strategy win out, or do the humans have the advantage, given that they can interview managements and avoid the really ugly stocks? We have selected only those who have a sufficiently long period of official *monthly* returns, so that we can compare risk-adjusted performance and drawdowns. For this analysis, we apply a hypothetical 1.5 percent management fee (paid monthly) and include trading and execution costs at 1 percent (paid monthly) in the Quantitative Value results. We do this so the returns are comparable to the returns net of management fees, 12b-fees, and fund transaction costs for the respective mutual funds we analyze. The three funds we examine are all legendary value investing funds: the Sequoia Fund, Legg Mason Value Trust, and Third Avenue Value Fund.

- On May 17, 1984, Warren Buffett delivered a speech to Columbia University commemorating the 50th anniversary of the publication of Graham and Dodd's *Security Analysis*. For value investors, the speech is the stuff of legend. Titled "The Superinvestors of Graham-and-Doddsville," [8] it was a full-throated defense of value investing delivered with the efficient market hypothesis in its ascendency. In it, Buffett identified several value investors sharing Benjamin Graham as a common intellectual patriarch, one of whom was William Ruane. When Buffett wound up Buffett Partners, he asked Ruane if he would set up a fund to handle all Buffett's former partners. That fund was the Sequoia Fund, and Ruane was the only person Buffett recommended to his partners.
- The Legg Mason Value Trust is best known for the incredible 15-consecutive-year streak that it beat the S&P 500 after fees from 1991 through 2005. Bill Miller managed the Legg Mason Value Trust from its inception in 1982 until he stepped down in November 2011. Miller was named by *Money* magazine as "The Greatest Money Manager of the 1990's." Morningstar named him 1998 "Domestic Equity Manager of the Year" and, in 1999, "Fund Manager of the Decade."[9]
- Martin J. Whitman founded the Third Avenue Value Fund in 1986, only stepping down in February 2012 at the age of 87. Whitman is best known as a pioneer of distress investing, and is a prolific writer,

authoring *Value Investing: A Balanced Approach* (2000), *The Aggressive Conservative Investor* (2005), and *Distress Investing: Principles and Technique* (2009).

Table 12.7 compares the performance of the Quantitative Value model against the Sequoia Fund, the Legg Mason Value Trust, and Third Avenue Value Fund. We assess returns from January 1, 1991, through December 31, 2011, because the Third Avenue Value Fund does not have historical data available prior to this date. All data are from the CRSP Survivor Bias-Free U.S. Mutual Fund Database.

TABLE 12.7 Performance Statistics for Quantitative Value (1991 to 2011)

	QV	Sequoia	Legg Mason	Third Avenue	S&P 500 TR
CAGR	13.32%	12.16%	9.14%	10.72%	9.02%
Standard Deviation	16.20%	14.62%	19.62%	16.49%	15.05%
Downside Deviation	10.52%	10.02%	14.28%	13.49%	10.89%
Sharpe Ratio	0.81	0.64	0.38	0.50	0.43
Sortino Ratio (MAR = 5%)	1.08	0.76	0.40	0.49	0.44
Worst Drawdown	−29.85%	−40.72%	−68.91%	−58.23%	−50.21%
Worst Month Return	−15.69%	−14.69%	−21.35%	−18.95%	−16.70%
Best Month Return	16.34%	16.36%	14.61%	18.85%	11.41%
Profitable Months	63.49%	60.71%	61.11%	62.30%	63.49%
Rolling 5-Year Win	—	65.28%	64.77%	76.17%	92.75%
Rolling 10-Year Win	—	86.47%	58.65%	92.48%	100.00%
Cumulative Drawdown	−4074.51%	−4358.42%	−6609.37%	−5116.35%	−5609.87%
Correlation	—	0.563	0.636	0.629	0.689

The Quantitative Value strategy performs well in comparison with these legends of investing. It generated a better CAGR, at one of the lower standard and downside deviations, which led to excellent Sharpe and Sortino ratios. The strategy also protected well against the downside, suffering a worst drawdown that was considerably better than those experienced by the other investors. The Quantitative Value portfolio has tended to outperform over rolling 5- and 10-year periods, beating out the other investors around two out of every three rolling 5-year periods, and between six and nine out of every ten rolling 10-year periods. Figure 12.13 shows the cumulative performance of the Quantitative Value strategy compared to the other well-known value investors.

Figures 12.13 and 12.14 shows the cumulative invested growth and annual performance of the Quantitative Value strategy. The Legg Mason Value Trust had a great run in late 1990s but crashed and burned in 2008. Legg Mason's valiant early run aside, Quantitative Value was in a close horse race with the three value-investing legends through most of the history we analyze. In 2002, about halfway through the race, the Quantitative Value portfolio pulled ahead and held its lead to the finish.

Figure 12.15 shows the market-cycle performance of the Quantitative Value strategy.

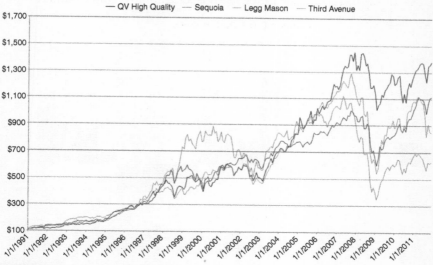

Value of $100 Invested

— QV High Quality — Sequoia — Legg Mason — Third Avenue

FIGURE 12.13   Cumulative Value for Quantitative Value (1991 to 2011)

	QV	Sequoia	Legg Mason	Third Avenue
1991	20.93%	40.00%	34.73%	34.18%
1992	24.78%	9.36%	11.44%	21.29%
1993	5.30%	10.78%	11.26%	23.66%
1994	15.98%	3.34%	1.39%	−1.46%
1995	54.26%	41.38%	40.76%	31.73%
1996	19.34%	21.74%	38.43%	21.92%
1997	58.12%	43.20%	37.05%	23.87%
1998	−1.62%	35.25%	48.01%	3.92%
1999	13.78%	−16.45%	26.71%	12.82%
2000	14.90%	20.06%	−7.14%	20.76%
2001	10.54%	10.52%	−9.29%	2.82%
2002	−10.44%	−2.64%	−18.92%	−15.19%
2003	39.92%	17.12%	43.53%	37.09%
2004	22.91%	4.66%	11.96%	26.60%
2005	15.94%	7.78%	5.32%	16.50%
2006	29.95%	8.34%	5.85%	14.69%
2007	24.66%	8.40%	−6.66%	5.76%
2008	−14.75%	−27.03%	−55.05%	−45.60%
2009	8.51%	15.38%	40.64%	44.51%
2010	0.44%	19.50%	6.67%	13.87%
2011	13.35%	13.19%	−4.00%	−20.68%

FIGURE 12.14   Annual Performance for Quantitative Value (1991 to 2011)

Figure 12.15 shows that the Quantitative Value strategy tended to deliver excellent returns through the business cycle, protecting capital in bear markets, and growing capital in bull markets. The relative performance is mixed for the three value investing legends. Quantitative Value outperforms

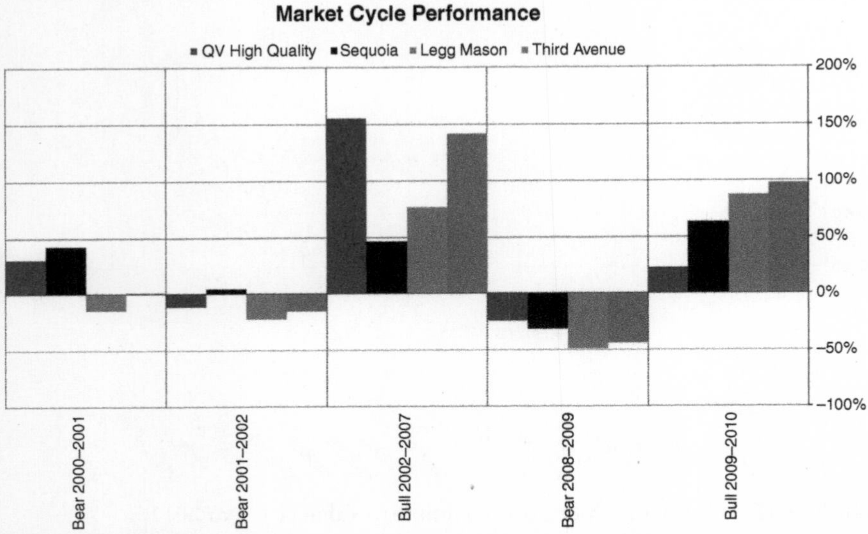

Market Cycle Performance

■ QV High Quality   ■ Sequoia   ■ Legg Mason   ■ Third Avenue

FIGURE 12.15   Market Cycle Performance for Quantitative Value (1991 to 2011)

by a wide margin in the bear market cycle, but then underperforms in the most recent 2009 to 2011 bull market cycle. This 2008 through 2011 period should be instructive for investors, illustrating that drawdowns matter to investment performance. Quantitative Value better protects capital through the 2008 financial crisis, and has a smaller recovery in the following 2009 to 2011 bull market. Quantitative Value wins over the full period because it compounds capital in the recovery from the larger capital base provided by the better downside protection in the bust.

Figure 12.16 shows the drawdown analysis of the Quantitative Value strategy.

Figure 12.16 demonstrates that the strategy tended to better protect capital in major market slumps. In the worst five-year period the S&P 500 was still down around 25 percent, while there was no five-year period from 1991 to 2011 where an investor would have finished down.

Figure 12.17 shows the risk/reward chart for Quantitative Value.

Figure 12.17 clearly shows that Quantitative Value delivers excellent risk-adjusted performance relative to the other investors. CAGRs are higher, and risk is roughly the same. Sequoia is the only manager that could conceivably compete on basic risk/reward metrics.

The Quantitative Value strategy performed well when compared with these top-flight investors. It generated a better CAGR, at one of the lower standard and downside deviations, which led to excellent Sharpe and Sortino ratios. The strategy also protected well against the downside, suffering a worst drawdown that was considerably better than those experienced

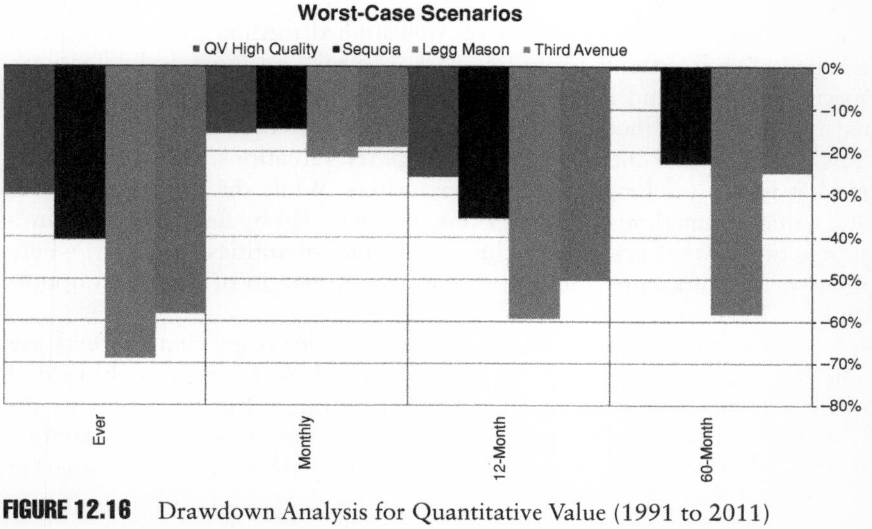

FIGURE 12.16 Drawdown Analysis for Quantitative Value (1991 to 2011)

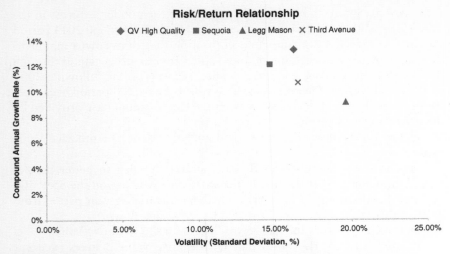

FIGURE 12.17   Risk/Reward Chart for Quantitative Value (1974 to 2011)

by the other investors. The strategy has tended to outperform over rolling 5- and 10-year periods, beating out the other investors around two out of every three rolling 5-year periods, and between six and nine out of every 10 rolling 10-year periods. Machine, it seems, beats man.

BEATING THE MARKET WITH QUANTITATIVE VALUE

Value investing is a highly effective, well-studied method of investing. It is a broad church, encompassing investors who take positions in liquidations, special situations, undervalued assets, and undervalued businesses, using a variety of valuation methods, from simple price ratios, to detailed discounted cash flow analyses, and intricate sum-of-the-parts valuations that seek current market values for long-term and fixed assets. While the investment styles and valuation methods run the gamut, all are united by Benjamin Graham's simple notion that price and value are distinct quantities, and that, where the two are sufficiently far apart to provide a margin of safety, an opportunity exists to invest.

Graham's credo runs counter to the orthodox view that markets are efficient, the proponents of which have applied increasingly sophisticated methods to discount the apparent market-beating returns to value by attempting to dissolve them in risk, size, momentum, and liquidity factors. We think Buffett's view on the debate is probably the right one: The market is frequently, but not always, efficient. Small inefficiencies persist because "naïve" investors are prone to cognitive errors, extrapolating poor earnings performance too far into the future, assuming a downward trend in stock prices will continue or simply overreacting to bad news, leading them to oversell stocks to the point they are undervalued. The inefficiencies can be exploited by investors prepared to invest contrary to these "naïve" investors and their own nature. Often, the slip twixt cup and lip occurs here. All of us, including value investors, are subject to cognitive biases that lead us to make behavioral errors. Our rational mind knows that value works, but exploiting the edge provided by value requires the subjugation of our own natures, which is exceptionally difficult to do.

We know, as Keynes did, that "the game of professional investment is intolerably boring and over-exacting to anyone who is entirely exempt from the gambling instinct; whilst he who has it must pay to this propensity the appropriate toll."[10] The power of the quantitative approach is both in the protection it affords us against our own gambling instinct and in its relentless exploitation of the small edges provided by others' errors. Rational exhortations against bad behavior don't work because behavioral errors are irrational—reliably and predictably so. As long as humans have cognitive biases, contrarian, mean reverting investment strategies like value will persist, creating opportunities for quantitative value investors to exploit.

There are many ways to identify value. Simple price ratios can be highly potent, so much so that we found it difficult to improve on the best of them, the EBIT variation of the enterprise multiple. All of the single-year price ratios, however, identified value stocks that outperformed the glamour stocks and the market in general. Other variations of the price ratios, including long-term "normalized" average price ratios, and composites of different price ratios, also identified value stocks that beat the market. Whichever way we slice it, the value effect seems to be robust to the technique we employ: over the long term, inexpensive value stocks have consistently outperformed expensive, glamour stocks.

As difficult as it is to outperform the best of the simple price ratios, we did find some logical and intuitive steps that we could take to improve the performance of the universe, and push up the returns to value. We found that by eliminating from the universe the stocks with no intrinsic value—the frauds, the financial statement manipulators, and those at high risk of financial distress—we could goose the performance of the universe. We also found that if we separated the value portfolio into high- and low-quality stocks using principles of security analysis, the high-quality stocks substantially outperformed the low-quality stocks. We quantitatively defined quality as financially strong stocks with franchises, evidenced by high returns on capital and high, stable, or growing margins.

It seems intuitive that the high-quality value stocks would outperform, but we don't want to make the mistake of confusing a good stock with a good investment. As investors have learned and relearned over the years, the attractiveness of a stock as an investment is a function of its price to its value. Overpaying for high quality leads to suboptimal performance, as this examination of the Magic Formula demonstrates. Value is always our dominant consideration. The deeper the discount from value we pay, the greater the margin of safety, and the better the returns will be. Graham, once challenged to distill the secret of sound value investment into three words, ventured the motto, "margin of safety." It is as true today as it was then, and the Quantitative Value strategy uses Graham's distillation to good effect.

NOTES

1. John Maynard Keynes, *The General Theory of Employment, Interest, and Money* (Palgrave Macmillan, 1936).
2. William F. Sharpe, "Capital Asset Prices: A Theory of Market Equilibrium under Conditions of Risk." *Journal of Finance* 19(3) (1964): 425–442.
3. Eugene Fama and Kenneth French, "Common Risk Factors in the Returns on Stocks and Bonds." *Journal of Financial Economics* 33 (1993): 3–56.
4. Mark Carhart, "On Persistence in Mutual Fund Performance." *Journal of Finance* 52 (1997): 57–82.
5. Lubos Pastor and Robert Stambaugh, "Liquidity Risk and Expected Stock Returns." *Journal of Political Economy* 111 (2003): 642–685.
6. James Simons, "Mathematics, Common Sense, and Good Luck: My Life and Career," MIT Seminar, January 24, 2011.
7. Warren Buffett, "Shareholder Letter," Berkshire Hathaway, Inc. Annual Report, 1996.
8. Warren Buffett, "The Superinvestors of Graham-and-Doddsville," *Hermes,* Columbia Business School alumni magazine, 1984. Available at *www7.gsb .columbia.edu/alumni/news/hermes/print-archive/superinvestors.*
9. Santa Fe Institute biography, *www.santafe.edu/about/people/profile/Bill%20 Miller.*
10. Keynes.

Appendix: Analysis Legend

The analysis legend below provides a definition of the words and symbols we use in the back-test.

Word/Symbol	Description
QV	Our quantitative value strategy.
MF	The Magic Formula strategy.
S&P 500 TR	Standard & Poor's 500 Total Return Index, the free-float, market capitalization–weighted index including the effects of dividend reinvestment.
MW Index	A total-return, market capitalization–weighted index that we construct from the universe of stocks included in our analysis. The index's returns represent a passive investment in the universe of all stocks we analyze.
CAGR	Compound annual growth rate.
Standard Deviation	Sample standard deviation (annualized by square root of 12).
Downside Deviation	Sample standard deviation of all negative observations (annualized by square root of 12).
Sharpe Ratio	Monthly return minus risk free rate divided by standard deviation (annualized by square root of 12).
Sortino Ratio (MAR=5%)	Monthly return minus minimum acceptable return (MAR/12) divided by downside deviation (annualized by square root of 12).
Worst Drawdown	Worst peak-to-trough performance.
Worst Month Return	Worst monthly performance.
Best Month Return	Best monthly performance.
Profitable Months	Proportion of monthly performances that have a positive return.
Rolling 5-Year Wins	Proportion of rolling 5-year periods that a designated strategy beats the identified benchmarks.

Word/Symbol	Description
Rolling 10-Year Wins	Proportion of rolling 10-year periods that a designated strategy beats identified benchmarks.
Cumulative Drawdown	Sum of the rolling 5-year period worst drawdowns for the designated strategy.
Correlation	Correlation coefficient for a designated strategy and the identified benchmarks, which demonstrates the extent to which a designated strategy and the identified benchmarks move together.

About the Authors

WESLEY R. GRAY, PhD, is the founder and executive managing member of Empiritrage, LLC, an SEC-Registered Investment Advisor, and Turnkey Analyst, LLC, a firm dedicated to educating and sharing quantitative investment techniques to the general public. He is also an assistant professor of finance at Drexel University's Lebow College of Business, where his research focus is on value investing and behavioral finance. Professor Gray teaches graduate-level investment management and a seminar on hedge fund strategies and operations. Dr. Gray's professional and leadership experiences include over 14 years building systematic trading systems, trading special situations, and service as a U.S. Marine Corps intelligence officer (Captain) in Iraq and various posts in Asia. Dr. Gray earned an MBA and a PhD in finance from the University of Chicago Booth School of Business. He graduated magna cum laude with a BS in economics from the Wharton School, University of Pennsylvania.

TOBIAS E. CARLISLE, LLB, B. Bus(Man), PLEAT, is the founder of Eyquem Investment Management LLC, portfolio manager of the Eyquem Fund LP and its precursor Eyquem Global Value Fund, and the author of the award-winning website greenbackd.com, which covers deep value, contrarian, and activist investment strategies. He has extensive experience in activist investment, company valuation, public company corporate governance, and mergers and acquisitions law. Prior to founding Eyquem, Tobias was an analyst at an activist hedge fund, general counsel of a company listed on the Australian Stock Exchange, and a corporate advisory lawyer. As a lawyer specializing in mergers and acquisitions he has advised on transactions across a variety of industries in the United States, the United Kingdom, China, Australia, Singapore, Bermuda, Papua New Guinea, New Zealand, and Guam, ranging in value from $50 million to $2.5 billion. He is a graduate of the University of Queensland in Australia with degrees in law and business (management).

About the Companion Website

This book includes a companion website, which can be found at www.wiley.com/go/quantvalue.

This website includes:

- A screening tool to find stocks using the model in the book.
- A tool designed to facilitate the implementation for a variety of tactical asset allocation models.
- A back-testing tool that allows users to compare performance among competing investment strategies.
- A blog about recent developments in quantitative value investing.

Index